FOUR
VIEWS
ON **THE APOSTLE PAUL**

Books in the Counterpoints Series

Church Life

Exploring the Worship Spectrum: Six Views

Evaluating the Church Growth Movement: Five Views

Remarriage after Divorce in Today's Church: Three Views

Understanding Four Views on Baptism

Understanding Four Views on the Lord's Supper

Who Runs the Church?

Bible and Theology

Are Miraculous Gifts for Today? Four Views

Five Views on Apologetics

Five Views on Law and Gospel

Five Views on Sanctification

Four Views on Divine Providence

Four Views on Eternal Security

Four Views on Hell

Four Views on Moving Beyond the Bible to Theology

Four Views on Salvation in a Pluralistic World

Four Views on the Book of Revelation

Four Views on the Spectrum of Evangelicalism

How Jewish Is Christianity? Two Views on the Messianic Movement

Show Them No Mercy: Four Views on God and Canaanite Genocide

Three Views on Creation and Evolution

Three Views on Eastern Orthodoxy and Evangelicalism

Three Views on the Millennium and Beyond

Three Views on the New Testament Use of the Old Testament

Three Views on the Rapture

Two Views on Women in Ministry

FOUR
VIEWS
ON
THE APOSTLE PAUL

Thomas R. Schreiner

Luke Timothy Johnson

Douglas A. Campbell

Mark D. Nanos

Stanley N. Gundry, series editor
Michael F. Bird, general editor

COUNTERPOINTS
▶ BIBLE & THEOLOGY ◀

ZONDERVAN®

ZONDERVAN.com/
AUTHORTRACKER
follow your favorite authors

ZONDERVAN

Four Views on the Apostle Paul
Copyright © 2012 by Michael F. Bird, Thomas R. Schreiner, Luke Timothy Johnson,
Douglas A. Campbell, Mark D. Nanos

This title is also available as a Zondervan ebook.

Requests for information should be addressed to:

Zondervan, *Grand Rapids, Michigan 49530*

Library of Congress Cataloging-in-Publication Data

Bird, Michael F.
    Four views on the Apostle Paul / general editor, Michael F. Bird; contributors,
Thomas R. Schreiner ... [et al.].
      p. cm.
    Includes index
    ISBN 978-0-310-32695-3 (softcover)
    1. Paul, the Apostle, Saint. — Theology. I Bird, Michael F. II. Schreiner, Thomas R.
BS2651.F68 2012
227'.06 — dc23   2012012196

Cover design: Tammy Johnson
Cover photography: M. Trischler
Interior design: Matthew Van Zomeren

Printed in the United States of America

HB 01.17.2024

CONTENTS

ABBREVIATIONS

Note: Standard abbreviations for classical and rabbinic sources are not included in this list, but are readily available in *The SBL Handbook of Style*.

AB	Anchor Bible
ABL	Anchor Bible Library
BBR	*Bulletin for Biblical Research*
BECNT	Baker Exegetical Commentary on the New Testament
BibInt	Biblical Interpretation
BZNW	Beihefte zur Zeitschrift für die neutestamentliche Wissenschaft
CBQ	*Catholic Biblical Quarterly*
ESV	English Standard Version
EvT	*Evangelische Theologie*
HBT	*Horizons in Biblical Theology*
HTR	*Harvard Theological Review*
JBL	*Journal of Biblical Literature*
JSNT	*Journal for the Study of the New Testament*
LNTS	Library of New Testament Studies
NAB	New American Bible
NIBC	New International Biblical Commentary
NIGTC	New International Greek Testament Commentary
NIV	New International Version
NovTSupp	Novum Testamentum Supplements
NTS	*New Testament Studies*
SJT	*Scottish Journal of Theology*
SP	Sacra pagina
TSAJ	Texte und Studien zum antiken Judentum
USQR	*Union Seminar Quarterly Review*
WBC	Word Biblical Commentary
WUNT	Wissenschaftliche Untersuchungen zum Neuen Testament
ZECNT	Zondervan Exegetical Commentary on the New Testament

INTRODUCTION

MICHAEL F. BIRD

The apostle Paul, writing about his ministry, said to the Corinthians:

> I have worked much harder, been in prison more frequently, been
> flogged more severely, and been exposed to death again and again.
> Five times I received from the Jews the forty lashes minus one.
> Three times I was beaten with rods, once I was pelted with stones,
> three times I was shipwrecked, I spent a night and a day in the open
> sea, I have been constantly on the move. I have been in danger from
> rivers, in danger from bandits, in danger from my own people, in
> danger from Gentiles. (2 Cor. 11:23–26)

Evidently, Paul was a controversial figure. He prompted vehement
opposition from Jewish Christians, violent reaction from his Judean
compatriots, and even criminal punishment from Greco-Roman
authorities. You do not get beaten, flogged, imprisoned, and stoned
without saying and doing things that are deemed controversial, offen-
sive, and even subversive.

Beyond the image of Paul the controversialist, we must remember
that Paul was responsible for shaping the early church in a significant
way.[1] His key theological motif, that the Gentiles are saved by faith
without adopting the Jewish way of life, won the day. Though he was
put to death by a Roman emperor, Roman emperors eventually came
to revere his letters as sacred Scripture. Despite the fact that he was
a Jewish Christian, he provided the framework that would later be
used to separate "Christianity" from "Judaism." While his letters were
occasional and even ad hoc, they came to form the basis of Christian
theology. It is not too much to say that Paul—the man, the mission,
and the martyr—was arguably the single, most driving intellectual
force in the early church, second only to Jesus. Church leaders in the

---

1. Cf. Michael F. Bird and Joseph A. Dodson, eds., *Paul and the Second Century* (LNTS
412; London: T&T Clark, 2011).

subsequent centuries, both orthodox and heretical, took inspiration and impetus from Paul. Indeed, it seems that spiritual renewal and theological reformation, from Augustine to Martin Luther to Karl Barth, have been largely driven by a fresh discovery (or recovery) of Paul for their day.

That said, Paul remains an inspirational and incendiary figure for our own times as well. By "inspirational" I mean that many still see themselves as Paulinists in trying to promote a theological vision and a Christian ethic, and to follow an evangelistic mandate that is distinctively Pauline. Others see themselves as furthering Paul's message of reconciliation in their own culture and context. And others regard Paul as the ultimate inclusivist, who was a prophet of postmodern values of diversity, tolerance, and pluralism. On the "incendiary" scheme, Paul's letters have facilitated heated debates inside and outside of the church as to what he meant by his few remarks on Israel, homosexuality, women, spiritual gifts, and the end times. Paul's letters have been quoted in endless theological fights, denominational splits, and mutual denunciations — all by people who claim that they hold to the proper interpretation of the true Paul.

In the attempt to get beyond the mass of debate that is Pauline studies, in both its historical and current forms, the modest aim of this volume is to contrast four competing perspectives on the apostle. In particular these contributors look at what Paul "meant" and what he continues to "mean" for contemporary audiences. To that end, assembled in this volume is a creative cast of Pauline scholars, well acquainted with Paul's writings and the vast scholarly literature that surrounds him, who will set forth their own perspectives on Paul. The aim is for each contributor to set forth his own portrait of Paul and then to have them engage with one another critically in a series of responses.

The commentators involved in this volume been carefully selected based on their reputation and expertise in their respective fields. The contributors involved in this exchange include an Evangelical, a Catholic, a mainline Protestant, and a Jew. A diverse bunch indeed! To keep the exchange to a containable and realistic set of topics, it was decided that each of the contributors would touch on four key areas in their respective essays. These topics are:

- What did Paul think about salvation?
- What was Paul's view of the significance of Christ?
- What is the best framework for describing Paul's theological perspective?
- What was Paul's vision for the churches?

These topics are controversial and thereby provide ample opportunity for the contributors to exposit their own distinctive understanding of Paul. These are questions where diversity, debate, and disagreement emerge precisely over what Paul taught in these areas. It is here that readers have the opportunity to learn and assess each essay as to how it properly accounts for the life and letters of the apostle Paul. Now obviously the contributors do not disagree over everything, and common ground was reached in some areas, but one does see the diverse ways in which Paul has been understood and appropriated. Readers are invited to listen and learn from the exchange as these scholars lock horns over Paul. Thankfully, the exchange, controversial and critical as is to be expected, has been undertaken with a spirit of generosity and charity that Paul himself would approve of.

Concerning our illustrious contributors, let me introduce them to you and summarize their positions. Thomas R. Schreiner, James Buchanan Professor at Southern Baptist Theological Seminary, is a veteran in Pauline studies, having written volumes on Paul and the law, a Pauline theology, a guide to Pauline interpretation, as well as commentaries on Romans and Galatians.[2] He writes from a Reformed Baptist position that is distinguished by a Calvinistic interpretation of Paul's letters with a due emphasis on God's sovereignty and God's passion for his own glory. Schreiner's position is representative of confessional Protestantism and an evangelical Reformed theology that is experiencing a resurgence in North America. In this theological scheme, Paul's letters are central as they establish key Reformed doctrines such as justification by faith, salvation by grace alone, and the assurance of salvation that believers may enjoy. Schreiner's writings have endeavored to show

2. Thomas R. Schreiner, *The Law and Its Fulfillment: A Pauline Theology of Law* (Grand Rapids: Baker, 1993); idem, *Paul, Apostle of God's Glory in Christ: A Pauline Theology* (Grand Rapids: Baker, 2001); idem, *Interpreting the Pauline Epistles* (2nd ed.; Grand Rapids: Baker, 2011); idem, *Romans* (BECNT; Grand Rapids: Baker, 1998); *Galatians* (ZECNT; Grand Rapids: Zondervan, 2010).

how these Reformed distinctives have ample biblical support especially in the Pauline corpus.

According to Schreiner, the framework for understanding Paul is eschatology. Paul believed that the Old Testament promises about a new exodus, a new covenant, and a new creation have been partially realized in the work of Jesus Christ and the gift of the Holy Spirit. Believers still look forward, however, to the final consummation of these promises in the future. As for the significance of Jesus Christ for Paul, Schreiner contends that Jesus is the heart and soul of Pauline theology and that he permeates every topic of Paul's theological thought. That centrality is evident in a number of areas, including Paul's testimony to the church's worship and sacramental life, the content of his gospel, and Paul's perspective that all life is lived under the aegis of Jesus' lordship. As such, Schreiner regards Christ as the center of Paul's framework since Christ is the goal of God's purposes.

Concerning Paul's view of salvation, in Schreiner's estimation, Paul identifies salvation as deliverance from the consequences of sin, namely, divine vengeance and eternal destruction. Salvation, then, is the manifestation of God's love by rescuing sinners from the retribution that their rebellion against God deserved. Persons are saved by the gracious mercy of God shown on the cross and do not merit salvation by their good deeds. The chief instrument of salvation is the substitutionary death of Jesus for the ungodly. In regards to the Pauline vision of the church, Schreiner identifies several constituent elements to Paul's thought. For a start the Pauline churches are considered to be a "true Israel" and "new temple" of sorts as they inherited the promises of the chosen nation. The church is the body of Christ, and Christ is the head of that body and the basis for unity among its many members.

Luke Timothy Johnson is a former Benedictine monk and priest; he presently is the Robert W. Woodruff Professor of New Testament and Christian Origins at the Candler School of Theology, Emory University.[3] He has specialized in the Greco-Roman contexts of the early church and the moral discourse of the New Testament with a particular focus on

---

3. Luke Timothy Johnson, *Letters to Paul's Delegates: A Commentary on 1 Timothy, 2 Timothy and Titus* (Valley Forge, PA: Trinity International, 1996); idem, *Reading Romans: A Literary and Theological Commentary* (Macon, GA: Smyth & Helwys, 1997); idem, *The First and Second Letters to Timothy: A New Translation with Introduction and Commentary* (AB; New York: Doubleday, 2001); idem, *The Writings of the New Testament: An Interpretation* (Minneapolis: Fortress, 2010).

Luke–Acts, the Pastoral Letters, the letter to the Romans, and the letter of James. He writes with a particular interest in the communal and experiential dimensions of the early church. Johnson represents a generation of post-Vatican II Catholic scholars who have embraced historical criticism while recognizing as well the importance of patristic and medieval interpretation.

In Johnson's perspective, the Pauline framework, though difficult to identify, is probably a matrix consisting of Paul's grounding in Greco-Roman culture, his religious sensibilities, and his loyalty to his Jewish heritage principally through the Jewish Scriptures. The significance of Christ for Paul lies in the fact that God's new creation is experienced through the experience of Jesus. As Lord, Jesus is the ruler and restorer of the Jews and all of humanity. With respect to salvation, Johnson emphasizes that salvation is chiefly about liberation and transformation—liberation from hostile powers, cosmic and social, and transformation in the empirical state of human beings into renewed persons, still awaiting the final triumph of God at the end of history. The vision of the church, as Johnson understands Paul, is that the New Testament church consisted of local assemblies who carefully tried to establish an identity in the Greco-Roman world and held on to their religious heritage with Israel. The churches were more than voluntary associations as they attributed the source of their life and power to the Holy Spirit. The church is united in a shared experience of the risen Lord, living out egalitarian ideals against hierarchical social norms and seeking the edification of the corporate group by following the pattern of Christ.

Douglas A. Campbell, Associate Professor of New Testament at Duke University, a native New Zealander and another specialist Pauline scholar, occupies a position that is a bit more difficult to describe. Campbell does not stand in any single school. In the end, however, we have labeled Campbell's position as "Post-New Perspective on Paul." The New Perspective on Paul sought to reinterpret Paul in light of a reinterpretation of Judaism as a nonlegalistic religion of works righteousness. This has led to a proliferation of debate in the last thirty years as to whether Paul was sufficiently "Lutheran" in his thinking or more concerned with ethnic issues related to Jewish and Christian identity.[4] Campbell gets

---

4. For an introduction to the debate, see Kent L. Yinger, *The New Perspective on Paul: An Introduction* (Eugene, OR: Cascade, 2011).

himself beyond this debate by taking the Jewish question of Paul's relationship to Judaism seriously, but also by incorporating a wider sway of theological resources into his reading of Paul, not least of which is the mission of the triune God that brings people to participate in Christ through the agency of the Holy Spirit. One can detect in his approach a kaleidoscope of theological and interpretive approaches to Paul.

Campbell was doctoral student of Richard Longenecker and follows Longenecker's style of biblical exegesis of Paul. There is a pervasive Barthianism that is conspicuous in Campbell's Christology and in his conception of divine freedom. He follows the Torrancian rejection of federal theology. There are echoes of Richard Hays in his books on Pauline studies too, especially on the "faithfulness of Jesus Christ." He is also indebted to the apocalyptic approach to Paul associated with Ernst Käsemann, J. C. Beker, and J. Louis Martyn. Campbell represents a type of Protestant Pauline scholarship that has drunk from the well of historical questions raised by New Perspective scholarship, but is intoxicated by the theological juices that run through Paul's letters.

Campbell offers a careful theological reading of Romans 5 – 8 as representative of Paul's thought and illustrative of what Paul thinks of salvation and the church.

1. Campbell believes that Paul envisages salvation as a trinitarian and missional activity mediated through Christ and the Spirit. As such, God's gift in salvation is the gift of God himself who enters into communion with human subjects who participate in the divine life. Its chief results are life, liberation, and community.
2. Concerning Christ, Campbell regards Paul as depicting Jesus as the self-disclosure of God. Jesus reveals the nature of the divine identity and the quality of divine action-in-love. Divine being and divine act are inseparable for Paul; Christ proves it.
3. The framework for understanding Paul is what Campbell calls, in other places, the "pneumatologically participatory martyrological eschatology" model.[5] This is simpler than it sounds.

---

5. Cf. Douglas A. Campbell, *The Quest for Paul's Gospel: A Suggested Strategy* (London: T&T Clark, 2005); idem, *The Deliverance of God: An Apocalyptic Rereading of Justification in Paul* (Grand Rapids: Eerdmans, 2009).

The Spirit places believers in both the martyrological and resurrection narratives of Christ where they experience faithfulness in present sufferings and a foretaste of the benefits of the new creation. This framework of participation links together Paul's view of apostleship, mission, Eucharist, worship, sexual and social ethics, and eschatological assurance.

4. Campbell proposes that Paul regards the church as an eschatological brotherhood, united as image bearers of the Son and practicing a panoply of virtues revolving around love while they live as part of the burgeoning new creation.

Mark D. Nanos is Soebbing Distinguished Scholar-in-Residence at Rockhurst University. He comes to the subject as a Jewish scholar who is a specialist in Pauline studies and in Jewish-Christian relations.[6] Nanos challenges both the Christian interpretation of Paul as the great denunciator of Judaism and the Jewish interpretation of Paul, largely in rejoinder, as an apostate. Nanos's thesis is that we should take Paul seriously as a first-century advocate and representative of Torah-based Judaism. This will help Jews and Christians become more aware of their common origins in spite of many eventual differences, leading to more respectful relations. In Nanos's view, Paul maintained that the end of the ages had at least begun in part because of the coming of Christ, and thus that Christ-believing Gentiles should be integrated into Jewish communities without becoming Jews in order to represent a key propositional truth — that is, to demonstrate in concrete social terms that God is the God of the nations as well as Israel. Simultaneously, Christ-believing Jews must not give up their Torah-observance and Jewish lifestyle based on the same propositional truth, for God is the God of Israel as well as of the other nations.

---

6. Cf. Mark D. Nanos, *The Mystery of Romans: The Jewish Context of Paul's Letter* (Minneapolis: Fortress, 1996); idem, *The Irony of Galatians: Paul's Letter in First-Century Context* (Minneapolis: Fortress, 2002); idem, "Paul and Judaism: Why Not Paul's Judaism?" in *Paul Unbound: Other Perspectives on the Apostle* (ed. Mark Given; Peabody, MA: Hendrickson, 2009), 117–60; idem, "'Broken Branches': A Pauline Metaphor Gone Awry? (Romans 11:11–24)," in *Between Gospel and Election: Explorations in the Interpretation of Romans 9–11* (eds. Florian Wilk and J. Ross Wagner; Tübingen: Mohr Siebeck, 2010), 339–76; "The Myth of the 'Law-Free' Paul Standing between Christians and Jews," *Studies in Christian-Jewish Relations* 4 (2009): 1–21; available at http://escholarship.bc.edu/scjr/vol4/iss1/4/; "Romans," in *The Jewish Annotated New Testament* (ed. Amy-Jill Levine and Marc Zvi Brettler; New York: Oxford Univ. Press, 2011), 253–86; idem, "Paul and Judaism," in ibid., 551–54.

Nanos sketches Paul's ideological position around the minority context of Jews and Judaism in the first-century Greco-Roman world. Concerning salvation, Nanos proposes that Paul viewed Gentiles to be in need of rescue from idolatry and sin. These members from the nations were outside of the covenant God made with Israel, wherein a relationship with God was established in the present age, and forgiveness could be obtained when one failed to live rightly according to the standards of that covenant. Jews did not need to be rescued (saved) on the same terms as Gentiles, since they were already in this covenantal relationship with God, which provided both instruction and atonement. Rather, in Paul's view, Jews needed to recognize what God had promised Israel had arrived in Christ, and those who were not persuaded yet of this "truth" needed to be restored to carrying out their covenantal responsibility (promised privilege) of announcing to the nations, alongside Paul and other Christ-following Jews, the "good news" that Gentiles can also be rescued and brought into a covenant relationship with God.

Christ in Nanos's reading of Paul was the promised one for Jews, for those already in the covenant but awaiting the promised age to come, when all of creation will be rescued from evil and restored to God's rule. Christ also brought mercy to the rest of the nations, the Gentiles, who had been previously outside the covenant, but who could now be rescued and restored to the worship of the one God of all humankind. Nanos finds the core of Paul's theology in his development of Israel's confession of the one God (cf. the Shema^c) and the covenants made with Abraham and Israel, and through them, with all of creation. Finally, Nanos argues that Paul's vision for the churches is based on the proposition that the end of the ages has arrived in midst of the present ("evil") age. To fulfill this utopian ideal, Christ-believers are to live empowered by the Spirit of the age-to-come now at work among them as equals, however different their relative rank may remain in this-age terms, and thereby to faithfully serve one another.

As you can observe, there are some very different views of Paul operating here. Unsurprisingly, the exchanges result in some big intellectual artillery being fired in four different directions all at once. Even so, what I think is to be truly appreciated is the honest and forthright attempts that these scholars make as they wrestle with Paul. In addition, they all agree that Paul matters. He matters immensely for the history of Christianity. He matters for relations between Jews and Christians. He matters for the faith of individual Christians and for the church corporately. It is our hope that from this exchange, readers will learn more about Paul and learn more about what Paul means to other interpretive communities too. Mostly readers will probably come away agreeing with the words of 2 Peter that Paul's letters contain things that "are hard to understand" (2 Pet. 3:15). But hopefully, they will strive to think Paul's thoughts after him and to find a way that they can better appreciate the Messiah and Lord whom Paul himself served. And I also hope that readers will afterward ponder ways to "do what leads to peace and mutual edification" (Rom. 14:19), as Paul would no doubt have wanted people who read his letters to do.

Michael F. Bird

PAUL: A REFORMED READING

THOMAS R. SCHREINER

In this essay I will attempt to explain the framework of Pauline thought, his view of Jesus Christ, his theology of salvation, and his view of the church. Obviously, given the space constraints of the essay, I can only sketch Paul's thought in these areas. Therefore, my goal is to try to show inductively from his letters what he thought; interaction with other views will be kept to a minimum.[1]

The Pauline Framework

What framework should we use for reading Paul's theology? And how should we derive that framework? Some scholars have read Paul in Gnostic or Hellenistic terms. Both approaches, however, fail to read Paul within his own historical context. If we read Paul inductively, it is clear that his theology was formed by the Old Testament. Martin Hengel has demonstrated that Judaism in the Second Temple period was influenced significantly by Hellenism.[2] Such a judgment does not falsify the truth that the Old Testament fundamentally shaped Paul's understanding of his gospel. I am not arguing that Paul came to the Old Testament with a blank slate and concluded that Jesus was the Messiah.

---

1. I am assuming in this essay that all thirteen Pauline letters are authentic. The Pastorals, of course, are the first letters that have been doubted. In defense of authenticity, see William D. Mounce, *Pastoral Epistles* (WBC; Nashville: Nelson, 2000), xlvi–cxxix; George W. Knight III, *The Pastoral Epistles* (NIGTC; Grand Rapids: Eerdmans, 1992), 21–52; Gordon D. Fee, *1 and 2 Timothy, Titus* (NIBC; Peabody, MA: Hendrickson, 1988), 1–31.

2. Martin Hengel, *Judaism and Hellenism: Studies in Their Encounter in Palestine during the Early Hellenistic Period* (London: SCM, 1974).

He believed that Jesus was the Messiah only after encountering him on the Damascus Road[3] (Acts 9:1–19; Gal. 1:11–17). Certainly Paul's experience with Jesus provoked him to read the Old Testament in a new way. And yet Paul was also convinced that the Old Testament *should* be read as pointing to Jesus, so that those who failed to see that Jesus was the fulfillment of Old Testament prophecies were not merely intellectually deficient. Their sin blinded them from seeing the truth of the fulfillment of Old Testament prophecy (2 Cor. 4:4–6).

Paul believed, then, that the great events of Christ's ministry, death, and resurrection, and the pouring out of the Spirit fulfilled Old Testament prophecy. Yet this truth must be held in tension with another truth. Not only was prophecy fulfilled in the coming of Christ, but it was also the case that a mystery was revealed.[4] In Pauline terms a "mystery" is something previously hidden but is now revealed. The full significance and the implications of the work of Christ were not evident simply by reading the Old Testament. Every reader, according to Paul, should see that Christ is the fulfillment of the Old Testament Scriptures. At the same time there are dimensions of the fulfillment that occurred in Christ that are only plain retrospectively. Both prophecy and fulfillment and mystery and revelation must be correlated and held in tension when articulating Paul's understanding of the Old Testament.

If we reflect on some of the central promises in the Old Testament, Paul clearly sees them as fulfilled in his gospel. For instance, the Old Testament prophesied that all nations would be blessed in Abraham (Gen. 12:3; 18:18, etc.). Paul maintains that this promise has been fulfilled in his gospel inasmuch as the Gentiles are justified by faith (Gal. 3:6–8). The great liberation of Israel from Egypt took place in the exodus, and Isaiah (Isa. 11:11–15; 40:3–11; 42:16; 43:2, 5–7, 16–19; 48:20–21; 49:6–11; 51:10) and other prophets looked forward to a new exodus in which the Lord would liberate and free his people from their enemies. When Paul refers to the "redemption" accomplished by Christ,

---

3. Cf. here Seyoon Kim, *The Origin of Paul's Gospel* (Grand Rapids: Eerdmans, 1982).

4. For the working out of this theme in Pauline thought, see D. A. Carson, "Mystery and Fulfillment: Toward a More Comprehensive Paradigm of Paul's Understanding of the Old and New," in *The Paradoxes of Paul*, vol. 2 of *Justification and Variegated Nomism* (eds. D. A. Carson, Peter T. O'Brien, and Mark A. Seifrid; WUNT 181; Grand Rapids: Baker/Tübingen: Mohr Siebeck, 2004), 393–436.

he draws on exodus language, signifying that believers have been liberated by the cross of Christ (Rom. 3:24; Eph. 1:7; Col. 1:14). Paul specifically ties the liberation accomplished by Christ to exodus motifs in proclaiming that Christ as the Passover was sacrificed (1 Cor. 5:7). Similarly, the Old Testament animal sacrifices anticipate and find their consummation in Christ's sacrifice on the cross (Rom. 3:25; 8:3; Gal. 3:13; 2 Cor. 5:21). The sacrifice of the Servant of the Lord prophesied in Isaiah (Isa. 53:4, 11–12) has become a reality with the self-giving of Jesus Christ on the cross (Rom. 4:25; 1 Cor. 15:1–4).

The new exodus that was promised includes the promise of the resurrection—the final vindication of God's people (Isa. 26:19; Ezek. 37:1–14; Dan. 12:1–3). The resurrection, which signifies the arrival of the end, has irrupted into history with the resurrection of Jesus from the dead (Rom. 4:25; 8:11; 1 Cor. 6:14; 15:1–23; 2 Cor. 4:14). That resurrection is another way of saying that the new creation has dawned, which Isaiah prophesied (Isa. 65:17; 66:22). The advent of the new creation signifies that death and sin have been defeated. And Paul teaches that Christians now enjoy victory over sin and death since they have died with Christ and have risen with him (cf. Rom. 6:1–14; Eph. 2:5–6; Col. 2:12, 20; 3:1). Believers are now a new creation (2 Cor. 5:17), and the old era of the law no longer rules over them (Gal. 6:15).

The Pauline perspective on the law and the claim that believers are no longer under the law (cf. Rom. 6:14–15; Gal. 3:10, 22, 25; 4:3–5; 5:18) show that the new creation has been inaugurated and the promised new covenant of Jeremiah is a reality (Jer. 31:31–34). Believers are no longer under "the old covenant" (2 Cor. 3:14), for a new covenant has begun with the death of Christ (1 Cor. 11:25) and the gift of the Spirit (2 Cor. 3:6). Those who argue that believers must continue to subscribe to the Mosaic law have failed to see that a new age has come, so that they are content to live in the "present evil age" (Gal. 1:4).

To summarize the Pauline framework, the apostle teaches that the new exodus, the new covenant, and the new creation have arrived in Christ. But a crucial proviso must immediately be introduced. Even though the new age has been inaugurated in Jesus Christ, it has not been consummated. The eschatological tension in Paul's gospel returns us to the theme of a mystery fulfilled. It is not apparent in reading the Old Testament that the promise of salvation would be fulfilled in an already but not yet fashion. Hence, the resurrection and the new age have entered history through Christ's resurrection, and believers are raised with Christ spiritually. Nevertheless, believers still inhabit mortal bodies (Rom. 7:24; 8:10). Their future resurrection is certain because of Christ's resurrection (Rom. 8:11; 1 Cor. 6:14; 2 Cor. 4:14; 1 Thess. 4:14), and yet there is an interval between Christ's resurrection and the resurrection of believers (1 Cor. 15:23–28). The new creation has dawned in Christ, but the old creation continues (Rom. 8:18–25), so that believers long for the day when God will raise them from the dead and renew the created universe.

In the Old Testament the coming of the Spirit signifies the fulfillment of God's promises and the advent of the new creation (Isa. 32:15; 44:3; Ezek. 11:18–19; 36:26–27; Joel 2:28). No wonder the apostles in Acts correlated the baptism of the Spirit with the coming of the kingdom in its fullness (Acts 1:6). Paul, in particular, emphasizes that believers are people of the Spirit.[5] If one lacks the Spirit, one is not a Christian (Rom. 8:9). Circumcision is not necessary to belong to the people of God, for the gift of the Spirit removes any doubt about whether one is a believer (Gal. 3:2, 5). Nevertheless, the gift of the Spirit does not entail the immediate consummation of all that God has promised. The Spirit is the seal and guarantee that God will redeem his people by raising them from the dead (2 Cor. 1:21–22; Eph. 1:13–14). The Spirit is the firstfruits, certifying that God will complete his adopting work on the day of resurrection (Rom. 8:23). The Spirit, in other words, demonstrates that believers live between the times. The blessings of the new exodus, the new covenant, and the new creation are theirs, and yet they await the day when death will flee forever. One of Paul's fundamental frameworks, then, is the already but not yet character of his eschatology.

The Centrality of Jesus Christ

We can scarcely do justice to this theme in such a short essay, for surely Jesus Christ is the heart and soul of Pauline theology. Every topic discussed here is Christ-centered, whether it is the Pauline framework or his teaching on salvation and the church. My goal here is to unfold the

---

5. See Gordon D. Fee, *God's Empowering Presence: The Holy Spirit in the Letters of Paul* (Peabody, MA: Hendrickson, 1994).

many texts that present the supremacy of Jesus Christ. Indeed, readers who are accustomed to reading the New Testament may start looking past Jesus, simply because he is present so pervasively in the warp and woof of the text.

The centrality of Christ is evident in the sacraments and liturgy of early Christians. The initiation rite by which someone joined the Christian church is described as baptism into Christ (Rom. 6:3; Gal. 3:27), and baptism was administered in Christ's name (1 Cor. 1:13–17). In the same way, Christians regularly celebrated a meal together in which they recalled the death of Jesus on their behalf (1 Cor. 10:16–17; 11:23–26). They participated in the blessings of Jesus' death in partaking this meal together. When Christians gathered in worship, they sang to Jesus Christ as their Lord—an act of worship that showed Christ's incredibly high stature (Eph. 5:20). Furthermore, they gathered together as believers in his name (1 Cor. 5:4). Hymns and confessional statements were written in praise of Christ (Phil. 2:6–11; Col. 1:15–20; cf. Eph. 5:14; 1 Tim. 3:16). Prayers were offered to him, just as prayers were offered to God (2 Cor. 12:8–9). All these practices are commended by Paul, who was nurtured in the Old Testament Scriptures and affirmed that there was only one God (cf. 1 Cor. 8:5–6). Apparently, Paul did not believe that worshiping Jesus Christ as Lord compromised monotheism. We have here the raw materials from which the theology of the Trinity developed.

Other features in the text point to the centrality of Jesus. We have already seen that Paul's gospel stands in fulfillment of the Old Testament (Rom. 1:2), but this good news centers on Jesus, the Son of God (Rom. 1:3–4), who is the Davidic Messiah and the resurrected Lord. In the Philippian hymn (Phil. 2:6–11), Jesus is identified as "being in the form of God" (v. 6 ESV), which is explained in terms of being equal with God. By virtue of his incarnation and suffering on the cross, God has exalted him as Lord over all (vv. 9–11). It is remarkable that Paul alludes to Isaiah 45:23 here, where every knee bows before Yahweh and confesses his name. Paul applies these words to Jesus, showing that Jesus is equal to God. Furthermore, the Isaiah text (45:20–22) contains one of the strongest affirmations of monotheism in the entire Old Testament. It is hard to believe that Paul did not know what he was doing in identifying Jesus Christ as Lord in the same terms we find in Isaiah.

Paul's instructions in Romans 14 are enlightening, where he admonishes the weak and the strong regarding the eating of foods and the observance of days; he emphasizes that both are subject to the lordship of God and Christ. Most commentators acknowledge that some of the references to "Lord" in this text refer to Christ while others refer to God. Indeed, in some cases it is difficult to know whether God or Christ is intended. The ambiguity of the text is itself illuminating. Paul does not carefully distinguish between the lordship of God and Christ, which suggests that Jesus shares the same authority as God. This is scarcely surprising, for Paul describes his gospel in terms of proclaiming Jesus as Lord (2 Cor. 4:5). Those who confess Jesus as Lord will be saved (Rom. 10:9, 13), and only those who are moved by the Holy Spirit are enabled to recognize Jesus' lordship (1 Cor. 12:3).

Indeed, one's entire Christian life is to be lived under Jesus' lordship (Col. 2:6). That lordship is no abstraction. It relates to what one eats and drinks (Rom. 14) and to the sexual lives of believers (1 Thess. 4:3–8). Wives are to submit to their husbands "as ... to the Lord" (Eph. 5:22), and children are to obey their parents "in the Lord" (6:1). Indeed, believers are called upon to rejoice in Christ as Lord (Phil. 4:4), and hence every moment of life is to be lived out joyfully as a servant of Christ. There is no crook or cranny of life separated from the lordship of Christ, for we read in Col. 3:17, "And whatever you do, whether in word or deed, do it all in the name of the Lord Jesus, giving thanks to God the Father through him." This statement is remarkably astonishing (cf. Eph. 5:20). There is no corner of life, no word or action, that should be carried out apart from Christ. Everything should be done in his name.

This idea of doing everything in Jesus' "name" is important to note. The reference points to the Old Testament, where the "name" refers to Yahweh, the God of Israel and the whole earth. Hence, a reference to Jesus' name also points to his deity. Similarly, the most likely reading of Romans 1:5 is that the mission to the Gentiles is carried out for the sake of Jesus' name. The context of 10:13, which clearly features faith in Jesus Christ, teaches that the name people must call on to be saved is that of Jesus Christ, and yet this text is taken from Joel 2:32, which clearly says that one must call upon Yahweh to be saved. Such a reading fits with 1 Corinthians 1:2, where believers are described as those "who call on the name of the Lord Jesus" (cf. Cor. 6:11). I have already mentioned the

Philippian hymn, and it should be pointed out here that Jesus is given a name above any other (Phil. 2:9–10).

We can turn the kaleidoscope and look at the beauty and preciousness of Christ from another angle. When Paul considers Jesus Christ, he can conceive of nothing that can compare with knowing and following him (Phil. 3:7–9). All Paul's previous accomplishments do not hold any attraction and are dismissed as excrement in comparison to Christ. The devotion to Jesus by the early Christians was not academic or sterile. Paul reminds the Colossians that "Christ ... is your life" (Col. 3:4). These words immediately call to mind Philippians 1:21, where Paul says, "For to me, to live is Christ and to die is gain." Loving Christ is not merely a duty; it brings intense pleasure, and it motivated early Christians even to die for his sake.

Paul's message in Colossians is significant in this regard. Apparently, outside teachers were promoting a variant teaching that promised fullness and completeness. There is no need to discern here the nature of the teaching that so attracted the Colossians, though a fascination with angels and asceticism seems be included (Col. 1:16; 2:10, 16–23). Paul counters by heralding the centrality and supremacy of Jesus Christ. He is "the image of the invisible God" (Col. 1:15; cf. 2 Cor. 4:4), and the sovereign ruler ("firstborn") over all creation. Any idea that Jesus is a created being is ruled out, for he is the creator of all (Col. 1:16), including those angels that so entranced those who promoted the deviant philosophy. Christ Jesus is sovereign over all, and all of creation coheres through him (1:17). Jesus is not only Lord over creation, but he is also Lord over the church, exercising his sovereignty over it as its head (1:18). For it is God's will that he have "supremacy" over all. That supremacy is rooted in who he is: "all [God's] fullness" dwells in him (1:19). It is also rooted in what he has done: he has accomplished reconciliation through the cross (1:20).

The Colossians were tempted to find sufficiency outside of Christ, seeing wisdom and power elsewhere, and hence Paul affirms that "all the treasures of wisdom and knowledge" are in Christ (Col. 2:3). The so-called knowledge and wisdom of the opponents were no wisdom at all, for it was "not according to Christ" (2:8 ESV). Since all the fullness of God dwells in Christ (2:9), the Colossians are filled in him (2:10). The deity of Christ is not an abstract doctrine for Paul here; the

Colossians have everything they need in Christ. Becoming entranced with foods and ascetic regulations may appear to be the path to spirituality, but these things are the "shadow" and Christ is the "reality" (2:17). Those who get distracted by such rules fail to hold fast to Christ as the head (2:19). In the new people of God one's social status or ethnic background is irrelevant, for "Christ is all, and is in all" (3:11).

The Corinthians were divided over preachers like Paul and Apollos (1 Cor. 1:10–17; 3:5–9; 4:1–6), assessing them on the basis of their wisdom. The reference to "wisdom" probably refers to the rhetorical ability of Paul and Apollos (1:17; 2:4). What was the antidote to their futile and vain discussions on wisdom? Paul reminds the Corinthians of the significance of Christ crucified (1:17). Those who grasp the meaning of the cross perceive in it the wisdom and power of God (1:18–25). This is why Paul centered on the message of the cross when in Corinth: "I resolved to know nothing while I was with you except Jesus Christ and him crucified" (2:2).

We can read Galatians in similar terms. Outside teachers were insisting that the Galatians get circumcised to become part of God's people (Gal. 5:2–4; 6:12–13; cf. 2:3–5). Paul could have responded in a number of ways. Presumably he could have dismissed the call to be circumcised by pointing out that the Galatians were baptized and that the latter sign replaced the former. Interestingly, Paul does not make this argument. Instead, he focuses on the death of Christ throughout the letter. By demanding circumcision the opponents have neglected or failed to see the significance of the cross. Christ by his death has delivered believers from "the present evil age" (1:4), and if they submit to circumcision, they will be reverting to the age that is passing away. Hence, the letter is framed by the cross, for Paul concludes with the call to boast only in the cross and in the new creation (6:14–15). Those who attempt to be righteous by circumcision teach that Christ died for nothing (2:21) and must have had a spell cast over them, for they have forgotten the significance of the cross (3:1).

The curse of the law is only removed through Christ's death on behalf of his people (Gal. 3:13) since no one does what the law commands (3:10). Jesus by his death has liberated those who were under the law and freed them from bondage (4:4–5). Therefore, there is no compromise. It is either Christ or circumcision (5:2), for justification through Christ is incompatible with justification through the law (5:4). Thus, the rumor that Paul preaches circumcision can be confidently rejected since Paul is persecuted because of his proclamation of the cross (5:11; 6:17).

How does Christ relate to the framework articulated in the first section of this essay? Clearly Jesus Christ fulfills Old Testament prophecy. But the mystery of God's will also centers on Christ, for it was God's purpose to unite all things in history in Christ (Eph. 1:9–10). The Christ was prophesied in the Old Testament, but the full significance of his work was hidden and is apparent only now that the fulfillment has come.

Paul's View of Salvation

In considering Paul's view of salvation, it is important to recall the framework set forth above. The saving work of God in Christ is a prophecy fulfilled and a mystery revealed. Another way of saying this is that there is an already but not yet character to the salvation accomplished by Christ. It almost goes without saying, but it must be said, that this salvation is also Christ-centered. Therefore, the Pauline framework and Paul's Christology play a major role in articulating the Pauline view of salvation.

Paul's View of Sin and Judgment

Before we can speak of salvation, however, we must discern why salvation is needed. Paul's answer is that human beings need to be saved from sin and from the judgment and wrath of God on the last day. A clear profile of Paul's theology of salvation can only be obtained by discerning what believers need to be saved from. Paul teaches that a final judgment is impending. God will assess all human beings on the final day according to what they have done (Rom. 2:6; 2 Cor. 5:10; 11:15; Eph. 6:8; Col. 3:25; 2 Tim. 4:14). Since God judges on the basis of works, his judgment is fair and impartial (Rom. 2:11). Those who do what is good will be vindicated, but those who practice evil will face his wrath and suffer distress forever (2:7–10). Those who transgress the Mosaic law will be judged on the basis of that law, and those who violate the law inscribed on their hearts will perish because of their failure to keep moral norms mediated through their conscience (2:12–16).

Jews who rely on circumcision for covenantal protection will not enjoy any advantage on the day of judgment, for transgression nullifies any shelter that circumcision might afford on the final day (Rom. 2:25–27). Similarly, Paul affirms in Galatians that those who practice "the acts of the flesh" will not inherit God's kingdom (Gal. 5:19–21). "Wrongdoers will not inherit the kingdom of God" (1 Cor. 6:9), and Paul proceeds to list vices that exclude one from the kingdom (6:9–10). A retribution that fits with what has been done is also evident in the assertion that those who sow to the flesh will reap eschatological corruption (Gal. 6:8). Those who are enemies of the cross will face eschatological destruction, for their god is their own appetite (Phil. 3:18–19; cf. 1 Tim. 6:9).

God's wrath is not exclusively eschatological. His wrath is expressed in his handing human beings over to the wide array of sins that blight human existence (Rom. 1:18, 24, 26, 28). Nor will it do to say that God's wrath can be limited merely to cause and effect. Such a view of God's wrath accords with modern Western sensibilities but does not reflect the biblical witness. Paul was tutored in the Old Testament, and it is clear from the Old Testament itself that God's wrath was his personal anger against sin (cf. Ex. 22:23–24; 32:10–11; Lev. 10:1–2, 6; Num. 16:45; Ps. 90:7–11, etc.). Wrath is God's personal, holy, and settled response to human sin, reflecting God's holiness and goodness in his opposition to evil. A deistic god that merely operates in terms of cause and effect strays severely from the biblical witness.

The wrath experienced by human beings now (Rom. 1:18–32) is a prelude to the wrath that will be unleashed on the day of judgment (2:5; 1 Thess. 1:10; 5:9). God will pour out his wrath on the last day on those who practice evil (Rom. 2:8). The final day will unveil his righteous judgment against sin (2:5). His wrath falls on those who practice evil and refuse to repent (Eph. 5:6; Col. 3:6). Human beings are by birth destined for wrath (Eph. 2:3). The notion that human beings are children of wrath fits with what Paul writes elsewhere. In Romans 5:12–19 sin and death are traced to Adam. Because of the one trespass of Adam all people die both physically and spiritually (5:15, 17). Condemnation is the portion of all because of Adam's one sin (5:16, 18). All without exception have become sinners because of Adam's sin (5:19).

What we have said about God's retributive judgment against sin is also communicated in 2 Thessalonians 1:5–9. Here Paul teaches that God's judgment is just and righteous. For God to "pay back [a very retributive word! *antapodounai*] trouble to those who trouble you" is "just" (v. 6). When will this just retribution take place? It will occur at the second coming of Christ, "when the Lord Jesus is revealed from heaven in blazing fire with his powerful angels" (v. 7). What will the punishment be? "He will punish those who do not know God and do not obey the gospel of our Lord Jesus" (v. 8). The word "punish" comes from the Greek word *ekdikēsis*, which has the same root as the word for "just" (*dikaios*) in v. 6. God's punishment on the disobedient, then, is an expression of his justice. The judgment is fierce since Jesus comes "in blazing fire" (v. 7). And what is the punishment to be exacted? "They will be punished with everlasting destruction and shut out from the presence of the Lord and from the glory of his might" (v. 9). The judgment is forever. They will be excluded from the Lord's presence permanently. Again, we should note that Paul emphasizes the justice of what God does in Christ. The word rendered by the NIV as "punished" (*dikē*) has the same root as the word "just" (v. 6) and "punish" (v. 8). The eternal punishment of the wicked is retributive and just.

The just judgment of God awaits all who do not repent and who fail to place their trust in Jesus Christ, for "all have sinned and fall short of the glory of God" (Rom. 3:23). No one (except for Jesus Christ, 2 Cor. 5:21) stands as an exception. Paul argues in Romans 3:9–18 that sin is universal, that no one is righteous, that "there is no one who seeks God" (v. 11), that "there is no one who does good, not even one" (v. 12). The law does not provide any help. Because of human transgression "every mouth" is "silenced" and all stand guilty before God (3:19). No one is vindicated before God by "works of the law," for all fail to practice what the law demands (3:20).[6] The law uncovers human sin (3:20), confirming that "every human being [is] a liar" (3:4).

What Paul concludes in Romans 3:9–20 about human sinfulness fits with the burden of his argument in 1:18–2:29. God's wrath is reserved even for those who are not familiar with the Mosaic law, for

---

6. Scholars have disputed vigorously what is meant by "works of law." I argue that it refers to all the deeds or actions commanded by the law. See Thomas R. Schreiner, "'Works of the Law' in Paul," *NovT* 33 (1991): 217–44.

all people understand via the created world that God exists and that he is supreme so that he deserves honor and praise (1:19–25). Unbelievers despise God's majesty and refuse to thank and glorify him, committing the fundamental sin of exalting the creature over the Creator. In Romans 2, as we have seen, Paul argues that even those who know God's law are not in a better position, for they have failed to keep the law they treasure and teach (cf. 2:21–22).

Is there a fly in the ointment in Romans 2? Doesn't Paul also refer to those who keep the law so that he contradicts the idea that all without exception are sinners (2:7, 10, 13–15, 27–29)? Space forbids tackling this question in detail.[7] Many scholars argue that the obedience described here is hypothetical; if that is the case, then no exception is contemplated. It seems more probable that Paul thinks of a genuine obedience here, but that obedience is the work of the Holy Spirit in those who have confessed Jesus as the Christ (2:28–29). Paul foreshadows here one of the main themes in Romans (7:6; 8:1–17). But if this latter interpretation is correct, the universality of human sin is not contradicted either. Those who have been transformed by the Holy Spirit entered the world as sinners. They did not come into the world as men and women of the Spirit; they received the Spirit when they confessed that Jesus is Lord (1 Cor. 2:6–16; 12:3).

The universality of sin is also taught in Galatians 3:10: "For as many as are of the works of the Law are under a curse; for it is written, 'Cursed is everyone who does not abide by all things written in the book of the law, to perform them'" (NASB). The meaning of the verse (like everything else in Paul!) is disputed. I would suggest, however, that the meaning is accessible. Why does a curse come for those who are of the works of the law? The curse is inflicted on those who do not comply with everything written in the law. The implied premise is that no one does what the law demands. This premise is not surprising, for Paul does not write like a professional philosopher by including every premise in his argument.

Indeed, the idea that all without exception are sinners is clear from the Old Testament (1 Kings 8:46; Ps. 143:2; Prov. 20:9; Eccl. 7:20). Nor will it do to say that Paul could not be demanding perfect obedience here since forgiveness was available for those who offered sacrifices in

---

7. See Thomas R. Schreiner, "Did Paul Believe in Justification by Works? Another Look at Romans 2," *BBR* 3 (1993): 131–58.

the Old Testament. That is precisely Paul's point! Those who rely on the law cannot appeal to Old Testament sacrifices for forgiveness now that Christ has come and atoned for sin (Gal. 3:13). If they rely on the law for atonement, they repudiate the sacrifice of Christ and end up saying that Christ died for nothing (2:21). Since Old Testament sacrifices no longer atone for sins, those who turn to the law for salvation must keep its prescriptions perfectly, which is impossible (cf. 5:3).

The pervasiveness of human sin is a regular theme in Paul's letters. We are not surprised to find that sin is described as a power that rules over human beings (Rom. 5:21). Before conversion human beings are slaves to sin (6:6) so that they are under its dominion and tyranny (6:17, 20). The law, which was in one sense designed to give life (7:10), has ended up bringing death (7:5, 9, 11), for sin drew the law into its orbit and used the law for its own ends. Human beings in Adam are "sold as a slave to sin" (7:14) and are "prisoner[s] of the law of sin" within them (7:23). Those who are "in the flesh" lack the Holy Spirit and hence do not belong to God's people (8:9).

The natural person cannot and does not welcome the things of the Holy Spirit (1 Cor. 2:14). Only those who receive the Spirit understand and accept the things of the Spirit (2:6–16; cf. 12:3). Those who are in the flesh and part of the old Adam do not and *cannot* keep God's law (Rom. 8:7). As Paul says, "those who are in the flesh cannot please God" (8:8 ESV). The utter inability of human beings shows the radical evil of human beings, for they are dead in trespasses and sin (Eph. 2:1, 5; Col. 2:13).

Some object that such a view does not make any sense. How can God command people to keep his law and to repent and believe when they are utterly unable to do so? Our first task is to explain Paul, even if his worldview is foreign to ours. We must beware of conforming him to our worldview and of only accepting what seems civilized and sensible to us. Paul teaches that people should refrain from sin even if they are unable to do so as sons and daughters of Adam. According to Paul, moral responsibility must not be tied to moral inability.[8] This too is part of the scandal of the gospel.

---

8. Jonathan Edwards make this argument effectively in his classic work, *The Freedom of the Will*. See Jonathan Edwards, *Freedom of the Will* (ed. by Paul Ramsey; New Haven, CT: Yale Univ. Press, 1957).

God's Saving Work in Christ

According to Paul, no one deserves to be saved. God would be just in excluding everyone from his presence forever (2 Thess. 1:9). But God is not only just; he is also loving. Because of his great love he saves human beings (Eph. 2:4). God's love is demonstrated supremely in the cross of Christ, for Christ died for those who were morally weak and ungodly, for sinners and enemies of God (Rom. 5:6–10; cf. 2 Cor. 5:14). Christ revealed his love for sinners by giving his life for them on the cross (Gal. 2:20; Eph. 5:2; cf. Eph. 5:25).[9] Paul emphasizes over and over that this love is undeserved.

Here, then, is one of the key words in Paul's theology: grace. Grace means that the salvation believers enjoy is a stunning gift. Paul's theology is nicely summed up in the phrase "by grace you have been saved" (Eph. 2:5, 8). He repeats this twice in a short compass to underline how amazing God's love is. As Paul says in Eph. 2:8, salvation "is the gift of God." Similarly, he affirms that justification is "by his grace" (Rom. 3:24; Titus 3:7). Salvation is not based on human obedience but depends entirely on God's grace (Rom. 4:16; 11:6; Gal. 2:21; Eph. 2:8). Everything believers end up accomplishing is by the grace of God (1 Cor. 15:10), and so they will praise God for his grace for all eternity (Eph. 2:7).

Paul especially emphasizes God's mercy (Rom. 9:16, 18, 23; cf. Eph. 2:4) and love (Rom. 9:13; Eph. 1:4–5; Col. 3:12; 2 Thess. 2:13) in electing people to salvation. Paul's teaching on election accords with his view of the evil of human beings. Human beings have no natural desire to turn to God and to repent of their sins. And they are unable to be saved by their works, for they do what is evil. Hence, Paul's theology of election, as Luther, Zwingli, and Calvin all taught, is tied irretrievably to the truth that human beings cannot be right with God by works (Rom. 9:11–13; 11:6; cf. Eph. 2:4–9). Election trumpets the truth that salvation is of the Lord. Election in Christ (Eph. 1:4), therefore, is "to the praise of his glorious grace" (1:6).

Paul is not interested in election for speculative or philosophical reasons. Election testifies that salvation is entirely the Lord's work, so that salvation is a matter of grace, not works. Hence all the praise and honor

---

9. The Father and the Son worked in concert in the Son's giving of his life. The Son was not forced by the Father to die for sinners.

go to God for salvation. Clearly, Paul does not believe that all without exception are saved (cf. Rom. 2:8–9; 3:5–6; 5:9; 6:23; 9:22; 1 Cor. 1:18; 9:24–10:12; 2 Cor. 2:15–16; Gal. 1:8–9; 5:21; 6:7–8; Eph. 5:5–6; 2 Thess. 1:5–10, etc.), so all are not elect (Rom. 9:13, 22–23). What amazes Paul, however, is that any are saved, since salvation stems from the tender mercy of God. Since he views God's election as a stunning act of undeserved love, not as a debt owed to human beings, he never ceases praising God for his electing grace.

The grace of God in Pauline theology is particularly manifested in the cross. I have already noted that in the cross God's love for sinners is displayed. The Pauline view of salvation is multifaceted, and it cannot be exhausted by one metaphor. Nor is it possible here to comment on every term or metaphor Paul uses to describe the salvation accomplished in Jesus Christ. It includes, among other truths: salvation, justification, reconciliation, redemption, sanctification, triumph over evil powers, and adoption. All of these blessings are secured in the cross of Jesus Christ.

How does the cross of Christ effect salvation? Christ died "for [*hyper*] the ungodly" (Rom. 5:6) and "for [*hyper*] us" (5:8). The idea that Christ gave his life "for" (*hyper*) his people or for our sins is a staple of Paul's theology (Rom. 8:32; 14:15; 1 Cor. 1:13; 11:24; 15:3; 2 Cor. 5:14–15, 21; Gal. 1:4; 2:20; 3:13; Eph. 5:2, 25; 1 Thess. 5:10; 1 Tim. 2:6; Titus 2:14). Clearly, Christ's death was for the benefit of his people. But how? In some of these texts sacrificial language is used. Justification is accomplished through Jesus' "blood" (Rom. 5:9; cf. 3:25). The Lord's Supper celebrates Jesus' self-offering in his blood (1 Cor. 11:25, 27; cf. 10:16). Jesus' death for the sake of his people is described as an "offering and sacrifice to God" (Eph. 5:2). It is most likely that the texts that describe Jesus' death "for" his people signify both representation and substitution. Jesus died as the representative of and substitute for his people. Those who put their faith in him are spared from the punishment they deserve.

That Paul thinks in terms of substitution (indeed of penal substitution) is suggested by the many statements that Christ died "for" believers or for sinners. The most natural way to take those texts is to read them to say that Christ died in our place. It is also the case, however, that Christ's substitutionary work is particularly emphasized in some crucial texts in his letters. One such text is Galatians 3:10–13. We have already seen from 3:10 that those who attempt to be right with God by works of law are cursed since God demands perfect obedience. How is the curse removed? Paul explains in 3:13, "Christ redeemed us from the curse of the law by becoming a curse for us." Though many interpreters try to explain it away, the substitutionary character of what Christ has accomplished is evident. Those who belong to Christ are liberated from the curse they deserved because Christ took the curse (the penalty!) in their place.

The substitutionary character of Paul's theology of the cross is also taught in 2 Corinthians 5:21: "God made him who had no sin to be sin for us, so that in him we might become the righteousness of God." Here we have the great exchange where Christ was made sin "for us" (*hyper hēmōn*), and believers partake of God's righteousness by virtue of their union with Christ. Substitution certainly seems to be involved here, for the sin that belonged to believers was placed on Christ and the righteousness that belonged to Christ (he "had no sin") is given to believers.

Romans 3:25–2 and 8:3 should also be interpreted along substitutionary lines. We saw above that God's wrath (1:18) and righteous judgment (2:5; 3:5) are directed against all people without exception because of human sin (1:18–3:20; 3:23). How can God's wrath be averted and sin be forgiven? Paul answers that question in Romans 3:25–26 by picking up sacrificial and atonement language from the Old Testament. He uses both *hilastērion* ("mercy seat" KJV; "atonement cover" NIV) and *haima* ("blood")—terms used frequently in Leviticus 16, which is the great Day of Atonement text in the Old Testament. If the blood were not properly applied during the atonement rituals, God's wrath would be manifested. Indeed, Leviticus is clear that blood signifies the surrendering of one's life by which atonement is secured (Lev. 17:10–11).

So too, Jesus' blood has secured forgiveness of sins, and Jesus' sacrifice is the "place" where God manifests his mercy to his people. His blood was shed instead of theirs. God's righteous wrath was poured out on Jesus (Rom. 3:25–26) instead of on believers. According to 8:3, God condemned sin in the flesh of Jesus because he gave himself as a sin offering. The words translated "for sin" in the ESV (*peri hamartias*) almost certainly refers to the Old Testament sin offering (cf. NIV 2011), for the phrase has that meaning forty-four out of fifty-four times it occurs in the Old Testament.[10] Once again we have a clear instance of substitution, for God condemned the sin of human beings in the flesh of Jesus. Hence, it seems clear that he took their sin on himself and bore the penalty they deserved.

The focus on God's grace, election, and the work of Christ on the cross does not rule out human response. In order to be saved, human beings must repent (Rom. 2:4) and believe in Jesus Christ. God's gracious election *secures* such a response in those whom God has chosen, but it does not make such a response unnecessary. Paul was not interested in providing a philosophical defense of how divine sovereignty correlates with human responsibility. We see in Romans 9–11 that he clearly teaches both. All those whom God elected will be saved, and yet human beings must and should believe in the gospel. Those who refuse to believe are held morally responsible, for they should believe.

What must be emphasized here is that Paul regularly teaches that human beings must believe in Jesus Christ to be saved. In recent years scholars have debated intensely whether the phrase *pistis Iēsou Christou* (e.g., Rom. 3:22, 26; Gal. 2:16; 3:22; Phil. 3:9)[11] refers to *faith in Christ* (objective genitive) or the *faithfulness of Christ* (subjective genitive).[12] I would argue for the former interpretation for the following reasons.

1. An objective reading is the most natural reading of the genitive "God" in Mark 11:22 (cf. also Jas. 2:1), so that the text should be translated, "Have faith in God."

2. A genitive object with other verbal nouns shows that an objective genitive with the verbal noun "faith" is normal grammatically: e.g., "knowledge of Christ Jesus" (*tēs gnōseōs Christou Iēsou*, Phil. 3:8 ESV). Just as Christ Jesus is the object of knowledge, so too he is the object of faith. Therefore, those who claim that the genitive *must* be subjective grammatically fail to convince.

---

10. For further discussion, see Thomas R. Schreiner, *Romans* (BECNT; Grand Rapids: Eerdmans, 1998), 402–4.

11. The phrase is not exactly the same in all these passages. I use the phrase above for convenience.

12. See the recent collection of essays on the topic, *The Faith of Jesus Christ: Exegetical, Biblical, and Theological Studies* (ed. Michael F. Bird and Preston Sprinkle; Peabody, MA: Hendrickson, 2009).

3. The texts that use the verb "believe" in a verbal construction and the noun "faith" with the genitive are not superfluous (e.g., Rom. 3:22; Gal. 2:16; 3:22) but emphatic, stressing the importance of faith to be right with God. Readers hearing the letter read aloud would pick up on the emphasis on faith in Christ, and thus this interpretation is to be preferred as the simpler of the two options.

4. Paul often contrasts human works and human faith in his theology. Therefore, seeing a polarity between works of law and faith in Christ—both *human activities*—fits with what Paul does elsewhere.

5. By contrast, nowhere else does Paul in speaking of Jesus Christ use the word "faith" (*pistis*) to describe his "obedience." There is not a single indisputable example.

6. Galatians 3:23, 25 refers to the coming of faith at a certain time in redemptive history. But such an observation hardly excludes faith in Christ, for faith in Christ becomes a reality when he arrives and fulfills God's saving promises. We should not pit redemptive history against anthropology.

7. Nor is the emphasis on faith in Christ somehow Pelagian, as if it detracts from God's work in salvation. A human response of faith does not undercut the truth that God saves, particularly if God grants faith to his own (Eph. 2:8–9).

The salvation Jesus accomplished fulfills Old Testament prophecy that the Lord would save his people, but we also have a mystery revealed here, for the saving work of Christ has an already but not yet character. I have used salvation as a general term to describe Paul's soteriology, but more technically the word denotes the rescue God accomplishes for his people. Paul often uses words denoting rescue and deliverance to denote what God will do in the *future*. Those who are *now* justified and reconciled through the death of Christ will be saved from the wrath of God on the final day of judgment (Rom. 5:9–10; cf. 13:14; 1 Thess. 1:10; 2 Tim. 4:18). Those who persevere in godly behavior and apostolic teaching will be saved on the last day (1 Tim. 2:15; 4:16). At the same time salvation can be described as a past reality. Believers are already saved by grace through faith (Eph. 2:5, 8; cf. 2 Tim. 1:5; Titus 3:5). The present participles in 1 Corinthians 1:18 and 2 Corinthians 2:15 also suggest that believers are in the process of being saved. Salvation, then, has an already but not yet character. Believers have already been saved, and yet they await the completion of their salvation on the final day.

Every dimension of the salvation Christ accomplished can be described in already but not yet terms. Here I will comment briefly on some of the features of Christ's saving work, noting the pervasiveness of inaugurated eschatology. Believers have been redeemed by the work of Christ on the cross (Rom. 3:24; Eph. 1:7; Col. 1:14), and yet they await the final redemption of their bodies on the day of resurrection (Rom. 8:23; Eph. 4:30). Believers are now in the realm of the holy ("sanctified") in Christ (1 Cor. 1:30; 6:11), but the consummation of sanctification awaits them (Eph. 5:26; 1 Thess. 5:23). Similarly, the theme of *Christus Victor* is prominent in Paul. Christ has triumphed over the devil and demonic powers through his work on the cross (Eph. 1:20–22; 4:8; Col. 1:20; 2:10, 15), but believers are still engaged in a conflict against demonic powers (Eph. 6:10–17) and await the day when Satan will be crushed forever (Rom. 16:20).

The Pauline theology of justification warrants more discussion since it continues to be controversial. The forensic and legal character of the term "justify" (*dikaioō*) derives from the verbal form of "justify" (*ṣdq*) in the Old Testament. Judges are to declare the righteous innocent and condemn the wicked (Deut. 25:1; cf. 2 Sam. 5:4; 1 Kings 8:31–32; 2 Chron. 6:23; Prov. 17:15; Isa. 5:23). Judges do not "make" anyone righteous. They pronounce on what is in fact the case — if they are righteous judges. In other words, the verbal form belongs in the forensic realm. For example, God will pass judgment on whether Paul is acquitted before the Lord on judgment day (1 Cor. 4:4). When Paul says the doers of the law will be justified (Rom 2:13), a declaration of righteousness is intended. God will pass judgment as to whether people are righteous, that is, as to whether they have done what is right and good. If they have lived righteously, according to Romans 2:13, he will declare them to be righteous.

Paul astonishes us, for he teaches that God declares those who are sinners to be in the right before him if they trust in Jesus Christ for their salvation. This is extraordinary because such a verdict violates the normal and just procedure for a judge. Judges who declare the guilty to be righteous violate the standards of justice. Paul, of course, does not think God violates any standard of justice, for Christ bears the curse that sinners deserved (Gal. 3:10–13), as we explained briefly above. Four other arguments support a forensic reading.

1. The law court background of "justify" is clear in Romans 8:33: "Who will bring any charge against those whom God has chosen? It is God who justifies." On the last day some may bring charges before God's chosen at the divine tribunal, but all charges will be dismissed because God has declared believers to be in the right before him. As the judge, he has declared that they are innocent of all accusations.

2. Paul often says that human beings are righteous by faith (e.g., Rom. 1:17; 3:22, 26; 4:3, 5, 9, 13; 9:30; 10:4; Gal. 2:16; 3:6, 11; 5:5; Phil. 3:9). In such contexts Paul contrasts righteousness by faith with righteousness by works. Righteousness by faith refers to the *gift* of righteousness given to human beings by God. Human beings are not righteous by virtue of doing but of believing. The righteousness given to them, then, is alien since it is not based on anything they have done but on God's work in Christ. This suggests that righteousness as a gift is granted to those who believe.

3. That righteousness is a forensic declaration is also supported by the link between righteousness and forgiveness. Paul slides easily from justification to forgiveness in Romans 4:1–8. David's forgiveness of sins is another way of speaking of his justification — his being in the right before God (4:6–8). The idea is not that David is transformed by God; the text calls attention to David's sin and his forgiveness by God, for he blots out his sins and declares him to be in the right.

4. The idea that righteousness is counted (*logizomai*) to believers indicates that righteousness is not native to human beings, that it is granted to them by God (Rom. 3:28; 4:3–6, 8–11, 22–24; 9:8; Gal. 3:6). This argument is strengthened when we add that righteousness is counted to those who believe — not to those who work. God does not "count" sins against those who have put their faith in Christ (2 Cor. 5:19). This is a strange reckoning or

counting indeed when those who have done evil are considered to be righteous. This fits with the notion, however, that believers have received "the free gift of righteousness" (Rom. 5:17).

Believers are righteous because they are united to Christ in both his death and his resurrection.[13] Because they are in Christ, they now enjoy the same vindication that Jesus enjoyed when God raised him from the dead (1 Tim. 3:16).

Is forensic righteousness a legal fiction? Certainly not. For God's verdict always creates reality, and so believers really are righteous since Christ, with whom they are united by faith, is their righteousness (1 Cor. 1:30). Paul typically uses righteousness to denote the standing believers already enjoy before God (cf. Rom. 5:1), but it also has an eschatological character (Gal. 5:5). The righteousness believers enjoy now is one that is grasped by faith. It is hidden from the world and is not visible to believers, but on the last day God will announce to the world those who are righteous, so that what is hidden will be revealed eschatologically.

Many objections have been raised against such a reading of forensic righteousness in Paul. Here I pause to answer only one. How does it account for ethics and life in the Spirit? The first thing that must be said is that the Pauline teaching on salvation must not be restricted to justification. Even if justification cannot be defined as the transformation of the sinner, it does not follow that there is no ethical transformation. One of the common false paths in Pauline theology is the attempt to derive all of his theology from justification. Justification is crucial in his thought, to be sure, especially since it explains how one can be right with God. It is a mistake, however, to conclude that the whole of Paul's soteriology is encompassed by justification. Paul also describes God's saving act in Christ as redemption, reconciliation, sanctification, transformation, adoption, victory over evil powers, and so on. We must guard against a one-dimensional reading of Paul that restricts his theology to one metaphor.

I would also suggest that Paul's argument in Romans itself supports the reading offered here. His opponents worried that the Pauline

---

13. See especially here Michael F. Bird, *The Saving Righteousness of God: Studies on Paul, Justification, and the New Perspective* (Eugene, OR: Wipf & Stock, 2007), 40–59.

theology of justification would lead to a life of license (Rom. 6:1). It is hard to see how they would think this if Paul's theology of justification emphasized the transformation of the sinner. The radical and gracious message that sinners and the ungodly are counted as righteous (4:5) caused them to worry that the Pauline gospel led to libertinism. Paul does not respond in Romans 6 by saying that righteousness actually means the transformation of the sinner. Instead, he argues that those who are righteous are also united with Christ in his death and resurrection. Believers are no longer slaves to sin (6:6). They are now enabled to live in a new way that pleases God.

There is a danger of defining words in Paul so that no distinction exists. All those who are justified are also transformed by God's grace, but it does not follow from this that the word justification means transformation. So too, all those who are justified are sanctified, but the words justification and sanctification do not mean the same thing. Justification is inseparable from life and the Spirit, and indeed is the foundation for such a life, but justification is still distinguishable from life in the Spirit. Paul argues in Romans 6, therefore, that all who are justified are also united with Christ and are no longer subject to the dominion and mastery of sin. Similarly, Romans 8 is clear that those who are justified also enjoy life in the Spirit. God gives his Spirit to those whom he has declared to stand in the right before him.

Justification, then, is God's free gift and is not based on human works or righteousness (Rom. 3:20, 28; 4:1–8; Gal. 2:16; 3:10–11; Titus 3:5). But all those who are justified will do good works (Rom. 2:7, 10; 8:13–16; 1 Cor. 6:9–11; 2 Cor. 5:10; Gal. 5:19–23; 6:8, etc.). Indeed, they must do good works. If good works are lacking, one will not inherit the eschatological kingdom. Hence, good works are not optional; they are necessary to receive eternal life. But we have already seen that such good works are not the basis of justification. It is probably best to say that the good works constitute necessary evidence that one is justified.

Paul's teaching on justification must not be read, then, as if it is the whole of his theology. God's free grace in Christ is foundational for Paul's gospel, and the forgiveness of sins never becomes a past reality since believers continue to sin until death. Nevertheless, there is also transformation by the Spirit (2 Cor. 3:18) for those who belong to Christ, and we are not surprised to learn that such transformation comes from beholding the beauty of Christ.

The Pauline Vision of the Church

Paul appropriates terms from the Old Testament to describe the people of God in the New Testament. For instance, the word "church" (*ekklēsia*, e.g., 1 Cor. 1:1; 10:32; 11:22; 2 Cor. 1:1; 1 Thess. 2:14) derives from the Old Testament, where the people of Israel were the "assembly of Yahweh" (*qāhāl yhwh*, Num. 16:3; 20:4; Deut. 23:1, 8; 1 Chron. 28:8, etc.) or "the assembly of Israel" (*qāhāl Yisrael*, Exod. 12:6; Lev. 16:17; Num. 14:5, etc.). Such appropriation suggests that it is fitting to say that the church of Jesus Christ is the "true" Israel for Paul.

Paul's response to the Galatians' opponents also fits with the church being the true Israel. Physical circumcision does not qualify one for salvation. Indeed, if one insists that circumcision is necessary for salvation (Gal. 2:3–5; 5:2–4; 6:12–13), then one proclaims a false gospel and stands under God's curse (*anathema*, 1:6–9). In Galatians Paul replaces circumcision, which was the initiation rite into Israel, with the cross of Christ (cf. 1:4; 2:21; 3:1, 13; 4:4–5; 5:11, 24; 6:12–14, 17). Hence, God's people consists of those who are truly circumcised, that is, those who trust in the cross of Christ for salvation instead of their obedience of the law.

The spiritual character of circumcision is more explicit in Philippians. The circumcision of the opponents is comparable to pagan mutilation (*katatomē*), which is surely one of the most shocking things Paul ever wrote. Those who are truly circumcised do not boast in themselves but worship in the Spirit and boast in Christ Jesus (Gal. 3:2–3). Similarly, we find in Colossians 2:11–12 that true circumcision is spiritual rather than physical, being rooted in Christ's work on the cross. Since those who trust in Christ's atoning work and worship in the Holy Spirit are truly circumcised (the entrance rite into the people of God), it seems legitimate to conclude that the church is the true Israel of God.

Such a judgment is confirmed by another theme related to circumcision in the argument of Galatians. The agitators insisted that one must be circumcised to be part of Abraham's family. In other words, one had to join the people of Israel to be a child of Abraham. Paul counters that the true children of Abraham are those who have the same faith as Abraham (Gal. 3:6–9). The blessing of Abraham is reserved, not for those who try to observe the law, but for those who trust in the work of Jesus Christ (3:10–14). All who belong to Christ through baptism and faith are the true offspring of Abraham (3:26–29).[14]

Indeed, Paul makes it clear in Romans 9:6–9 that being mere physical descendents from Abraham does not make one a true child of Abraham. Indeed, ethnic Jews who fail to believe in Jesus are not saved (9:30–10:21, esp. 10:1) and hence do not belong to God's people. Because they do not belong to Christ, Paul is willing to be cursed (*anathema*) on their behalf (9:3). Such a wish cannot be fulfilled, of course, but Paul's desire clarifies that Jews who do not put their faith in Christ are destined for eternal judgment. Paul's final word in Romans 9–11 is that "all Israel will be saved" (11:26). The meaning of this verse is controversial. I have defended elsewhere that Paul looks forward to an end-time salvation of ethnic Israel.[15] But such a promise does not mean that all Israelites who ever lived will be saved. Only those who trust in Christ belong to the true people of God. The true "Israel of God" (Gal. 6:16), then, consists of all those, Jews or Gentiles, who put their faith in Jesus Christ and hence belong to the church of Jesus Christ. It seems legitimate to conclude that Paul sees the church as the true Israel, and all ethnic Jews and Gentiles who believe in Christ belong to the Israel of God.

Paul does not often call the church God's temple (*naos*).[16] Yet the fact that he does occasionally do so (1 Cor. 3:16–17; 2 Cor. 6:16; Eph. 2:21) is significant since the temple was so central to Judaism, one of the pillars on which Judaism rested. For Paul, however, the Jerusalem temple no longer holds any importance. There is no reference to priests serving as cultic functionaries, nor are any sacrifices recommended since the one definitive sacrifice is the sacrifice of Christ. To have a "religion" without a temple, priests, or sacrifices would have seemed strange in the Greco-Roman world. The newness of the gospel emerges at this very point. God's new building cannot be confined to a physical structure but is the church (1 Cor. 3:9) — that is, the people of God is his dwelling place. The foundation of this building is Jesus Christ, and minis-

---

14. The centrality of Christ is evident when it comes to ecclesiology as well!

15. See Schreiner, *Romans*, 611–23.

16. The sections on the church as a temple and body come from my Pauline theology with some modifications.

ters build on this superstructure either with quality materials or with materials that will perish on the day of judgment (1 Cor. 3:10–15). The Spirit lives in believers, not in the temple in Jerusalem (3:16). In 3:16 the focus is not on the Spirit indwelling believers individualistically. What Paul emphasizes is the Spirit's indwelling believers corporately. The Jerusalem temple pointed to and anticipated the church of Jesus Christ, which fulfills what the former temple envisioned.

Second Corinthians 6:16 makes it clear that the temple imagery of the Old Testament is fulfilled in God's dwelling in his people corporately. The only uncleanness to worry about now does not relate to food or other Levitical regulations but the uncleanness of sin (7:1). Temple imagery is also present in the word "access" (*prosagōgē*). Access to God is available not through some cultic process but through faith in Christ (Rom. 5:2). Believers now have access to God, not through the sacrificial system and the temple in Jerusalem, but in the Spirit on the basis of the cross of Christ (Eph. 2:18). Since Gentiles are now part of God's temple, they are members of his household (*oikeioi*, 2:19). In God's new temple Jewish and Gentile believers are no longer alienated from one another but are equal members of the same house.

Paul is distinctive in identifying the church as Christ's body. The centrality of Christ is evident in this metaphor, even if it is understood in diverse ways. In Paul's earlier letters the body metaphor is used to emphasize the unity of the church. In 1 Corinthians 10:16–17 Paul forges an analogy between the one loaf shared at Communion and the body of Christ. Sharing the cup involves sharing in the benefits of Christ's blood, and sharing in the loaf involves sharing in the benefits of Christ's death (10:16). Paul detects significance in the fact that there is "one loaf" (10:17). The unity of the loaf demonstrates that believers are one body, united in Christ. This unity stems from the source of their life since all believers partake of the same loaf. The life of believers derives from their feeding on the crucified and resurrected Lord; that is, their new life derives from believing in the crucified and risen Christ. Only by partaking in the benefits of his death are believers made members of Christ's body.

An extended discussion on the church as a body ensues in 1 Corinthians 12. Divisions over spiritual gifts were creating havoc in Corinth (chs. 12–14). Paul attempts to provide perspective without quenching the use of such gifts in the community. His main theme is unity in diversity. Paul reminds the Corinthians that diversity does not cancel out unity but is instead an expression of it. First Corinthians 12:12 says, "Just as a body, though one, has many parts, but all its many parts form one body, so it is with Christ." What is surprising here is that instead of saying "so also is the church," Paul says, "so it is with Christ." Why does Paul insert Christ instead of the church? This idea is similar to what we saw in 10:16 – 17. The church is one body because it eats of the one loaf, Christ. The individual members of the church, in other words, are the body *of Christ*. Christ, not the church, has priority. The fundamental reality in the people of God is Christ, not the diversity of gifts. Paul wants the Corinthians to take their eyes off their so-called dazzling gifts and focus on Christ.

The unity of the body is realized at baptism, where believers are baptized into one body (1 Cor. 12:13). Baptism fundamentally involves being baptized into Christ (Rom. 6:3), in which believers are plunged into his death (6:3 – 4). "For all of you who were baptized into Christ have clothed yourselves with Christ" (Gal. 3:27). To be baptized into one body, then, is to be baptized into Christ. He is the one body. But by definition the one body is characterized by diversity (1 Cor. 12:14), for bodies are made up of many members. No member of the body should feel inferior (12:15 – 16), for every member is needed. The foot and ear may appear less useful than a hand or an eye, but they are just as crucial to the body as the latter two parts. Indeed, if the body were composed of only one member, it would be grotesque. It would be a monstrosity if the body were a giant eye or a giant ear (12:17).

The variety of the body is "appointed" (ESV) and determined by God (1 Cor. 12:28). The diversity of the church is not contrary to his will but an expression of it. By definition a body is comprised of not one but many members (12:19 – 20). If some members of the church are tempted to exalt themselves, thinking that they are superior to other members, they are sadly mistaken (12:21). The eye cannot dispense with the hand, nor can the head dispense with the feet, for without the so-called inferior parts there is no body. The various parts of the body are needed for the body to function properly (12:22 – 24; cf. Rom. 12:4 – 5), and God has constituted the body as a unified whole (1 Cor. 12:25). This unity manifests itself in caring for one another, so that all participate in each other's joy or sorrow (12:25 – 26).

In Ephesians and Colossians Paul speaks of Christ as being the "head" of the body (Col. 1:18; 2:19; Eph. 1:22–23; 4:16; 5:23). Paul shifts the metaphor to emphasize Christ's lordship over the church. Christ at his resurrection was exalted over all angelic powers and seated at the right hand of God, and he presently reigns over the church (Eph. 1:19–23). Similarly, the Colossian hymn (Col. 1:15–20) features Christ's supremacy in creation and redemption. Since Christ is the Lord of the church, the church must submit to him as her Lord and Master (Eph. 5:23–24). There is no doubt here that the word *kephalē* refers to Christ's authority over the church. Yet there may also be the idea that the head is the source from which the body derives its strength, nourishment, and growth.[17]

Paul uses the metaphor of "head" in a twofold way. Those swept away by the asceticism of the "philosophy" (Col. 2:8) are "not holding fast to the Head" (2:19 ESV). It is from the head that growth comes (2:19), which suggests that the head is the source of nourishment and of a well-functioning body. Perhaps Paul conceives here of food entering the body through the head. Similarly, in Ephesians 4:15 the church is exhorted to grow up into the head, which is clearly an example of mixing metaphors!

Unity is also a theme in Colossians and Ephesians. Believers must let Christ's peace have dominion in their corporate life, for they were called to such harmony as the body of Christ (Col. 3:15). In Eph. 2:11–3:13 Paul emphasizes the unity of Jews and Gentiles in Christ. By virtue of Christ's work on the cross, Jews and Gentiles are no longer estranged from one another, nor are they estranged from God. They have both been reconciled to God "in one body through the cross" (2:16 ESV). The inclusion of Gentiles is highlighted since they were formerly cut off from the covenant people and separated from the promises of Israel. Christ has come and broken down the barrier that separated Jews and Gentiles from each other (cf. Rom. 11:17–24). The peace established between Jews and Gentiles, manifested in the "one body," is rooted in the gospel, namely, the message of the crucified and risen Lord (Eph. 2:17–18). It is this gospel that proclaims peace to those who are near

---

17. Clinton E. Arnold, "Jesus Christ: 'Head' of the Church (Colossians and Ephesians)" in *Jesus of Nazareth: Lord and Christ: Essays on the Historical Jesus and New Testament Christology* (ed. J. B. Green and M. Turner; Grand Rapids: Eerdmans, 1994), 346–66.

and who are far. The mystery revealed to Paul is that Gentiles are "are heirs together with Israel, members together of one body [*syssōma*], and sharers together in the promise in Christ Jesus" (Eph. 3:6).

Paul's focus on the unity of the body is not surprising, for the church is at center stage in Ephesians. God has chosen and predestined a people for his glory (Eph. 1:3–14). After saying that Christ is the head of the church (i.e., his body), the church is said to be "the fullness of him who fills everything in every way" (1:23). Although the meaning of this is debated, the participle *plēroumenou* should probably be construed as a middle that functions like a verb in the active voice. This judgment is supported by the theology of Ephesians as a whole, where the church receives its fullness from God, Christ, and the Spirit (3:19; 4:10, 13; 5:18). The power of the church is not inherent but comes from God himself, who has filled it on the basis of Christ's death, resurrection, and exaltation.

Since the church is so extraordinary, we are not surprised to learn that it is "through the church" that "the manifold wisdom of God" is displayed (Eph. 3:10). Paul was not a Western individualist who indulged in a privatized Christianity. Nor did he conceive of the church as an embarrassment or a necessary evil. The church enshrined God's plan for history, revealing to all creation the wisdom and depth of God's saving plan. The church is the locus of God's glory, the theater in which he displays his grace and love. The church features God's wisdom and declares to the whole universe that the outworking of history is not arbitrary but fulfills God's plan.

Since the church is at the center of God's purposes, Paul summons it to live up to its calling (Eph. 4:1–3). When the church follows her Lord, she brings honor to God and to the Lord Jesus Christ. The church fulfills its calling in particular when it maintains "the unity of the Spirit through the bond of peace" (Eph. 4:3). We have already seen from 2:11–3:13 that the unity of the church was established through the blood of Christ. The church is not called upon to create unity but to preserve the unity that already exists (4:4–6). Paul does not summon people to unity who are fractured by irreconcilable differences. He calls the church to peace because enmity and hatred ended at the cross of Jesus Christ. He summons the church to enjoy the peace and harmony already won. The imperative, as always, is grounded in the indicative.

The unity of the body continues to be a theme in the discussion of spiritual gifts (Eph. 4:7–16). Various gifts are given to the church so that the body will be edified (4:12). This edification is defined further as "unity in the faith" (Eph. 4:13). Such unity is realized when believers come to the knowledge of God's Son, when they grow up into maturity and reach the full stature of Christ. This vision for the church will not be fulfilled perfectly until the day of redemption, but Paul expects that it will be attained in some measure in this age. The church will be stabilized so that it will not be rocked by every new and deviant teaching (4:14). The unity Paul envisions, therefore, cannot be described merely as feelings of harmony and love, as important as the expression of love is. The unity demanded is rooted in truth and jeopardized by false teaching. Unity will be realized only if the church is faithful to the truth of the gospel and avoids teachings contrary to this gospel.

Hence, the church will grow up into its head only through the proclamation of the truth of the gospel (Eph. 4:15). This verse is not simply saying that we should speak the truth in love—as right as that thought is—but that the truth of the gospel should be heralded with love. The unity of the body, then, coincides with the growth of the body. And the body grows when it is rooted in the truth of the gospel. Paul has no place for those who proclaim unity but disparage truth.

Conclusion

What is most striking about Paul's theology is its Christ-centeredness. Whether we speak of the framework of his thought, his soteriology, or his ecclesiology, the saving work of Jesus Christ is the focus. Hence, what it means to be a believer is to embrace Jesus Christ for the forgiveness of sins, to give up all things for the sake of knowing Christ (Phil. 3:7–9), and to do everything in his name (Col. 3:17).

LUKE TIMOTHY JOHNSON

Of the three essays to which I am responding, that by Professor Thomas Schreiner is the easiest for me to engage, partly because his conception of the assigned task corresponds to my own—he tries to account for the Paul of all the letters rather than of just a few—and partly because on some points of his presentation I am in substantial agreement, while on others I take only partial exception. His account of the importance of Christ for Paul, for example, is impressive; I especially applaud his polythetic approach to the subject, as he asserts that Christ's significance is not to be weighed only by Paul's propositions, but in the many modes through which Christ permeates Paul's experience and practice—and, to be sure, the experience and practice of Paul's readers—so that "one's entire Christian life is to be lived under Jesus' lordship."

The first issue on which I take partial exception is Professor Schreiner's locating the framework for Paul's thought in Scripture, and specifically the fulfillment of Torah in the new creation that is life in Christ. It is, to be sure, a reasonable choice. Certainly, the conviction that the good news is "according to the Scriptures" is one that dominates some of Paul's letters (1 and 2 Corinthians, Galatians) and is virtually the theme of his longest (Romans). But if I were to claim that "the fulfillment of Scripture" was in any comparable way present in the other letters—Philemon, Philippians, 1 Thessalonians, 2 Thessalonians, Colossians—I should be considerably overstating the case. Scripture is not only absent by way of citation from these Pauline compositions, but it is difficult to see how the fulfillment of Scripture is a framework for them. Other letters that do contain scriptural citations or allusions (such as 1 and 2 Timothy) do not display a scriptural "framework" in the manner so obvious in Romans.

More important, I think, is that Professor Schreiner's depiction of the "fulfillment of Scripture" misses the complexity of Paul's engagement with Torah. Please note that I am not disputing Professor Schreiner's basic point; it is well supported by such passages as Romans 15:4 and 1 Corinthians 10:11. Rather, I am suggesting that Paul's relationship is much more tensely dialectical than Schreiner proposes. He captures some of this when he notes that Paul proclaims a "mystery" not fully anticipated by Scripture; but he restricts this to the "already but not yet" character of eschatology. In fact, Paul's rereading of Torah in light of the crucified and exalted Messiah is strong and at times subversive. His claim in Galatians 3:1–14 that those who receive the Holy Spirit are in fulfillment of God's promise to Abraham completely reinterprets the meaning of Genesis; his allegory concerning the two sons of Abraham in Galatians 4:21–29 does more than a little violence to the plain sense of the same composition. And his shocking twist of Exodus 34:29–35 and the veiling of Moses' face is at the least interpretively high-handed. In the Pauline dialectic, Scripture is at least as much read in light of Christ as Christ is read in light of Scripture.

The second of Professor Schreiner's emphases with which I take issue concerns sin, which he makes, without qualification, "what believers need to be saved from." This is itself an odd formulation—what do "believers" need to be saved from?—but still stranger statements follow. He says, "The just judgment of God awaits all who do not repent and fail to place their trust in Jesus Christ, for 'all have sinned and fall short of the glory of God'" (Rom. 3:23). This collapse of Paul's humanity (Jews and Greeks) into "believers" and sin into "failure to place their trust in Jesus Christ" strikes one as an unusual reading of Romans 1–3, but it appears to be no accidental reading, for Schreiner states that Paul's declarations concerning those who kept the law (written or not) in Romans 2 points to "the work of the Holy Spirit in those who have confessed Jesus as the Christ" (2:28–29).

Schreiner appears to contradict his recognition that Paul makes an exception when he states in the next paragraph that "the universality of sin is also taught in Galatians 3:10," and interprets it to have as an implied premise "that no one does what the law demands." This statement flies in the face of Paul's plain statement in Philippians 3:6, in essence, that "I was above reproach when it came to justice based on the law." Schreiner avers that "those who rely on the law cannot appeal to

Old Testament sacrifices for forgiveness now that Christ has come and atoned for sin (Gal. 3:13). If they rely on the law for atonement, they repudiate the sacrifice of Christ and end up saying that Christ died for nothing (2:21) ... those who turn to the law for salvation must keep its prescriptions perfectly, which is impossible (5:3)." Not only is this a reading of Paul from a perspective like that of Hebrews, but the texts cited by Schreiner are twisted to support his assertions.

Schreiner continues to advance the universality of sin, saying that "the pervasiveness of human sin is a regular theme in Paul's letters," and even speaks of "the radical evil of human beings." But is it true to say that sin is a regular theme in Paul's letters? Paul's diction suggests otherwise. Of the eighty instances where Paul uses cognates for "sin," fifty-four appear in the sixteen chapters of Romans. Across the seventy-one chapters of Paul's other letters, such cognates occur only twenty-six times; they do not appear at all in Philemon, Philippians, and Titus.

As with the claim made about the fulfillment of Scripture, Schreiner's treatment of sin depends entirely on Galatians and Romans rather than a reading of Paul's letters as a whole. And against the grain of those letters, he captures little of the personified, cosmic dimension of sin or its social realizations in the world. Sin appears as an individual offense, a matter of not keeping the law or disobeying the commandments. Little of Paul's radical treatment of sin and faith in Romans survives this treatment.

Corresponding to his treatment of sin is Schreiner's insistence on the "substitutionary character of Paul's theology of the cross" and his privileging "forensic righteousness" as the governing metaphor for understanding salvation. I do not object to Schreiner's making such judgments, but I regard his treatment as an unnecessary narrowing of Paul's richer and more multivalent understanding both of the cross and of salvation.

The final point I find problematic in Schreiner's essay is his section on *pistis Christou* ("faith in/faith of Christ"). First, I think that he mischaracterizes the issue. The choice is not, as he states, between "believers have been redeemed by the work of *Christ* (objective genitive) or the *faithfulness of Christ* (subjective genitive)." It is, rather, which faith places humans in a condition of righteousness: the faith they place in Christ, or the faith that Christ showed toward God.

Second, in my own treatment of the subject, I have made it clear that *both* meanings are clearly found in Paul: believers certainly have "faith in Christ" as they profess him to be both Messiah and Lord; such confession is the specific articulation of the obedience of faith, which, for Paul, must always be directed to God. The issue, rather, is whether in some of his arguments concerning righteousness (above all in Galatians and Romans), Paul also speaks of Jesus' human faith in God as the critical response of God's Son that established other humans in a condition of righteousness—to be received by them with a faithful response to such a gift. Is the "faith of Jesus," in short, a key part of Paul's argument concerning God's way of making humans righteous?

Third, those who have made the argument concerning the faith of Jesus Christ in these letters have done so not on the basis of theological presuppositions, but on the basis of strict exegesis: there are cases— Romans 3:26 is the outstanding example—where an objective reading of the genitive is grammatically impossible. The statement that God makes righteous *ton ek pisteōs Iēsou* ("the one out of the faith of Jesus" or "shares the faith of Jesus") cannot be twisted to mean "the one who has faith in Jesus" (compare Rom. 4:16).

Fourth, the argument concerning the faith of Jesus in no way compromises the *extra nos* character of salvation; in fact, it enhances it, since it is the faith of the Son of God who makes us righteous prior to our faith in the Son of God.

Fifth, it is plain from a serious reading of Romans 5:12–21 that the meaning of the faith of Jesus in 3:21–26 is to be found in his obedience to God. In light of these observations, I confess that I do not find in the least convincing the five points that Schreiner adduces in favor of his position.

Readers of Professor Schreiner's essay will find much that is familiar in its vision of Paul, because it is basically the treatment that most of them will have heard in sermons and Sunday school classes, and therefore it is unlikely that they will sense any deficiencies in his account. It is only when his reading is checked against the evidence of the entire Pauline correspondence that its highly selective character becomes clear. In the end, it is a reading of Paul that centers on Romans and Galatians (finding support only marginally, if at all, in other letters), that views the drama of sin and salvation in fundamentally individualistic terms, and that adopts certain understandings as essential (substitutionary death/forensic justification), not because they force themselves on the reader because of the pervasiveness of their use, but because they fit beautifully a highly specific Christian theology.

RESPONSE TO THOMAS R. SCHREINER

DOUGLAS A. CAMPBELL

My main response to Schreiner's essay is glad agreement with its main claim—that Paul's thought is utterly Christ-centered. My main concern with Schreiner's essay is that he does not always take his own advice; Schreiner's account of Paul's thinking is not always Christ-centered. But I am grateful in an ironic sense that he makes this mistake because this is a common modern and largely Protestant error in the interpretation of Paul, and it gives me an opportunity to indicate here—very briefly—where (in my view) he goes wrong.

I need to reiterate first that I concur completely with Schreiner that Christ is central for Paul (and most of Schreiner's essay argues this). Moreover, the triune God revealed by Christ is gracious, loving, and elective, as he suggests. Schreiner goes on to show how this God and his eschatological gathering of a people are the mystery contained in the Old Testament Scriptures. I could not agree more with all this.

But from this point on Schreiner's account falls off the Reformed wagon, so to speak. It does so by introducing an unnecessary question that opens up his unfolding description to a set of categories that are important in any ultimate theological account of Paul, but that are now explored by Schreiner in an a priori way *and hence not in a way that is reshaped by the Christ event.* He states: "Before we can speak of salvation ... we must discern why salvation is needed." And this question correlates with a later issue: "how we are made right with God." In view of these concerns Schreiner essentially *makes a new theological start.*

Oriented now by different texts from Paul and the Old Testament from the ones he cited before—and, in fact, by a different view *of* the OT—he proceeds to articulate positions that Paul supposedly held on sin, judgment, and justification, and on the atonement. Related positions on Israel, unbelievers, and faith are shortly described as well. Most scholars will not have any difficulty recognizing here what New Testament scholars often call the "Lutheran" reading of Paul, although it is rather more accurate to call it "Melanchthonian." Luther was not committed to all aspects of the model that Schreiner now inserts into Paul's description, nor was Calvin. But Melanchthon was. So straightaway we see that Schreiner is no longer providing *the* Reformational account of salvation in Paul. Three further brief observations on this account can now be made.

First, there is clearly not enough space to describe Schreiner's Melanchthonian model in full here, but I have done so several times elsewhere. I initially called this model "the JF model" because of its key slogan, "Justification by Faith,"[18] and more lately have called it "Justification Theory," abbreviated to JT.[19] Unfortunately, further debate of the entire situation has been hampered when scholars like Schreiner have denied that my description of this model is accurate; they deny that they do commit to JF theory or to JT as I describe it. But Schreiner's essay illuminates nicely that my descriptions are in fact accurate. He clearly reproduces all the key moves in Justification Theory. So we can now lay this false objection to my work to rest.

The material that I want to target as unhelpful and ultimately false, which has been supplied for the description of Paul by Schreiner and scholars like him, is summarized neatly by JT—a presentation of Paul's "gospel" initially as a problem generated by God's (retributive) justice and a general human failure to obey the law, which self-evidently elicits divine wrath in the form of punishment. This is followed by a solution composed of a penal substitutionary atonement and an appropriation of that solution by an individual act of faith. In short, Schreiner encapsulates JT nicely (mainly in the sub-section "Paul's View of Sin and Judgment"). So with this false objection out of the way, the really important conversation can hopefully now begin.

My second observation is that the switch by Schreiner to this new approach creates several extremely awkward problems, two of which can be elaborated here a little more specifically.[20] (a) This model of

---

18. See esp. my "The Contractual (JF) Construal of Paul's Gospel, and Its Problems," ch. 8 in my *The Quest for Paul's Gospel: A Suggested Strategy* (London: T&T Clark, 2005), 146–77.

19. See esp. "The Heart of the Matter: The Justification Theory of Salvation," ch. 1 in my *The Deliverance of God: An Apocalyptic Rereading of Justification in Paul* (Grand Rapids: Eerdmans, 2009), 11–35.

20. For fuller accounts see *Quest*, 132–45, 164–73; and *Deliverance*, 36–218, 338–411.

the gospel *clashes* with the model that he has *already* committed to—a model grounded in Christ, God's love, and election, and that is carried through in the life of the Christian primarily by the Spirit in transformational terms (and that looks very Reformed).[21] We can grasp the nature and depth of this clash quickly by observing that the approach to theological knowledge in Schreiner's Melanchthonian model, or JT, is essentially *Arian*. It relies on people reaching critical insights about God naturally and sometimes even from nature, largely unassisted (i.e., from within the problem, in order to establish that). But the alternative model that we both share is *Athanasian*—or, as Pauline scholars tend to say, apocalyptic—relying on *revelation*, and in particular, *the revelation that is Christ* to impart all the key insights about God, including about what God thinks of sin and how it is actually judged.

Now no compromise is really possible here. These are two completely different theological modes, and the church has generally dubbed one of them, in the end, heretical. Moreover, many Pauline scholars in the modern period have been grappling with this epistemological collision for some time.[22] Yet Schreiner simply muddles these two modes together, apparently unaware that this is a big mistake.[23]

(b) A second problem is similar to the first one. JT begins with an account of the problem, from within which certain insightful individuals proceed to grasp the Christian solution. But this entails that the construction of the problem must be universal and harsh—clearly in order to propel everyone to the solution. As a result of this, however, any people who continue to live on within the problem in defiance of the Christian gospel will be held implacably accountable for their irrationality and immorality.

---

21. See esp. James B. Torrance, "The Vicarious Humanity of Christ," in *The Incarnation: Ecumenical Studies in the Nicene-Constantinopolitan Creed, A. D. 381* (ed. T. F. Torrance; Edinburgh: Handsel, 1981), 127–47; but Richard Gaffin makes much the same point in much of *By Faith, Not By Sight: Paul and the Order of Salvation* (Waynesboro, GA: Paternoster, 2006).

22. Sanders grasps the issue well, relying on earlier work by Schweitzer. But I find Wrede's account especially clear; see his *Paul* (trans. E. Lummis; London: Philip Green, 1907), esp. 74–154.

23. A more detailed account of these dynamics is supplied by my essay "What Is at Stake in the Reading of Romans 1–3? An Elliptical Response to the Concerns of Gorman and Tilling," *Journal for the Study of Paul and His Letters* 1/1 (2011): 113–37; see also Alisdair Heron, "Homoousios with the Father," in *The Incarnation: Ecumenical Studies in the Nicene-Constantinopolitan Creed A. D. 381*, 58–87.

Now there is a truth here, but it is partial. God's *primary* attitude in Christ toward those "on the outside" is, as Schreiner notes, one of engagement and love. "While we were yet sinners, Christ died for us" is a crucial text that he quotes (cf. Rom. 5:6, 8). If you are prepared to offer up your only beloved Son for your enemies while they still hate you, then you love them. However, the Melanchthonian account of the gospel introduced by Schreiner essentially overrules this insight (!), claiming that God's fundamental posture toward outsiders is punitive. Schreiner is clear about this. Moreover, this category includes unbelieving *Jews*, at which point we stumble on one of the most inaccurate and sinister aspects of Schreiner's Melanchthonian model. (And I will have much more to say about this when responding to Mark Nanos's essay.)

The Old Testament does not describe Judaism in fundamentally negative terms; it is not just one long characterization, in representative form, of sinners. It is this, but it is so much more. Hence to *reduce* it to a flat and awful story of sin and its establishment is to give a deeply impoverished account of the Old Testament, of salvation history, and of Judaism. Yet this is where Schreiner's Melanchthonian reading takes us. Jews *must* be legalists, according to this schema, even if they say they are not and the sources support their protests. That is, Schreiner's Melanchthonian account of parts of Paul leads the apostle straight into the jaws of the post-Holocaust critique. The only solution he offers worried Pauline interpreters at this point is denial that this is really a problem, which is small comfort "in the presence of the burning children." We learn here, rather, that something is deeply wrong with Schreiner's account of Paul.

My third observation is that Schreiner does not need to do any of this. He creates these difficulties for himself by raising questions that do not need to be put, and by generating answers to key theological issues here that should be answered in the light of Christ, at which point they receive rather better answers.

The trouble starts, as we have already seen, when Schreiner states, "Before we can speak of salvation ... we must discern why salvation is needed." And it just needs to be said here clearly that this is not true, *and his other material tells us why.* God acts *electively, before* humans know anything (a strong Reformed claim). He does so, moreover, not because people are sinful, but because he loves them. Indeed, Ephesians says this clearly, the key text—which is often overlooked—reading " ... *in love* he predestined us for adoption through Jesus Christ [and for him]" (Eph. 1:4b–5a). Ephesians then goes on to tell us at some length that God desires to create people and to have fellowship with them from and for eternity. *Because* he loves them, he will intervene to rescue them when they have fallen into trouble, and the order of his actions here is crucial.

There is no impossible "plan A" followed by a remedial "plan B" in this Reformed elective understanding of God as Melanchthonians suggest, and mercifully so! This would suggest that God was lacking in foreknowledge, or fundamentally inconsistent and fickle, or perhaps powerless—all appalling theological options. There was only ever plan A, which was and is elective, rooted in the positive divine purposes, and this will stay on track and ultimately triumph despite human corruption, stupidity, and sinfulness—something Calvin appreciated better than most. In short, a proper understanding of God's election in Christ entails that Schreiner does not need to ask the question that launches the secondary discordant system that disorders his broader description of Paul. But a proper respect for human sinful depravity reinforces this judgment to refrain from asking an anthropocentric question and beginning theology there as Melanchthon does.

Depraved humans, corrupt and fallen in every aspect *including their minds*, cannot reach accurate judgments about God unassisted in and from the cosmos until they have been enlightened by grace (see Rom. 12:1–2; Col. 1:21). They can only appreciate the truth about God and the world *in retrospect*, as they look back with a clarifying mind, informed by the Spirit, on their former corrupt and distorted existence. This is how Paul talks in critical passages like Romans 7:7–25 and Philippians 3:1–11. Such lost figures need help first, not judgment (while a strict introduction of judgment "up front" because they deserve it will be both ineffective and unjust). Hence depravity does not establish the need for election in Paul, as Schreiner suggests (*quelle horreur*). Paul's consistent point is, rather, that election triumphs over even human depravity and so speaks of the glorious love and grace of God.[24]

---

24. Grounded more firmly in these insights, Schreiner needs to let his accounts of divine judgment, divine justice, and human freedom or agency be *shaped* by these revelations and Christology—processes I have gestured toward in my principal essay in this book.

There is so much more to say but space unfortunately precludes it. All I can do is refer readers—in some frustration—to helpful things that have been said elsewhere.[25] I would like to end my response to Schreiner, however, on the note of affirmation that I began with.

Schreiner and I concur that the heart of Paul's gospel, life, and theology is Christ crucified, resurrected, and enthroned, who reveals a divine love that is really past understanding. And since we agree on this, any disagreements between us must be over secondary matters; we disagree on how exactly this central truth plays out in relation to other theological questions in Paul. But these must then be, at bottom, disagreements not between enemies, but between friends and fellow servants of a gospel that proclaims a God of love revealed in Christ.

---

25. Some key studies have been indicated in my principal essay.

MARK D. NANOS

Thomas Schreiner's construction of Paul repeats a well-known traditional interpretation modified by his own tradition's perspectives and emphases. But does that construction of Paul and of his message, or his Reformed modifications thereof, represent the most probable interpretation of the original meaning, and thus, for the cross-cultural implications drawn thereafter in these interpretive traditions?

The way Schreiner approaches the topics raised in his essay is historically or rhetorically evaluative only when it is supposed by him to be supportive of what he already knows must be the case; not surprisingly, it corroborates the views of his tradition. It represents more of an ideological than historical position; it does not explain sufficiently what needs to be explained to someone who does not already share his views as if self-evident. While in this essay he only reveals that implicitly by the way he proceeds, elsewhere he makes that case explicit: not without significance for my response here, he does so by specifically objecting to my approach to interpreting Paul's language by way of privileging historical methodology.

In his recent *Galatians* commentary, Schreiner briefly mentions my work on that letter only to dismiss it as impossible for one who knows the answers as he does, which is based on an appeal to the point of view he presumes that his target reader shares:

> Nanos strives *to be fair* to the opponents and hence shrinks back from negative language to characterize them. *But for those of us who accept Paul's language as inspired Scripture and as God's viewpoint of the opponents*, the Pauline stance regarding the opponents should be accepted as an accurate depiction, and hence it is legitimate to designate them as agitators, troublemakers, opponents of the gospel, and deserving God's eschatological curse (1:8–9).[26]

---

26. Thomas Schreiner, *Galatians* (ZECNT; Grand Rapids: Zondervan, 2010), 52; emphasis added). I do not "shrink back," but challenge internalizing polemical perspectives rather

As I read Schreiner's essay in this book, I cannot escape the glaring difference in his approach and judgment about how to proceed to discover what most probably represents any given situation that provoked Paul to write a given letter, and thus what he likely sought to communicate therein. That topic seems to me more important to discuss than the few particulars I could engage in the space available, not least because throughout his essay this matter of method is fundamental, and thus it would need to be discussed anyway.

I am pleased, of course, that Schreiner acknowledges my entry into the conversation about Galatians, but more than perplexed at the purpose to which he put introducing some of my views: dismissal of them out of hand on the basis of his ideological stance, not their historical merit, and the attribution of his stance to Paul, and more than that, to God. This is not the venue to discuss at any length my views or Schreiner's brief dismissal of their merits on either side of his statement without actually engaging the arguments I offered, or his merely restating what he already upholds as if my argument had not engaged those views and shown them to be inadequate. But it cannot be beside the point to note a few problems with what he does state, which includes observing how he operates.[27]

Schreiner's criticism involves a claim to speak authoritatively for Paul and God, and thus for historical truth. Following such a remarkable methodological claim, one might expect his dismissal to be closely based on what Paul wrote—but it is not. To put this bluntly: Paul may well have been inspired to speak for God (which is not historically verifiable), but unless Schreiner claims the same inspiration for himself, he should accept that he is, like everyone else, limited to engaging in the interpretation of Paul's texts. Consider briefly each of the details of his summary description.

(1) Paul does not actually name those whose influence in Galatia whom he opposes "agitators" or "troublemakers." Instead, he writes that the position they uphold is unsettling or troubling the Galatians (Gal. 1:7; 5:10), as well as other similar statements about the effect they are having (I will refer to them more fairly and neutrally as the "influenc-

---

than evaluating them. My work under discussion is *The Irony of Galatians: Paul's Letter in First-Century Context* (Minneapolis: Fortress, 2002).

27. It should also not go unmentioned that he compels the naive reader into agreement with him by this rhetorical method.

ers," as discussed at length in the argument he dismisses). At the same time, Paul intends his letter to unsettle and trouble the Galatians too! Would that make it appropriate to call Paul an agitator or troublemaker?

(2) Paul does not call them "opponents of the gospel" (or of Paul). He accuses them of seeking to "undermine" the gospel in their interaction with the Galatians, that is, according to Paul's understanding of what it should be. Paul opposes their "good news," but he does not define what it discloses beyond completion of the rite of proselyte conversion (circumcision of males; 1:6–7; 6:12–13).

(3) Paul does not write that they deserve "God's *eschatological* curse." Paul wishes a curse on anyone who would present "a different good news" (which, he states, "is not another [good news]") in such a way as to undermine the good news about Christ as he presents it, even himself (1:8–9). Paul also wishes that anyone advocating circumcision of these non-Jews would cut off the whole thing (5:12). But neither of these curse or castration wishes are presented as eschatological; they are his wishes for the *present time*.

Much more could be said here about the details of the information in Galatians, but I have done so already. These simple observations about what is revealed in Scripture rather than in Schreiner's construction will be apparent to anyone who explores what Paul actually wrote (in Greek). Since Schreiner knows Greek, this suggests that he knows what it says already when he approaches the text. In short, it is this kind of presentation that leads me to see his approach as ideologically driven — as eisegesis, not exegesis.

Schreiner states in his objection, "the Pauline stance regarding the opponents should be accepted as an accurate depiction." I agree that a rhetorical point of view for Paul is expressed: we thus can discuss *Paul's stance* on the matter. The question is whether one has accurately assessed what Paul's *stance* was; that requires interpretation. Moreover, the way Schreiner has stated his claim is problematic even if one supposes that one is not interpreting but merely parroting what Paul depicted; what that reveals can only properly be described as Paul's *rhetorical* stance regarding *those whose influence he opposes*. Whether Paul's expressed view, which is constructed to influence his addressees, provides certainty about the historical identity or stance of *the influencers themselves* is a different matter.

What will also strike any *fair*-minded reader as remarkable in Schreiner's commentary is the double standard he applies to this methodological matter. When he discusses the identity of those whom Paul calls "false brethren" in Jerusalem in Galatians 2:4, Schreiner instead equivocates, noting the difference between rhetorical and historical information, even if he will take Paul's side: "Obviously, the false brothers themselves did not think they were advocating slavery. What we find here is Paul's perspective on their theology."[28] That is simply what I advocate as a standard, although one that should be executed more carefully, for it is what Paul writes about his perspective, which will not likely reveal as much about what he thinks about them as what he wants to highlight in the service of his objectives for the letter's communication goals.

Although much more could be discussed about the matters raised there, let us consider some similar problems in the essay herein. Schreiner baldly states that for Paul, "Jews who do not put their faith in Christ are destined for eternal judgment" (which he qualifies as "are not saved" and "do not belong to God's people" and "are cursed"), as he drives toward the conclusion that "it seems legitimate to conclude that Paul sees the church as the true Israel, and all ethnic Jews and Gentiles who believe in Christ belong to the Israel of God." One can readily see that Paul has not clearly stated what Schreiner decides in the way that he has proceeded in the argument and admitted at its conclusion ("such a wish cannot be fulfilled, of course" and "it seems …"). Reasoning from what is written to what one suspects to be implied is not methodologically objectionable to me! However, since this constitutes a conclusion that goes beyond what Paul states, it cannot be said to represent Paul's or God's viewpoint according to Schreiner's own methodological bias.

It is thus worth raising the question why one would choose to take the path of replacement theology and declare that anyone who does not share Schreiner's beliefs is destined for eternal judgment. In contrast, many Christian interpreters have reconsidered whether that was the best interpretation of the texts of Paul or reflected the ethos of the God they believe he sought to communicate therein, or would seek to communicate if writing to Christians today— that is, whether it is exegetically or hermeneutically appropriate to perpetuate after the history of

---

28. Schreiner, *Galatians*, 125.

harm to which it so obviously contributes, which runs contrary to the ideals these Christians uphold. And many today would refrain from making judgments about the eternal destiny of anyone, even if it had been clearly stated.

I have come to the opposite conclusion after detailed investigation of the relevant texts concerning whether Christ-following non-Israelites become members of Israel in Paul's teaching: they do not. As my essay briefly explains, that is important to the propositional logic of Paul's gospel proclamation; it is part of why he opposes proselyte conversion for them: Israelites must remain Israelites just as those from the other nations must remain those from the other nations.

Schreiner also argues that "those who failed to see Jesus was the fulfillment of Old Testament prophecies were not merely intellectually deficient. Their sin blinded them from seeing the truth"; and "every reader, according to Paul, should see that Christ is the fulfillment of the Old Testament Scripture," even if qualified as "only plain retro-spectively." Putting aside whether that represents what Paul was writing about in the texts Schreiner cites, or whether he correctly speaks for Paul's view of "every reader," Paul's own experience puts that conclusion in serious doubt!

Paul himself required more than reading the Tanakh or the words of some follower of Jesus. It took a miraculous revelation to come to this realization. So why should it be so self-evident to anyone who has not had a similar encounter? Can someone whose expectations for the future are derived from the prophecies in the Tanakh really be expected, on the basis of empirical evidence, to recognize that they have been fulfilled fol-lowing the death of Jesus anymore than it was evident to Paul before his miraculous experience: e.g., that the Davidic kingship has been reinstated to rule Israel, that Israel has been freed from the hands of her enemies, that peace has been established on earth, that the righteous are vindi-cated and the wicked punished, that sin and death have been defeated, that non-Jews who claim to become the people of God by believing in a Judean martyr of the Roman regime should be accepted as full members apart from becoming Israelites through undertaking proselyte conver-sion, that Jesus was resurrected and ascended to heaven. Which prophe-cies unambiguously point toward the claims made about the suffering and death of Jesus being related to the arrival of the Messiah?

According to the Gospels and Acts, even those who were with Jesus in his ministry failed to see that it was self-evident that he had brought the kingdom following his death, until they received a special disclosure from the resurrected Jesus. It was only thereafter that they found warrant from the Tanakh for their new interpretation of Jesus as the Messiah, and for what this meant for themselves, their fellow Jews, and the rest of humankind. Paul took a miraculous encounter that few other Jews can claim. Is failure to be convinced by reading or hearing such claims (assuming one has) really a sufficient basis for concluding that someone is not only intellectually deficient, but worse than that, that one has sinned against God so as to have blinded oneself, and thereby earned eternal damnation?

It is clear in Romans 11 that Paul does not yet hold many of his fellow Israelites accountable in the terms that Schreiner attributes to Paul. Paul even argues that the reason some of them have not yet, in Paul's view, come to share his views is the result of God's sovereign design, including that it is necessary in order for God to accomplish the ends in view for the nations. (I have written extensively on the topics that arise in Romans 11; some are listed in my own essay herein.) In the spirit of Pauline ideals, I ask Schreiner to reconsider his approach and judgments, at least the certainty with which he represents them and expects everyone else who is concerned about God's will or the integrity of Scripture to capitulate to his opinions as if they are also inspired and beyond doubt.

THE PAUL OF THE LETTERS:
A CATHOLIC PERSPECTIVE

LUKE TIMOTHY JOHNSON

Although the term "Roman Catholic" suggests a range of highly specific concepts and practices shaped by Reformation controversy, it is not at all clear how any list of such particularities—Marian piety, for example, or papal authority, or celibate priesthood—derives from or provides a perspective on the letters of Paul. The "Catholic tradition" as such, however, is both broader and deeper than a set of polemical postures, embodying the sort of "universal and inclusive" connotations suggested by the term. This is the tradition that very much derives from the canonical Scriptures, that is shaped by the creed, that is enlivened by the work of the Holy Spirit, and that expresses itself in a variety of individual and communal practices proper to what Paul calls "the body of Christ." It is a tradition that expresses its interpretation of Scripture above all in forms of worship and piety, but that also draws on all the resources of a splendid intellectual tradition formed over some 1,500 years prior to Reformation battles.

In this essay, I approach the letters of Paul as a Catholic in this older and broader tradition, defined not by a single standpoint (either in Paul or in the interpreter) but in a conversation among standpoints, trying to avoid whenever possible the sharp alternatives of "either-or" in favor of a more balanced (even when dialectical) "both-and." I am perhaps the least likely person able to identify what is distinctively Catholic in this reading of Paul, although I suspect that the attention I give to the resurrection and the power of the Holy Spirit, as well as to the church as the body of Christ, may owe something to the tradition in which I was raised and which I still embrace.

Selection of Sources

Every construal — or "vision" — of Paul involves decisions concerning which sources are to be considered and how they are to be read. Most scholars seeking to describe Paul's life, for example, depend on a critical assessment of the Acts of the Apostles and his letters. Claims to ignore Acts and rely solely on Paul's letters always turn out to be exaggerated — Acts is indispensable for reconstructing Paul's life.[1] In contrast, the search for Paul's "thought" requires ignoring Acts — those are Luke's speeches, not Paul's[2] — and focusing exclusively on Paul's own literary productions as the expression of his thought. These are in general sound decisions, and I agree with them. I do think it important, however, to state my own understanding of them.

First, the process is inevitably selective. Selection from among the sources is necessary, precisely because the sources do not agree in every respect. Acts and the letters are distinct in authorship, genre, and purpose.[3] The thirteen canonical letters ascribed to Paul are no less diverse in circumstance, rhetorical form, style, and function.[4] But selection also arises from the predilections of readers, who inevitably approach "Paul" with presuppositions concerning the apostle that derive from factors other than the close exegesis of the sources.[5] A preference for certain letters as more revealing of Paul's thought than others is difficult to avoid and may even have heuristic value. The legitimate construction of Paul based on such selection, however, can easily turn into an illegitimate exclusion of other constructions based on other selections. The nature of the sources demands that every construction of Paul should be regarded as work in progress rather than a finished edifice.

Second, scholars need to be wary of abstraction. "Paul's thought" or "Paul's theology"[6] does not exist apart from and prior to the com-

---

1. See, e.g., J. Murphy-O'Connor, *Paul: A Critical Life* (Oxford: Oxford Univ. Press, 1996).

2. M. L. Soards, *The Speeches in Acts: Their Content, Context, and Concerns* (Louisville, KY: Westminster John Knox, 1994).

3. The failure to account for these is the critical flaw in Philip Vielhauer, "Zum 'Paulinismus' der Apostelgeschichte," *EvT* 10 (1950–51): 1–15.

4. For a treatment of each letter, see L. T. Johnson, *The Writings of the New Testament: An Interpretation* (3rd ed.; Minneapolis: Fortress, 2010), 231–401.

5. As an example, see D. Boyarin, *A Radical Jew: Paul and the Politics of Identity* (Berkeley: Univ. of California Press, 1994).

6. The efforts under this title run from the modest, as J. Fitzmyer, *Pauline Theology: A Brief Sketch* (2nd ed.; Englewood Cliffs, NJ: Prentice-Hall, 1989), to the massive, as in J. D.

positions that alone serve as evidence. We make contact with "Paul's thought" only through the rhetoric of specific letters. Like other writers, Paul probably discovered what he thought in the process of composition. Certainly, the diversity of expression and argument found in his letters shows that Paul was not a systematic thinker. As occasional responses to specific circumstances in his churches or in his ministry, the letters elicit specific modes of expression and argument. A romantic, individualistic notion of Paul's authorship needs revision.

Third, I differ from the majority of critical scholars in the selection of relevant Pauline compositions. Since the late nineteenth century, a broad consensus of scholars has considered only seven of the canonical letters "authentic," that is, written by Paul himself during his ministry, with the six remaining letters "disputed" to a greater (1 Timothy, 2 Timothy, Titus) or lesser (Colossians, Ephesians, 2 Thessalonians) degree, and assigned to one or more "Pauline schools" writing after Paul's death.[7] So broad is this consensus that the other "visions of Paul" in this volume may be based exclusively on the so-called "undisputed letters": Romans, 1 and 2 Corinthians, Galatians, Philippians, 1 Thessalonians, and Philemon.

I find the reasons for rejecting six letters to be both formally and materially flawed.[8] There are as many variations in style and theme among the undisputed letters as between the undisputed and disputed. The Pauline corpus, in fact, falls into a number of clusters. Each group has strong internal connections and strong differences from the other clusters: (1) Romans/Galatians; (2) 1 and 2 Thessalonians; (3) 1 and 2 Corinthians; (4) Philemon, Colossians, Ephesians, Philippians; (5) 1 and 2 Timothy, Titus. The differences between the six rejected and the seven accepted by the majority of scholars are a matter of degree rather than of kind. The two Thessalonian letters are as different in style and theme from Romans and Galatians as 1 and 2 Corinthians are different from 1 and 2 Timothy. The differences across the entire collection, moreover, are just as likely to be due to circumstance, subject matter,

---

Bassler, D. M. Hay, and E. E. Johnson, eds., *Pauline Theology* (4 vols.; Minneapolis: Fortress, 1994–1997).

7. For a short history of the debate that led to the present consensus, see L. T. Johnson, *The First and Second Letters to Timothy: A New Translation with Introduction and Commentary* (AB 35A; New York: Doubleday, 2001), 42–54.

8. For a close consideration and critique of the criteria, see Johnson, *First and Second Timothy*, 55–90.

and rhetoric, as they are to a difference in authors.[9] The evidence of the letters as well as what can be known of the patterns of Paul's ministry in the end support the position that Paul's coworkers and delegates formed a "school" even during his lifetime, significantly shaping the correspondence. All thirteen letters should be considered as authored by Paul during his lifetime, in the sense that he "authorized" their composition, even if he did not directly write any of them.[10]

The Letters

If statements made about "Paul" in this essay are drawn from the thirteen canonical letters written in his name, it is appropriate briefly to characterize that correspondence.

1. Paul's letters are occasional in the sense that they respond to specific circumstances that evoke the treatment of topics and the rhetoric deployed. They are real letters for actual readers, not literary exercises that happen to use the epistolary genre.[11]

2. They are official correspondence from the leader of a religious movement to assemblies of that religious movement. Even the letters written to individuals (Philemon, Timothy, Titus) have at least a semipublic function, dealing with religious experiences, convictions, and behavior.[12]

3. The letters are the least-favored response to community issues by the apostle. His instinct is to visit communities in person, and when that is not possible, to send personal delegates to represent him. Visits, delegations, and letters form a complex web of communication between Paul and his churches. The letters represent only a portion of a larger conversation.[13]

---

9. New insight is yielded when individual disputed letters are put in conversation with undisputed letters individually; see, e.g., L. T. Johnson, "*Oikonomia Theou*: The Theological Voice of 1 Timothy from the Perspective of Pauline Authorship," *HBT* 21/2 (1999): 87–104, and "1 Timothy 1:20: The Shape of the Struggle," *1 Timothy Reconsidered* (Colloquium Ecumenicum Paulinum 18; Leuven: Peeters, 2008), 19–39.

10. Johnson, *Writings of the New Testament*, 239–42.

11. See S. K. Stowers, *Letter Writing in Greco-Roman Antiquity* (Philadelphia: Westminster, 1986).

12. See L. T. Johnson, *Religious Experience in Early Christianity: A Missing Dimension in New Testament Studies* (Minneapolis: Fortress, 1998).

13. M. M. Mitchell, "New Testament Envoys in the Context of Greco-Roman Diplomatic and Epistolary Conventions: The Examples of Timothy and Titus," *JBL* 111 (1992): 641–62.

4. Given such a small sample, Paul's letters are remarkably diverse with respect to length and letter type.[14] The diversity in rhetorical style, invention, and arrangement is as obvious in the undisputed as it is in the disputed letters.
5. The letters are complex in composition. They contain elements of standard rhetorical formulations,[15] community traditions,[16] and authoritative texts,[17] as well as stances taken by readers to which the letter responds,[18] all of which help shape the "thought" of each composition. They are complex also in terms of production: the letters are sometimes dictated,[19] they are often cosponsored,[20] and they contain elements (such as midrash and diatribe) that suggest a communal setting for the formation of certain complex arguments within them (see, e.g., Rom. 9–11; Gal. 3–4).[21]

While such observations steer us away from a romantic notion of authorship and the expectation of finding Paul's personality or the systematic theology of a religious genius, they steer us at the same time toward an appreciation for an apostle who establishes and nurtures churches and responds to them by letter when he cannot visit them in person, and who works out arguments demanded by diverse circumstances within the fellowship of coworkers. Still, the letters do allow some judgments concerning the religious sensibility and intelligence that authorize and guide their composition. The test to which such judgments must be held is simple: Are they supported sufficiently by

14. See H. J. Klauck, *Ancient Letters and the New Testament: A Guide to Context and Exegesis* (Waco, TX: Baylor Univ. Press, 2006).

15. Such as lists of virtues and vices (e.g., Rom. 1:29–32); lists of hardships (e.g., 2 Cor. 11:21–29); catalogues of household ethics (Eph. 5:21–6:9).

16. E.g., creeds (1 Cor 8:4–6); hymns (Col. 1:15–20; 2 Tim. 2:11–13).

17. A still helpful survey of Paul's usage is E. E. Ellis, *Paul's Use of the Old Testament* (Grand Rapids: Baker, repr. 1981).

18. The classic example is 1 Corinthians: Paul responds to queries (and perhaps slogans) of the assembly; see J. C. Hurd, *The Origin of 1 Corinthians* (London: SPCK, 1965).

19. See E. R. Richards, *The Secretary in the Letters of Paul* (WUNT 2/42; Tübingen: Mohr Siebeck, 1991).

20. Paul writes eight letters with others: 1 Cor. 1:1; 2 Cor. 1:1; Gal. 1:2; Phil. 1:1; Col. 1:1; 1 Thess. 1:1; 2 Thess. 1:1; Phm. 1:1.

21. Midrash is a social activity involving a teacher, students, and texts of Torah in a lively exchange; diatribe also has as its first social setting the classroom in which teacher and students are dialogically engaged.

evidence drawn from across the canonical letters, and conversely, are they contradicted by any of the canonical letters?

The Search for a Center

The history of Pauline scholarship is to a significant degree the quest for a central composition, influence, idea, or perspective that can control the diversity of the correspondence. Excluding six letters is itself an expression of the search for a singular, internally coherent Paul.[22] But since even the seven "undisputed" letters resist homogenization, some scholars focus exclusively on the so-called "great" letters (Romans, Galatians, 1 and 2 Corinthians),[23] or they simply decide to take Romans as the least "occasional" and most "systematic" of Paul's letters[24] and treat it as representing the essential Paul, with the other six undisputed letters read in light of Romans.

Other scholars have sought leverage in some aspect of Paul's cultural and religious context — his "symbolic world." From the Greco-Roman side, researchers examine the possible links between Paul and Epicureanism[25] or Paul and Stoicism.[26] The argument has been made that Paul most resembles Hellenistic Jews like Philo, especially in his understanding of the law.[27] Others exploit Paul's roots in Palestinian Judaism,[28] specifically in the perceptions specific to a Pharisee,[29] or the dualistic understanding of history provided by apocalyptic.[30] Finally, some have

---

22. Consistency in style and theme was the driving force in determining the "authentic" letters from the start; see F. Schleiermacher, *Über den sogennanten Ersten Brief des Paulus an den Timotheus: Ein kritisches Senschreiben an J. C. Gass* (Berlin: Realschulbuchhandlung, 1807).

23. The classic theological studies of Paul by Bultmann and Käsemann focus almost exclusively on these letters: R. Bultmann, *Theology of the New Testament*, vol. 1 (trans. K. Grobel; New York: Charles Scribner's Sons, 1951); E. Käsemann, *Perspectives on Paul* (trans. M. Kohl; Philadelphia: Fortress, 1971).

24. See J. D. G. Dunn, *The Theology of Paul the Apostle* (Grand Rapids: Eerdmans, 1998).

25. See N. W. Dewitte, *St. Paul and Epicurus* (Minneapolis: Univ. of Minneapolis Press, 1954).

26. E.g., T. Engberg-Pedersen, ed., *Paul in His Hellenistic Context* (Minneapolis: Fortress, 1995).

27. See H.-J. Schoeps, *Paul: The Theology of the Apostle in the Light of Jewish Religious History* (trans. H. Knight; Philadelphia: Westminster, 1961).

28. E. P. Sanders, *Paul and Palestinian Judaism: A Comparison of Patterns of Religion* (Philadelphia: Fortress, 1977).

29. Classically, W. D. Davies, *Paul and Rabbinic Judaism: Some Rabbinic Elements in Pauline Theology* (New York: Harper and Row, 1967).

30. J. C. Beker, *Paul the Apostle: The Triumph of God in Life and Thought* (Philadelphia: Fortress, 1980).

made the kerygma of the pre-Pauline Hellenistic church the basis for Paul's thought.[31]

Efforts have not been lacking to find a thematic center that might enable some control over the disparate evidence. Scholars who select Romans and Galatians as the essential Paul, especially when they read from a Lutheran perspective, have found Paul's struggle with the law and the theme of righteousness by faith as the center of his thought.[32] Remarkably enough, scholars reading the same compositions from the standpoint of the so-called "new perspective" find Paul's engagement with the story of Israel as the key to his thinking.[33] Still other readers of Romans and Galatians see an implied story about Jesus as the "narrative substructure" of Paul's theology.[34] Another classic option argues that Paul is defined by eschatological categories and that participation "in Christ" is the central Pauline conviction.[35]

Each effort has served to highlight things that might otherwise not have been seen. But none of the proposed "centers" meets the evidentiary test: faith and works are absent from the Corinthian and Thessalonian correspondence, for example, and the story of Israel seems of little concern in Colossians, the Thessalonian letters, Philippians, or 2 Timothy. A strong case can be made for an implied story of Jesus lying behind Romans, Galatians, the Corinthian letters, and Philippians, but it is less obviously a premise in the Thessalonian or Prison Letters.

If the correspondence discourages us from seeking a single proposition, perspective, or premise as the center of Paul's thought or concern, we are nevertheless able to characterize the sensibilities at work in its production. Here, the positive results of the quest for a Pauline center can be affirmed. His grounding in Greco-Roman culture is evident in his writing rhetorically crafted letters to communities,[36] in

---

31. W. Bousset, KYRIOS CHRISTOS: *A History of the Belief in Christ from the Beginnings to Irenaeus* (trans. John E. Steely; Nashville: Abingdon, repr. 1970).

32. See S. Westerholm, *Perspectives Old and New on Paul: The "Lutheran" Paul and His Critics* (Grand Rapids: Eerdmans, 2004).

33. N. T. Wright, *The Climax of the Covenant: Christ and the Law in Pauline Theology* (Minneapolis: Fortress, 1992).

34. The pioneering figure is R. B. Hays, *The Faith of Jesus Christ: The Narrative Substructure of Galatians 3:1–4:11* (2nd ed.; Grand Rapids: Eerdmans, 2002).

35. A. Schweitzer, *The Mysticism of Paul the Apostle* (New York: Holt, 1931).

36. See, e.g., M. M. Mitchell, *Paul and the Rhetoric of Reconciliation: An Exegetical Investigation of the Language and Composition of 1 Corinthians* (Louisville: Westminster John Knox, 1991).

his—acquaintance with commonplaces of moral philosophy,[37] and above all in a religious sensibility that builds on experience, yet insists on the use of reason.[38] Paul's loyalty to his Jewish heritage is marked by his explicit concern for the destiny of Israel as God's people and his intense engagement with Torah; his symbolic framework and specific diction are shaped by the Jewish Scriptures.[39] The influence of Hellenistic Judaism is found in his use of the Greek Septuagint (LXX) as Scripture,[40] and in his concern for strong boundaries separating the community from paganism. Palestinian Judaism appears in his claim to be a Pharisee, in his interpreting the LXX according to modes that are recognizably proto-rabbinic,[41] and in an apocalyptic understanding of history.[42]

Much more difficult is the question of what holds these dimensions together. What distinguishes this authorial voice from that of a Philo or of a Hillel? An answer must be adequate to account for Paul's turn from persecutor to an apostle, his preaching and founding of communities, and the experiences, convictions, and commitments he shares with such communities as he addresses their problems. I speak of experiences, commitments, and convictions, because the matrix out of which Paul's correspondence emerges is first of all not conceptual but existential, less a matter of abstract thought than of religious concern.[43] Paul put his mind and heart to work in the interpretation of three religious realities.

First was his *personal religious experience*, which included not only his encounter with the risen Jesus and his call to be an apostle (1 Cor. 9:1; 15:8; Gal. 1:15–16; 1 Tim. 1:12), but also his mystical experiences of prayer—including speaking in tongues (1 Cor. 14:18) and a vision of

---

37. See esp. A. J. Malherbe, *Paul and the Popular Philosophers* (Minneapolis: Fortress, 1989).

38. The similarity between Paul and Epictetus owes at least something to the fact that they shared the same type of religious sensibility, that of moral transformation; see L. T. Johnson, *Among the Gentiles: Greco-Roman Religion and Christianity* (ABL; New Haven, CT: Yale Univ. Press, 2009).

39. See the detailed expositions in R. B. Hays, *Echoes of Scripture in the Letters of Paul* (New Haven, CT: Yale Univ. Press, 1989), and *The Conversion of the Imagination: Paul as Interpreter of Israel's Scripture* (Grand Rapids: Eerdmans, 2005).

40. See C. D. Stanley, *Arguing with Scripture: The Rhetoric of Quotations in the Letters of Paul* (Edinburgh: T&T Clark, 2004).

41. See N. A. Dahl, "Contradictions in Scripture," in *Studies in Paul* (Minneapolis: Augsburg, 1977), 159–77.

42. See D. A. Campbell, *The Deliverance of God: An Apocalyptic Rereading of Justification in Paul* (Grand Rapids: Eerdmans, 2009).

43. See J. B. Wallace, *Snatched into Paradise (2 Cor 12:1–10): Paul's Heavenly Journey in the Context of Early Christian Experience* (Berlin: De Gruyter, 2011).

heavenly places (2 Cor. 12:1–5)—and a continuing sense of empowerment through the Holy Spirit that came from the exalted Christ (Phil. 4:13). When Paul speaks of being "in the Lord" (1 Cor. 4:17; 9:1–2) or "in Christ" (1 Cor. 15:31; 2 Cor. 2:14, 17), he is not referring to concepts but to personal experience that binds him mystically to Jesus.[44]

Second was the *religious experience of his readers*, whom he saw as existing in the energy field of the Holy Spirit, who also placed them "in Christ" (1 Cor. 1:2; Gal. 3:26) and Christ "in them" (Rom. 8:10). His letters assume and appeal to the presence of the Spirit not as an ideal to be desired but as a factual reality.

Third was the *complex of traditions and practices of the community already in place* when Paul became a founder of churches and writer of letters: the practices of baptism (Rom. 6:1–11; Gal. 3:27; Eph. 4:5; Col. 2:12; Titus 3:5) and the Lord's Supper (1 Cor. 11:17–34), confessions of faith (Rom. 10:9; 1 Cor. 8:4–6; 12:3; 1 Tim. 3:16), and above all traditions concerning Jesus: the facts of his life and death, the witnesses to his resurrection, and the shape of his human character (see below). Paul's appreciation for antecedent traditions is found not only in his use of them in his letters but in his explicit statements concerning conversation and communion with the church in Jerusalem and its leadership (Rom. 15:19, 25; 1 Cor. 15:3–8; 16:1–4; 2 Cor. 8–9; Gal. 1:18; 2:7–10).

The combination of these elements makes Paul's letters distinctive among other first-century religious and philosophical literature, as well as other New Testament compositions. Paul's teachings move into, out of, and around such experiential and traditional elements. They are present in diverse degree and manner in all the letters. Together they characterize the distinctive voice that we recognize as Paul's. These realities, called "gospel of God" or "gospel of Christ" (Rom. 1:1; 1 Cor. 15:1; 2 Cor. 2:12; Gal. 1:7; Eph. 1:13; Phil. 1:27; Col. 1:23; 1 Thess. 2:2; 2 Thess. 1:8; 1 Tim. 1:11; 2 Tim. 1:8; Phlm. 13), are foundational for Paul and his communities. They create also a real tension with

---

44. Note the intensely personal character of Paul's statements in Galatians: "I live, no longer I, but Christ lives in me; insofar as I now live in the flesh, I live by faith in [or: the faith of] the Son of God, who has loved me and given himself up for me" (Gal. 2:20); "May I never boast except in the cross of our Lord Jesus Christ, through which the world has been crucified to me, and I to the world" (6:14); "I bear the marks of Jesus on my body" (6:17). In this essay, I use the New American Bible translation of the New Testament.

elements of Paul's symbolic world — above all his prior understanding of Torah — that demands resolution through interpretation. Everything is read through the religious experience of Paul and his readers.

The Significance of Christ

All these religious experiences and traditions center on the figure of Jesus Christ.[45] It is Christ who inaugurates the new age, indeed the new creation. It is in light of Christ that all previous understandings of God must be evaluated. Christ marks both the end and the goal of history: he is the "eschatological Adam." He is more than simply another human leader; he is "God's Son," whose existence carries with it the destiny of humanity as a whole. Because Christ is so important, Paul's understanding of him is complex. Paul can speak of Jesus Christ in several modes of discourse. He uses historical language, mythical language, even ontological language, sometimes side by side.[46]

Paul's perception of Jesus begins with and is shaped by the resurrection. There is no evidence that Paul knew Jesus before his death, and his encounter with the risen Lord is the start of his apostolic ministry: "I have seen the Lord Jesus" (1 Cor. 9:1). Paul lists himself as the last (and least) of those to whom Jesus appeared after his death (15:3–8). His own experience of Jesus as the risen one, however, has more than merely personal significance: Paul experienced the truth of the good news and the power that was at work in the community that preceded him. "Whether it be I or they," he declares of the resurrection, "so we preach and so you believe" (15:11).

Jesus' resurrection is more than resuscitation or simple vindication. With other early believers, Paul above all proclaims Jesus to be "Lord," with the term *kyrios* bearing all of the theophoric resonances established by the LXX's use of the title for the proper name of God.[47] The resurrection is Jesus' exaltation "to the right hand of God" (Ps. 110:1), where he "intercedes for us" (Rom. 8:34). It is because the exalted Jesus exists

---

45. An older but splendid treatment of Pauline Christology is L. Cerfaux, *Christ in the Theology of Saint Paul* (New York: Herder and Herder, 1959).

46. Historical: Jesus was "born of a woman, born under the law" (Gal. 4:4); mythological: "God was in Christ reconciling the world to Himself"(2 Cor. 5:19); ontological: when Christ hands over the kingdom to God, then "God will be all in all" (1 Cor. 15:28).

47. E.g., Gen. 2:4; Ex. 3:15, 16; 34:6; Pss. 24:1; 25:1; Isa. 53:1.

now as Lord, sharing fully both the presence and the power of God,
that he is able to help those whom he has chosen (Phil. 4:13; 1 Thess.
3:11–13; 1 Tim. 1:12; 2 Tim. 4:17–18), that makes him share as well in
the divine role of judge over humans (Rom. 2:16; 2 Cor. 5:10), and that
makes his future *parousia* a revelation of the full triumph of God in the
world (1 Cor. 15; 1 and 2 Thessalonians).

For Paul, then, the title *Christos* ("Messiah") captures only a part
of Jesus' significance. His exaltation as Lord extends his dominion far
beyond the bounds of Israel. Paul takes pains to establish the real if
paradoxical role of Jesus as Israel's Messiah (Rom. 9–11)—paradoxical
not least because in human terms (i.e., in the terms of contemporary
Jewish expectation, "according to the flesh"), Jesus appeared as a failed
if not a false Messiah, and the majority of Jews failed to recognize him
in any sense as their Anointed One. For Paul and his readers, however,
Jesus is Messiah or Christ precisely as "Lord," for he exercises God's
rule over all things. Jesus is more than the ruler or restorer of the Jewish
people; he is the ruler and restorer of all humanity.

Central to the understanding of Christ's resurrection in Paul's letters is the work of the Holy Spirit. Believers can proclaim "Jesus is
Lord" because they are "in the Holy Spirit" (1 Cor. 12:3). The resurrected Jesus, in turn, has become "a life-giving spirit" (15:45), a description that evokes the distinctive attributes of God within Scripture.[48]
The realm of the Spirit within which Christians exist—which, in fact,
"indwells" them (Rom. 8:9)—and the realm of the resurrected Lord
therefore coincide, so that Paul can speak of the Holy Spirit being in
them (Rom. 8:11) and of their being in the Holy Spirit (8:9), of Christ
being in them (8:10) and of their being in Christ (8:1).

At times, Paul speaks of the Spirit in explicitly personal terms
(1 Cor. 2:11); at other times, the term suggests an energy field or power
that touches and transforms (12:13). In both usages, the Spirit appears
as a medium that serves to connect subjects who would otherwise seem
impossibly distant: the Spirit links an executed Messiah as risen Lord
both to God and to humans (see esp. 2 Cor. 13:13). The Spirit transcends space and time to join persons across space and time, enabling
Paul to speak of the resurrection not simply as a past event, but as an

48. See 2 Kings 5:7; Neh. 9:6; Job 36:6; Ps. 70:20.

existential reality of the present suffusing both Jesus and the believers with the power and presence of God. The Holy Spirit provides humans with access to God through Christ, and the Holy Spirit works to transform humans into the image of Christ (3:17–18).

Jesus' resurrection can be considered "historical" in the sense that witnesses can testify to his appearances within time and space (1 Cor. 15:5–8). But it far transcends the historical, because Jesus now shares the life and power of God (15:24–28, 45). The resurrection is therefore an eschatological event; it transcends the categories of ordinary historical sequence and introduces a radically new element into human existence. It is a "new creation" (*kainē ktisis*), in which "old things have passed away; behold all things are new" (2 Cor. 5:16–17). The God who "raised Jesus our Lord from the dead" (Rom. 4:25) is the one who "gives life to the dead and calls into being what does not exist" (4:17). Understanding Jesus as cosmic Lord (Phil. 2:10–11) motivates Paul's mission to the Gentiles. If Jesus is Lord of all, then the God revealed by Jesus is the God of all humans: "Does God belong to Jews alone? Does he not belong the Gentiles, too? Yes, also to Gentiles, for God is One" (Rom. 3:30).

Paul's letters do not therefore portray Jesus as a new lawgiver like Moses. In fact, Paul tends to compare himself to Moses (Rom. 9:1–3; 2 Cor. 3:7–18; 2 Tim. 3:8–9). Jesus instead reveals a new form of humanity, and the "new covenant" that he institutes "in his blood" (1 Cor. 11:25) is inscribed in human hearts through the power of the Spirit (2 Cor. 3:3–6). Paul speaks of Jesus as the "last Adam" and compares him to the original human in Genesis. Whereas the first Adam established humanity in sin and disobedience, Christ established humanity in grace and obedience (Rom. 5:12–21); whereas the first Adam was merely human ("a living being"), the eschatological Adam has, through resurrection, become "a life-giving spirit" (1 Cor. 15:45). Those who are "in Christ," therefore, have assumed a new form of humanity as well (Gal. 3:26; 6:15; Eph. 4:22–24; Col. 3:9–11).

But why does Jesus, among all humans, have this distinctive representative significance? In Romans 1:4, Paul contrasts Jesus' human existence ("descended from David according to the flesh") and his divine exaltation: "established as Son of God in power according to the spirit of holiness through resurrection from the dead." In other passages, however, Paul uses language that suggests the fullness of God's presence in Jesus before the resurrection and even before his human birth. In Galatians 4:4, he states that the Son, "born of a woman, born under the law," was "sent by God," which suggests a prior existence; likewise in Romans 8:3, Paul speaks of God sending "his own Son." Paul's midrashic interpretation of the wilderness experience in 1 Corinthians 10:1–4 identifies the rock that followed the ancient Israelites with Christ.[49]

Christ even has a role in creation (1 Cor. 8:6; Col. 1:16) and participates fully in the divine, being "in the form of God" (Phil. 2:6), and being "the image of the unseen God" (2 Cor. 4:4; Col. 1:15; 3:10). In Christ "dwells the whole fullness of the deity bodily" (Col. 2:9), and "God was reconciling the world to himself in Christ" (2 Cor. 5:19). Jesus is not for Paul just another human. He is, in a way no one else is, God's Son (see especially Rom. 8:29, 32; 1 Cor. 1:9; 2 Cor. 1:19; Gal. 1:16; 2:20; Eph. 4:13; Col. 1:13; 1 Thess. 1:10). Within twenty-five years of Jesus' execution, Paul makes this affirmation of belief: "For us there is one God, the Father, from whom all things are and for whom we exist, and one Lord, Jesus Christ, through whom all things are and through whom we exist" (1 Cor. 8:6). Similarly, he states: "For there is one God. There is also one mediator between God and the human race, Christ Jesus, himself human, who gave himself as a ransom for all" (1 Tim. 2:5).

Precisely such a strong position concerning the status of Christ as God's Son makes more dramatic Paul's depiction of his human condition as an "emptying out" (*kenōsis*), in which Christ does not regard being in the form of God as "something to be grasped" but takes on the form of humans as an expression of humility (Phil. 2:7–8). This classic statement in Philippians is matched by a series of reversal declarations in 2 Corinthians: "For our sake he made [Christ] to be sin who did not know sin, so that we might become the righteousness of God in him" (2 Cor. 5:21); "for your sake he became poor although he was rich, so that by his poverty you might become rich" (8:9); "he was crucified out of weakness, but he lives by the power of God" (13:4).

The frequent assertion in Paul's letters that Christ "gave himself" for humans (Gal. 1:4; 2:20; Eph. 5:2; 1 Tim. 2:6; Titus 2:14), therefore, can

---

49. W. A. Meeks, "'And Rose Up to Play': Midrash and Paraenesis in 1 Corinthians 10:1–22," *JSNT* 16 (1982): 64–78.

legitimately be read also as God's "giving himself" to humans through Christ (Rom. 8:31–39). From such statements concerning "God's Son," the reader can properly infer conclusions concerning the character of God. But they also point us to the last important aspect of Christ's significance in Paul's letters, namely, his human character.

On this point it is particularly important not to draw a false inference from Paul's statement in 2 Corinthians 5:16, "even if we once knew Christ according to the flesh, yet now we know him so no longer." Paul here refers to the perception of Jesus apart from his encounter with the risen Lord, a perception that regarded Jesus simply in human terms and not "according to the spirit." That Paul does not indicate thereby his present unconcern or even disregard for the humanity of Jesus is shown by his statement in 1 Corinthians 12:3, "nobody speaking by the spirit of God says, 'Jesus be accursed.'" In fact, Paul's positive appreciation for the humanity of Jesus is impressive.

It is true that Paul's letters do not contain substantial portions of gospel material, which is not surprising in occasional letters addressing specific circumstances. We find no reports concerning Jesus' miracles and few of Jesus' sayings in Paul's letters. Still, simply at the level of fact, the letters reveal a significant knowledge of the human Jesus. Paul asserts that Jesus had a human birth, was Jewish, and had a mission to the Jews: "God sent forth his Son, born of a woman, born under the law, to ransom those under the law" (Gal. 4:4). Similarly, he declares that "Christ became a servant to the circumcised to show God's truthfulness, to confirm the promises to the patriarchs" (Rom. 15:8). Jesus is legitimately, "according to the flesh," the Jewish Messiah (9:5). Indeed, Jesus is descended from David "according to the flesh" (1:3; see also 2 Tim. 2:8). Paul considers as authoritative the few sayings of Jesus to which he refers, concerning divorce (1 Cor. 7:10), payment for preaching (9:14; see also 1 Tim. 5:17), and the end times (1 Thess. 4:15). It is highly likely that in Galatians 4:6 and Romans 8:15–16, Paul refers to shared community traditions concerning Jesus' distinctive Aramaic prayer to *Abba*.

Paul's letters are particularly dense in their references to the end of Jesus' human life. He explicitly quotes the words that Jesus spoke over the bread and the cup "on the night he was handed over," initiating a new covenant in his blood—identifying these words as a tradition received by him and handed on to his readers (1 Cor. 11:23–25). He also explicitly connects the death of Jesus to the Passover celebration of the Jews: "Our paschal lamb, Christ, has been sacrificed" (5:7). That Jesus underwent a trial before human judges is the best reading of 1 Cor. 2:8: "none of the rulers of this age knew; for if they had known it, they would not have crucified the Lord of glory." A trial before Pontius Pilate is explicitly reported in 1 Timothy 6:13. Paul's allusion to Psalm 69:9 in Romans 15:3 suggests that Jesus underwent abuse and humiliation: "For Christ did not please himself; but as it is written, 'The insults of those who insult you fall upon me.'"

That Jews in Jerusalem were actively involved in Jesus' death is explicitly stated in 1 Thessalonians 2:13–16, a passage whose authenticity has been challenged but which surely derives from early Pauline tradition: " ... the Jews, who killed both the Lord Jesus and the prophets and persecuted us; they do not please God, and are opposed to everyone."[50] The letters attest to Jesus' death by crucifixion (1 Cor. 1:23; 2:2; 2 Cor. 13:4; Phil. 2:8; Gal. 3:1; Eph. 2:16; Col. 1:20), his burial (Rom. 6:4; 1 Cor. 15:4), and his appearance to a variety of witnesses, including Paul himself (1 Cor. 9:1; 15:4–8; Gal. 1:15–16).

Such statements of fact do not appear as part of a sustained narrative but occur incidentally, which makes them all the more impressive as evidence for Paul's knowledge of and appreciation for the human Jesus. They attest as well to Paul's enmeshment within the larger Christian movement and to the ubiquity as well as antiquity of the story of Jesus. Ubiquity is as significant as antiquity: Paul can assume that his readers in Rome are as familiar with the facts concerning Jesus as are his readers in Corinth or Galatia. That these facts can be ordered to correspond to the gospel sequence also supports the hypothesis that Paul knew, alluded to, and applied aspects of the story of Jesus in his letters.[51]

The crucifixion of Jesus — in the social/symbolic world of the Roman Empire the most shameful of all deaths[52] — is particularly

---

50. See J. A. Weatherly, "The Authenticity of 1 Thess. 2:13–16: Additional Evidence," *JSNT* 42 (1991): 79–98.

51. See L. T. Johnson, *Living Jesus: Learning the Heart of the Gospel* (San Francisco: HarperSanFrancisco, 1999), 99–115.

52. M. Hengel, *Crucifixion in the Ancient World and the Folly of the Message of the Cross* (trans. J. Bowden; Philadelphia: Fortress, 1977).

important in Paul's letters. First, the cross is a scandal or stumbling block preventing Jews from accepting Jesus as their Messiah (Rom. 9:30–33; 1 Cor. 1:23). This is so, as Paul declares in Galatians 3:13, because the manner of Jesus' death certified that, by the standards of Torah, he was cursed by God: "For it is written, 'Cursed be everyone who hangs on a tree'" (Deut. 21:23). In the ancient world, the manner of one's death indicated the character of one's life. If Jesus died as one cursed by God, then he could not be the source of righteousness and life, and any claim by believers that he was the Messiah was invalidated. The issue of "Christ and the law," which plays such a central role in Galatians and Romans—and to a much lesser degree and in a slightly different manner in Philippians, Colossians, Ephesians, 1 Timothy, and Titus—arises precisely out of the cognitive dissonance created by the experiential claims of the resurrection and the brutal fact of crucifixion. In those letters, consequently, "the cross of Christ" functions as the key hermeneutical lens for the reinterpretation of Torah (see especially Rom. 9–11 and Gal. 3–4).

Second, the cross is the supreme sign that God "did not spare his own Son" for the sake of humans, but "handed him over for us all" (Rom. 8:32). Jesus' death was a sacrifice (1 Cor. 5:7), in which "God set [him] forth as an expiation … by his blood" (Rom. 3:25), an act that sealed a new covenant between God and humans in his human blood (1 Cor. 11:25; see 2 Cor. 3:6). Jesus' death was a sacrifice "for our sins" (1 Cor. 15:3; cf. Rom 3:25), the complete proof of God's love for humans: "God proves his love for us in that while we were still sinners Christ died for us" (Rom. 5:8). As such, the cross represents God's power present in human weakness (1 Cor. 1:18–24; 2 Cor. 13:4), the pure "grace/gift" of God that constitutes, with the resurrection, the "gospel" (Rom. 1:16; 1 Cor. 15:1–4; Eph. 2:8–14).

Third, the cross is also an expression of the human Jesus' character, namely, the faith he shows toward God and the love he displays toward other humans. Scholars debate the difficult expression *pistis Christou*. Should it be taken as believers' faith in Christ or as Christ's faith in God?[53] There are strong reasons for holding that in some key

---

53. See the various essays in M. F. Bird and P. M. Sprinkle, eds., *The Faith of Jesus Christ: Exegetical, Biblical, and Theological Studies* (Peabody, MA: Hendrickson, 2009).

passages—above all in Rom. 3:21–26—Paul speaks of the faithful human response of Jesus to God as an essential dimension of his sacrificial death.[54] The expression "obedience of faith" in Romans 1:5 and 16:26 indicates how Paul understands the equivalence between the two terms, and the development of the statements made concerning faith in 3:21–26 in terms of obedience in 5:12–21 indicates that Paul thinks of faith in terms of obedience.[55]

The most convincing evidence is provided by Philippians 2:8, where Paul speaks of Jesus' self-emptying in this fashion: "he humbled himself, becoming obedient unto death, even death on a cross" (see also Gal. 2:16, 20; 3:22; 26; Phil. 3:9; 1 Tim. 3:13; 2 Tim. 1:13; 3:15). Paul understands the human character of Jesus in terms of faithful obedience revealed above all in his death on a cross. In similar fashion, Jesus' human character is shown by his "giving himself" in death for others: thus Paul speaks of "liv[ing] by the faith of the Son of God who loved me and gave himself up for me" (Gal. 2:20; see also 2 Cor. 5:14; Eph. 3:19; 5:2; Phil. 2:3–4; 1 Tim. 1:14; 2 Tim. 1:13).

Finally, the cross—as shorthand for the manner and disposition of Jesus in his death—appears in Paul's letters as a pattern for community behavior.[56] Paul speaks of acting according to "the mind of Christ" (1 Cor. 2:16) in the context of a reminder of the cruciform character of life in the community, in which strength expresses itself in service to the weak (1 Cor. 1:18–2:16). Similarly, he tells the competitive Galatians that they should "bear one another's burdens, and so you will fulfill the law of Christ" (Gal. 6:2). His recounting of the *Kenosis* of Christ in Philippians 2:6–8 has the purpose of encouraging readers to think as Christ did (2:5) in order to shape a community ethos in which "each look[s] out not for his own interests, but [also] everyone for those of others" (2:1–4). The faith and love displayed by Christ in his death is the pattern for moral dispositions within Paul's communities.

The understanding of Jesus in Paul's letters is richly complex, embracing Jesus' relationship with God—even in creation and in the

---

54. L. T. Johnson, "Romans 3:21–26 and the Faith of Jesus," *CBQ* 44 (1982): 77–90.

55. L. T. Johnson, *Reading Romans: A Literary and Theological Commentary* (Macon, GA: Selwyn and Helwys, 2001), 83–99.

56. See W. A. Meeks, *The Origins of Christian Morality* (New Haven, CT: Yale Univ. Press, 1993), 61–65, 86–88.

history of Israel—his human life, and his exalted present existence; his status as God's Son and his kenotic life for others; his presence in the Holy Spirit and in the hearts of believers. All these aspects of Jesus are for Paul "grace," the distinctive gift that God gives to those in the new creation.

The Meaning of Salvation

Among the most important of the experiences, convictions, and commitments that bound Paul and his readers was that the living God was acting on and for them through the risen Lord Jesus, and that their existence had been and was still being altered through the power of God. The good news from God in which they stood was also saving them (1 Cor. 15:2); the good news was the "power of God for the salvation of everyone who believes" (Rom. 1:16). Although expressions of it vary, the conviction that God was at work to save humans is constant across Paul's letters.

Two basic aspects of the conviction should be emphasized from the start. First, salvation is not something accomplished by humans by their own efforts, but is accomplished by God through the death and resurrection of Jesus and the power of the Holy Spirit. Second, salvation has to do not with the accidental circumstances of life so much as the essential conditions of human existence; liberation is not from social or political oppression,[57] but from forces that constrain and distort personal freedom and community integrity. The basic human problem lies less in the inadequate or even harmful structures and systems of society than in the twisted recesses of the human heart. The solution must therefore apply primarily to personal transformation and secondarily to social change.

At the most basic level, the terms for salvation (*sōzō, sōtēria*) point to a change from a negative to a positive condition.[58] Paul's letters do not envisage humans in the manner common since the Enlightenment,

---

57. Paul is more conservative than not regarding social institutions (see Rom. 13:1–7; 1 Cor. 7:17–31). It is possible to infer anti-imperial nuances from Paul's language, but it is impossible to conclude that Paul considered the empire to be the root cause of human alienation. For a summary of the inferences, see N. T. Wright, "Paul and Empire," in *The Blackwell Companion to Paul* (ed. S. Westerholm; Oxford: Wiley-Blackwell, 2011), 285–97.

58. See Johnson, *The Writings of the New Testament*, 85–94.

as independent agents; rather, they view humans as always defined by relationship to powers that either enhance or diminish their authentic existence. Humans are either ruled by powers that hold them captive (see Rom. 5:14, 17; 6:12) or establish them in freedom by "the reign of God" (Rom. 14:17; 1 Cor. 4:10; Gal. 5:21; Eph. 5:5; Col. 1:13; 1 Thess. 2:12; 2 Thess. 1:5; 2 Tim. 4:1, 18). The good news proclaimed by Paul is that God's power to rule is superior to that of hostile forces and, through the death and resurrection of Jesus, has brought believers within the sphere of power exercised by the Holy Spirit.

Thus, Paul speaks of "the Lord Jesus Christ, who gave himself for our sins that he might rescue us from the present evil age" (Gal. 1:3–4); similarly, the Thessalonians await the Son who "delivers us from the coming wrath" (1 Thess. 1:10). The rule of God is not theoretical but actual; it is a matter of power (*dynamis,* see Rom. 1:16; 1 Cor. 1:18; 2 Cor. 13:4; Gal. 3:5; 2 Tim. 1:7), authority (*exousia,* see 1 Cor. 8:9; 9:4; 2 Cor. 10:8; 13:10; 2 Thess. 3:9), and energy (*energeia,* see 1 Cor. 12:6, 11; Gal. 3:5; 5:6; Eph. 3:20–21; Col. 1:29; 1 Thess. 2:13; Phlm. 6).

Paul can speak of slavery or captivity to cosmic powers (Rom. 8:38; Gal. 4:3; Eph. 2:1–10; Col. 1:13), to death (Rom. 5:21; 1 Cor. 15:26; 2 Tim. 1:10), to the flesh (Rom. 7:25; 8:3; Gal. 5:13, 16), to sin (Rom. 6:6; 7:11; 1 Cor. 15:17; Gal. 2:17; 3:22; Eph. 2:1; 1 Thess. 2:10; 1 Tim. 5:24; 2 Tim. 3:6), and to law (Rom. 6:15–23; 2 Cor. 3:6–18; Gal. 5:1; Col. 2:8–23). Rescue from such negative forces, in turn, can be expressed in terms of freedom (Rom. 6:18, 20; 8:2; Gal. 5:1, 13), spirit (Rom. 5:5; 7:6; 8:2; 1 Cor. 2:4; 12:13; 2 Cor. 1:22; 3:17–18; Gal. 3:2–3; 4:6; Eph. 1:17; 2:18; Phil. 1:19; 2:1; Col. 1:8; 1 Thess. 1:5–6; 2 Thess. 2:13; 2 Tim. 1:7; Titus 3:5; Phlm. 25), and life (Rom. 5:2; 8:2; 2 Cor. 2:16; 4:10; Col. 3:3–4; 1 Tim. 4:8; 6:19; 2 Tim. 1:1). Salvation is not, however, simply a matter of repair or of restoration in the human condition; it is a matter of elevation to a higher state of being. Thus, Paul emphasizes in his contrast between Adam and Christ "how much more" is the gift of God in Christ than was the harm done by Adam (Rom. 5:12–21). Humans are not simply rescued from physical death to enjoy empirical life. They are rescued from the death that stands for alienation from God and are given a share in the life that is distinctive to God. Paul thus speaks of the gift of "eternal life" (Rom. 2:7; 5:21; 6:22–23; Gal. 6:8; 1 Tim. 1:16; 6:12; Titus 1:2; 3:7).

The change that God effects in the world is a reality greater than any single discourse can capture. Paul's letters use several metaphors drawn from the social and religious realities of Greco-Roman and Jewish culture.[59]

1. In diplomatic language, the condition of distance from God is expressed in terms of alienation (2 Cor. 5:18–20; Eph. 2:12); God's action is expressed in terms of reconciliation (Rom. 5:10–11; Eph. 2:16); Christ is an ambassador (Rom. 5:11; 2 Cor. 5:18) or mediator (1 Tim. 2:5) who effects peace between God and humans (Rom. 5:1; Eph. 2:14–17; 2 Thess. 3:16).

2. In economic language, the condition of distance from God is expressed in terms of slavery (Rom. 6:6, 17; 8:21; Gal. 4:1, 8–9; Titus 2:9); God's action is expressed as redemption (Rom. 3:24; 8:23; 1 Cor. 1:30; Eph. 1:7; Col. 1:14); Christ's death is a ransom (1 Tim. 2:6) that "purchases" believers (1 Cor. 6:20); the result is freedom (Rom. 6:18; 8:21; 2 Cor. 3:17; Gal. 5:1).

3. In forensic language, God is the righteous judge (2 Tim. 4:8) who responds to the deeds of humans with wrath (Rom. 1:18; 2:5; 9:22; Eph. 2:3; Col. 3:6; 1 Thess. 1:10) or mercy (Rom. 9:23; 11:31; Gal. 6:16; 2 Tim. 1:16–18, 3:5), but judges without respect to appearances (Rom. 2:11; 3:22; Eph. 6:9; Col. 3:25). The condition of alienation from God is expressed as unrighteousness (Rom. 1:18, 29; 6:13; 2 Thess. 2:10; 2 Tim. 2:19), lawlessness (Rom. 6:19; 2 Cor. 6:14; 2 Thess. 2:7; 1 Tim. 1:9; Titus 2:14), transgression (Rom. 2:23; 5:14; Gal. 3:19; 1 Tim. 2:14), faithlessness (Rom. 3:3; 11:20; 1 Tim. 1:13), or disobedience (Rom. 11:30–32; Eph. 2:2; 5:6; Col. 3:6). Christ is the one who is righteous (1 Cor. 1:30) through faith (Rom. 1:17; 3:22, 25; Gal 3:11); the result of God's action through Christ is human righteousness—being in right relationship with God (Rom. 5:17, 21; 6:13–20; 8:10; Gal. 5:5; Eph. 4:24; Phil. 3:9; Titus 3:5).

---

59. My thought here is influenced by M. E. Boring, "The Language of Universal Salvation in Paul," *JBL* 105 (1986): 269–92.

4. In cultic language, the human condition of separation from God is expressed by sin (Rom. 3:9; 5:12, 21; 1 Cor. 15:56; Gal. 3:22; Eph. 2:1; Col. 1:14; 1 Thess. 2:16; 1 Tim. 5:24; 2 Tim. 3:6); the work of Christ is found in a sacrificial death for sins and a covenant in his blood (Rom. 3:21–25; 8:32; 1 Cor. 11:25; 15:3; 2 Cor. 5:21; Gal. 1:4; Col. 1:14), leading to atonement and human "access" to God (Rom. 3:25; 5:2; Eph. 2:18; 3:12), with the result being "sanctification" or "holiness" (Rom. 6:19, 22; 15:16; 1 Cor. 1:2, 30; 6:11; Eph. 1:4; 5:26; Col. 1:22; 1 Thess. 4:3, 7; 5:23; 2 Thess. 2:13; 1 Tim. 2:15; 2 Tim. 1:9; 2:21).

5. In kinship language, humans are potential heirs of God (Eph. 1:14, 18), who while children are like slaves not yet in possession of the promise (Gal. 3:15–29; 4:1–3). Christ is the Son whom God sends to ransom/liberate humans (4:4), and through the Holy Spirit, makes them adopted children of God (Rom. 8:15, 23; Gal. 4:5–6), conformed to the image of the Son, who is the "firstborn among many brothers" (Rom. 8:29).

No single metaphor is the most important or governs the others. Paul uses them rather as roughly equivalent symbolic modes for expressing a reality that cannot be fully communicated by any of them. Indeed, Paul mixes the metaphors, so that the language from one logically distinct set finds a place within another (see, e.g., Rom. 5:1–8).

The theme of salvation as treated in Paul's letters also has a distinctive temporal dimension.[60] Emphasis on the present reality of God's rule in the world—made manifest in the resurrection of Jesus and the work of the Holy Spirit among believers—is everywhere attested. Paul employs the past and present tenses when speaking of this work, and he constantly iterates the word "now" (*nyn*) to stress the presence of the new creation (see, e.g., Rom. 3:26; 5:9; 8:1; 13:11; 16:26). There is an "already" to God's triumph in the world, a point that Paul needs to make particularly to believers who worry that those who have died

---

60. The expression "already/not yet" is commonplace in Pauline studies and is perhaps most classically associated with O. Cullmann, *Salvation in History* (New York: Harper and Row, 1967).

will miss out on that victory. Paul tells the Thessalonians that their hope for the future is grounded in the fundamental triumph of God over death as demonstrated through the resurrection of Christ (1 Thess. 4:14; 5:9–10).

Paul is forceful in his assertions concerning the present reality. The Galatians have experienced and can point to works of power among them (Gal. 3:1–5), as have the Corinthians (1 Cor. 1:5; 4:20; 12:27–28; 2 Cor. 12:12), the Thessalonians (1 Thess. 1:5), and the Colossians (Col. 1:11). At the most basic level, the cosmic forces inimical to humans have been thwarted through the death and resurrection of Christ (Rom. 8:31–39; 1 Cor. 3:22–23; Eph. 2:1–10; 3:10; 4:7–8; Phil. 2:10; Col. 2:14–15), and "those who have been saved" have a freedom given by the Holy Spirit to live in a new way of obedience to God (Rom. 6:1–14; 8:1–13). More than that, they are gifted with new capacities of faith, hope, and love (see 1 Thess. 1:2–3; cf. 1 Cor. 13:13), as well as diverse manifestations of the Spirit (Rom. 12:3–8; 1 Cor. 12:1–11; Eph. 4:1–16).

Yet, God's triumph is not complete in the empirical order; the new creation is not fully realized among humans. A sense of reservation is demanded by the hard facts on the ground: sin continues within communities (1 Cor. 5:1–5; Gal. 5:16–21; Col. 2:16–23; 1 Tim. 4:1–4; 5:20–25; 2 Tim. 2:15–26; 3:1–9; Titus 1:10–11), death and illness remain powerful (1 Cor. 11:28–32; 1 Thess. 4:13), and cosmic forces continue to threaten (1 Cor. 5:5; 2 Cor. 11:14; 1 Thess. 2:18; 2 Thess. 2:9; 1 Tim. 1:20; 5:15). Just as Paul needed to remind the Thessalonians that God's victory had been won in principle, so he was required to remind the Corinthians that their arrogant behavior — as though they "have already grown rich ... become kings" (1 Cor. 4:8) — was inappropriate. The resurrection of Christ was the "firstfruits" of God's triumph (1 Cor. 15:23), in which they participated through the gift of the Holy Spirit (12:12–13). But their own behavior revealed how much they had still to mature to become fully "spiritual" rather than "fleshly" (3:1–4), adult rather than childish (13:11–13; 4:20). They still had to change (15:53). God's full triumph over sin and death must still be accomplished (15:25–26, 54–57). Paul declares, "in hope we were saved" (Rom. 8:24), precisely because God's rule has not yet fully been experienced.

Paul's letters are strikingly diverse concerning that future triumph.[61] Three letters sketch fairly elaborate apocalyptic scenarios. First Thessalonians 4:13–18 expects both the living and the dead to be caught up in the clouds to meet the Lord in the air and always be with the Lord; 2 Thessalonians warns against a panic generated by the announcement of the Lord's arrival and sets out the public events that must occur before the climactic moment (2 Thess. 2:1–12); 1 Corinthians lays out the stages between the resurrection of Jesus and the handing over of the kingdom by the Son to God, who will then be "all in all" (1 Cor. 15:20–28). Less elaborately, Philippians 3:20–21 speaks of waiting for "a savior, the Lord Jesus Christ [who] will change our lowly body to conform with his glorified body by the power that enables him also to bring all things into subjection to himself."

Language about an "appearance from heaven" of Jesus Christ is found also in 1 Timothy 6:15–16 and 2 Timothy 4:1, as well as Titus 2:13, which speaks of awaiting "the blessed hope, the appearance of the glory of the great God and of our savior Jesus Christ." The link between that appearance and the destiny of believers is asserted by Colossians 3:4, "When Christ your life appears, then you too will appear with him in glory"; and by 2 Timothy 2:12, which affirms that "if we have died with him we shall also live with him; if we persevere we shall also reign with him." All such statements connect a visible appearance and a public participation.

But Paul can speak of the "revelation" of God's children through the groaning birth pangs of creation with no reference to a visible "coming of the Lord" (Rom. 8:18–25), and he is also capable of using strongly platonic terms when he speaks of individuals "going home to the Lord" at the point of leaving the body, with no reference at all to a public, apocalyptic, appearance (2 Cor. 5:1–9).[62] Similarly in 2 Timothy 4:18, Paul says that God "will bring me safe to his heavenly kingdom." In 2 Corinthians 5:10, Paul concludes with a thoroughly traditional statement of Jewish eschatology, in which God judges the deeds of humans, except that the role is now played by Christ: "For we must all appear

---

61. See J. Plevnik, *Paul and the Parousia: An Exegetical and Theological Investigation* (Peabody, MA: Hendrickson, 1997).

62. See J. Dupont, SYN CHRISTOI: *l'union avec le Christ suivant Saint Paul* (Bruges: Editions de l'Abbaye de Saint Andre, 1952).

before the judgment seat of Christ, so that each one may receive recompense, according to what he did in the body, whether good or evil" (5:10). Similar statements about God's judgment of human deeds occur in Romans 2:2–11 and 14:10.

Paul's eschatological language is so diverse in part because he could not possibly know what the future would be and was forced to use a variety of available dictions to express his confidence in God's full victory, and in part because his sketch of the end times was fitted to the specific sort of pastoral issues he was addressing. Paul had the hope that his fellow Jews would hear the good news and become part of the restored people of God, so that "all Israel" might be saved (Rom. 11:26); he expected that the final enemies of death and sin would be swallowed up in victory (1 Cor. 15:55–57); he was convinced that believers would be transformed so that they could "be with the Lord always" (2 Cor. 5:8; Col. 3:4; 1 Thess. 4:17; 2 Tim. 4:18) and share in his glory (Rom. 8:30). But it is in the nature of the topic that such expectations and desires must remain fluid, even for one whose experience of the resurrection was personal and direct (1 Cor. 9:1).

Paul's concern for the future is concentrated primarily on the victory of God in the world and only secondarily on the participation of believers in that victory. Apart from a handful of statements, his letters evince little interest in the destiny of believers after the moment of victory, and none in the eternal destiny of individuals. His language about salvation is almost entirely social in character. In distinction from Paul's diction concerning righteousness, which addresses the character of the human relationship with God—and is available to Abraham as well as Jesus, to Gentiles as well as to Jews (see Rom. 3:21–4:23)—his discourse concerning salvation connotes participation in a presently-being-rescued community. To "be saved" in Paul's letters does not indicate one's future destiny with God, but one's present inclusion in God's visible people.[63] Thus, Paul's discussion of God's call and "predestination" (8:29–30) in Romans 9–11 is misread when understood as dealing with the destiny of individuals, and Paul's expectation that "all Israel will be saved" (11:32) does not mean that all Jews will go to heaven, but indicates

---

63. L. T. Johnson, "The Social Dimensions of *soteria* in Luke-Acts and Paul," *Society of Biblical Literature Seminar Papers*, ed. E. H. Lovering (Atlanta: Scholars, 1993), 520–36.

Paul's hope that all Jewish people will eventually be included in the people whom God is presently shaping out of Jews and Gentiles.

Paul focuses most on the "in-between-time" of salvation, when believers are to "conduct [themselves] as worthy of the God who calls [them]" (1 Thess. 2:12; Eph. 4:1), and to "work out [their] salvation with fear and trembling" (Phil. 2:12). In the present, they are to "stay alert and sober" (1 Thess. 5:6); they are to engage the world "as though it were not," knowing that the frame of this world is passing away (1 Cor. 7:29–31); they are to be "separate" from the world of idolatry and corruption (2 Cor. 6:14–18); and they are to be "children of God without blemish in the midst of a crooked and perverse generation, among whom you shine like lights in the world" (Phil. 2:15).

Protected by the armor of faith, hope, and love (1 Thess. 5:8), and wearing "the helmet of salvation and the sword of the Spirit, which is the word of God" (Eph. 6:17), believers must engage in spiritual combat with the cosmic powers that continue to oppress, corrupt, and destroy humans (6:12–15; Rom. 16:17–20; 2 Cor. 10:2–6; 2 Thess. 2:5–12; 1 Tim. 4:1; 5:15), and they seek to be educated by the gift of God in Christ so that they might "reject godless ways and worldly desires and to live temperately, justly, and devoutly in this age" as they await the appearance of Jesus Christ (Titus 2:12–13). Refusing to conform themselves to the present age, they are renewed in mind so that they can "discern what is the will of God, what is good and pleasing and perfect" (Rom. 12:2).[64] Such efforts are not in service of "saving one's [individual] soul," but in service of building a saved community.

The Role of the Church

The term "church" (*ekklēsia*) occurs in all of Paul's letters except 2 Timothy and Titus, and even in these letters, Paul's concern for the congregation of believers is evident. Believers gathered in groups that were much like the associations (*ekklēsiai*) common in Greco-Roman culture.[65] The Pauline *ekklēsia* drew from and used the basic structure of

---

64. See L. T. Johnson, "Transformation of the Mind and Moral Discernment in Paul," *Early Christianity and Classical Culture: Comparative Studies in Honor of Abraham J. Malherbe* (ed. J. T. Fitzgerald; NovTSupp 110; Leiden: Brill 2003), 215–36.

65. See esp. P. Harland, *Associations, Synagogues, and Congregations: Claiming a Place in Ancient Mediterranean Society* (Minneapolis: Fortress, 2003).

such associations, just as the Diaspora synagogue already had. As many other voluntary associations, Paul's communities met in households (Rom. 16:5; 1 Cor. 16:15, 19; Col. 4:15; Phlm. 2).[66]

In Paul's letters, *ekklēsia* refers primarily to the local assembly; only in Ephesians does the term take on a greater, more cosmic, meaning. Nevertheless, Paul made efforts to link local associations in a variety of ways: he wrote to churches throughout a region (Gal. 1:2); he reminded local assemblies of common belief (1 Cor. 1:2), teaching (15:11), and practice (11:16; 14:33 – 36); he encouraged the exchange of letters among communities (Col. 4:16); he wrote a circular letter to a number of churches (Ephesians);[67] he reminded readers of his (and their) connection to a larger movement leading out from Jerusalem (Rom. 15:19 – 20; Gal. 1:18 – 2:10). He worked to create a larger sense of fellowship (*koinōnia*) among assemblies through organizing and completing a collection from among Gentile communities for the Jerusalem church (Rom. 15:25 – 33; 1 Cor. 16:1 – 4; 2 Cor. 8 – 9; Gal. 2:10).[68]

With an important exception (Romans), Paul either directly (in the case of the Thessalonians, Corinthians, Galatians, Ephesians, and Philippians) or indirectly (as in the case of Colossians) founded the assemblies to which he wrote, and he appointed the delegates (Timothy, Titus, Tychichus) who represented him in churches. Consistent with his calling (Gal. 1:16; 2:7; Eph. 3:1; 1 Tim. 2:7), Paul's foundations were either exclusively or dominantly Gentile (Galatians, Thessalonians, Philippians, Colossians), although he never foreswore care for his fellow Jews, with the result that some of his churches were ethnically mixed (1 Corinthians). Paul claims the authority that came to him with his prophetic/apostolic calling (2 Cor. 10:7 – 11; Gal. 1:15 – 16) as a witness to the resurrection (1 Cor. 9:1; 15:8 – 10), and as one who possessed the Spirit of God (7:40). He did not tolerate the interference of rival missionaries in churches established under his apostolic authority (e.g., 2 Cor. 10:12 – 11:15; Col. 2:16 – 23; 1 Tim. 1:3 – 11, 19 – 20; 4:1 – 3; 2 Tim. 2:16 – 26; Titus 1:10 – 14).

---

66. W. A. Meeks, *The First Urban Christians: The Social World of the Apostle Paul* (New Haven, CT: Yale Univ. Press, 1983).

67. Johnson, *Writings*, 359 – 71.

68. See now, D. J. Downs, *The Offering of the Gentiles: Paul's Collection for Jerusalem in Its Chronological, Cultural, and Cultic Contexts* (WUNT 2/248; Tübingen: Mohr Siebeck, 2009).

Paul's churches also had local leadership that managed the community in the apostle's absence. The letters do not reveal much about such leadership, and there is no reason to think that arrangements were absolutely consistent in every church, but the evidence contained in the letters corresponds with what is known about the social structure of first-century associations and synagogues. A board of elders (*presbyterion*, 1 Tim. 4:14) administered the community by exercising leadership (Rom. 12:7–8; 1 Cor. 16:15; 1 Thess. 5:12), teaching (Gal. 6:6; 1 Thess. 5:12; 1 Tim. 5:17–18), settling disputes (1 Cor. 6:1–8; 1 Tim. 5:19–22), and managing finances — as in collecting for and distributing to the needy (1 Tim. 5:3–16). The position of superintendent (*episkopos*, Phil. 1:1; 1 Tim. 3:2; Titus 1:7) probably involved special leadership obligations — such as hospitality (1 Tim. 3:2–5) — within the framework of the board.

Practical chores were carried out by male and female helpers (*diakonoi*, Rom. 16:1; Phil. 1:1; 1 Tim. 3:8, 11), who may well have made possible by their practical assistance the community acts of worship. The most obvious candidates for leadership positions in the assembly were the heads of the households within which the association met and who supported the movement financially (see 1 Cor. 16:15–17, 19; Phlm. 7). Paul expected recognition and submission to be paid to such local leaders (1 Cor. 16:16; Col. 1:7; 4:13; 1 Thess. 5:12–13).[69]

Although Paul's churches can be identified in terms of their geographical location, they are more than simply voluntary associations gathered because of shared occupations or interests. Paul sees them as brought into being by the call of God (see 1 Cor. 1:9; Eph. 4:1, 4; Col. 3:15; 1 Thess. 2:12; 2 Thess. 2:14; 2 Tim. 1:9). They are therefore "the church of God" (*ekklēsia tou theou*, 1 Cor. 1:2; 10:32; 11:16, 22; 15:9; 2 Cor. 1:1; Gal. 1:13; 1 Thess 2:14; 1 Tim. 3:5, 15) or "the church of Christ" (Gal. 1:22). God's Holy Spirit, therefore, should be not only the source of its life and power (Rom. 8:9–10, 14–15; 1 Cor. 2:4–14; 12:13; Gal. 3:2–5; 4:6; Eph. 2:18–22; Phil. 1:12, 27; 1 Thess. 1:5–6; 4:8; 2 Tim. 1:7; Titus 3:5), but also the guide to its behavior (Rom. 7:6; 8:4–6; 1 Cor. 14:2–32; 2 Cor. 12:18; Gal. 5:16–25; Eph. 4:3–30; Phil. 2:1–4; 1 Thess. 5:19; 2 Tim. 1:14).

---

69. See Johnson, *First and Second Timothy*, 218–25.

Since the same Holy Spirit was also the source of knowledge and speech within communities (1 Cor. 12–14), it is no surprise to find that Paul's letters reveal a tension between the ordinary processes of association governance and charismatic authority (1 Cor. 11:3–16; 14:33–40; 1 Thess. 5:19–20).

Because Paul's churches were intentional communities that had powerful religious experiences and convictions but only a fragile place within their social world, they inevitably experienced a variety of tensions that Paul had to address in his letters. These problems, much more than any theoretical positions, shape Paul's thought. He is not a systematic but a practical or pastoral theologian, whose best thought is given to tracing the links between religious experience and conviction and consistent community practice.

Some tensions had to do precisely with the boundaries of the community vis-à-vis the surrounding culture. Take the necessity to be "holy," that is, "different." With regard to Gentile culture, some requirements were obvious: Paul says that believers should "turn from idols" (1 Thess. 1:9), and he demands of his readers that they separate from idolatry completely (2 Cor. 6:14–18), refusing to participate in "the table of demons" (1 Cor. 10:21) or to return to the spiritual activities associated with "dumb idols" (12:2; 14:23). Yet he puzzles with his Corinthian readers over the legitimacy of eating meat that had been sacrificed to idols if it does not cause a brother to stumble (8:1–13). Although Paul explicitly rejects philosophy as a wisdom contrary to the cross (1:18–31; Col. 2:4–8), he makes use of the commonplaces of Greco-Roman moral teaching. And although he eschews powerful rhetoric for the same reason (1 Cor. 2:1–5; 2 Cor. 10:10–11), even such disavowals reveal a rhetorical strategy. Most significant is the fact that Paul does not envisage the community as "going out of the world" (cf. 1 Cor. 5:9–10); the disposition of eschatological detachment ("as though not") is compatible—indeed, demands—continued engagement in the ordinary social activities of the earthly empire (7:17–35).

Establishing "holiness" with respect to Judaism was more delicate, above all since holiness was the defining characteristic of Jews in the ancient world. Because of their commitment to the one God who was "different" from all other gods, Jews were demonstrably "different" from all other nations (Gentiles). Paul's churches are both continuous and discontinuous with Judaism.[70] Discontinuity is due to the majority of Jews not recognizing Jesus as Messiah (Rom. 9:31–33) and the majority of Paul's converts being Gentiles (9:25–30). But by defining the promise made by God to Abraham in terms of the Holy Spirit, Paul argues a form of continuity: the Gentiles, who have received the Holy Spirit, are also children of Abraham and children of the promise (Gal. 3:7–18; 4:1–7). They belong, in short, to the "Israel according to the Spirit" (cf. 4:21–31) that God uses in his mysterious dialectical plan to save even Israel "according to the flesh" (Rom. 11:1–36), in accord with his faithfulness to his promise (15:8–13). It is in this dialectical sense that Paul can speak of the Gentile churches in Galatia as "the Israel of God" (Gal. 6:15–16).

The church's relationship to Torah is correspondingly complex. It is impossible to understand "Christ" without the symbols of Torah, impossible to understand the significance of God's promises without the stories and prophecies of Torah. Paul therefore appropriates for his readers all the narratives, prophecies, and wisdom traditions of Torah, reading them all, to be sure, through the lens of a crucified and raised Messiah. The sticking point is the law in the proper sense. Paul has no difficulty with Jewish believers keeping the commandments, which he declares are "holy and righteous and good" (Rom. 7:12). The gift of the Holy Spirit, indeed, enables believers to fulfill "the righteous decrees of the law" (8:4). Obedience to what God commands is basic: it is not circumcision or uncircumcision that counts, but keeping God's commands (1 Cor. 7:19); God makes such obedience the basis of judgment for both Jews and Gentiles (Rom. 2:1–29).

At the same time, Paul is adamant that Gentiles not be required to keep the Mosaic law, the symbol for which is the ritual of circumcision (1 Cor. 7:17–20; Gal. 2:3, 15–21; 5:2–6; Phil. 3:2–4; Col. 2:11). Gentiles are also not to observe all the ritual observances by which Jews marked themselves as distinctive among the Gentiles (Gal. 4:9–10; Col. 2:16–18; 1 Tim. 4:3–4; Titus 1:14–16). What Paul means by the righteous requirement of the law seems to be the moral commands that continue to have validity in the new creation, namely, the Decalogue

---

70. See J. M. G. Barclay, "Paul, Judaism, and the Jewish People," in *The Blackwell Companion to Paul* (ed. S. Westerholm; Chichester, West Sussex; Malden: Wiley-Blackwell, 2011), 188–201.

and the law of love from Leviticus 19:18 (Rom. 13:8–10; Gal. 5:14; see 1 Tim. 1:8–11).[71]

Other issues in Paul's churches arise from the internal tensions created by the gap between utopian ideals and social realities. Paul subscribes to the ideal expressed by the baptismal formula in Galatians 3:28, that "you are all one in Christ Jesus," with a breakdown of the status markers of ethnicity, class, and gender: "neither Jew nor Greek ... neither slave nor free person ... not male and female" (see also 1 Cor. 12:13; Col. 3:10–11). These egalitarian ideals, however, conflicted with deeply embedded conventions—above all in the conservative institution of the household, where the associations met.

The tension is obvious in the case of "Jew/Greek." Paul himself asserts the primacy of Jews in God's call and ultimate plan (Rom. 1:16; 11:1–36) and declares that Jews have an advantage (3:1–4; 9:1–3). Why should this advantage not apply to community practice? Why should Gentiles not seek to be included in such an advantage (Galatians)? In mixed communities, furthermore, the ideal of "neither Jew nor Greek" would seem to mean the Jewish believers' disadvantage, especially in matters of table fellowship: Gentiles give up nothing, but Jews must give up being Jewish in order to eat with Gentiles (Rom. 14; 1 Cor. 8–10; Gal. 2:11–14).

The ideal of "neither slave nor free" found little practical realization in Paul's churches. Paul considered the condition of actual slavery negligible in terms of God's call (1 Cor. 7: 21–24), and although he considered the escaped slave Onesimus a brother rather than a slave (Phlm. 16), he nevertheless returned him to Philemon, his owner (v. 12). And his household instructions do little to mitigate the harsh realities of social captivity (Eph. 6:5–9; Col. 4:22–25; 1 Tim. 6:1–2).[72]

The case with "not male and female" is more complex. In one respect, Paul is more liberated than any other ancient author. He recognizes the role of women in the missionary field (Rom. 16:1–16; 1 Cor. 16:19; Phil. 4:1–2); he asserts mutual rights of women and men in marriage (1 Cor. 7:1–6) and acknowledges the legitimacy of celibate existence dedicated to the Lord (7:7–11, 25–40); he recognizes the practice of

---

71. See A. J. Hultgren, "Paul and the Law," in *The Blackwell Companion to Paul*, 202–15.
72. See D. Martin, *Slavery as Salvation: The Metaphor of Slavery in Pauline Christianity* (New Haven, CT: Yale Univ. Press, 1990).

women praying and prophesying in the community (11:3–16). But the more female activity takes place within the conventions of the household, the more restrictive Paul becomes; he wants them to pray and prophesy with heads covered (11:3–16), forbids them teaching in the assembly (14:33–36; 1 Tim. 2:11–15); encourages domestic roles for them (1 Tim. 5:3–16; Titus 2:3–5), and within marriage wants wives to show submission to their husbands (Eph. 5:21–33; Col. 4:18; 1 Tim. 2:11).[73] Part of the difficulty, and also the excitement, in reading Paul is found in the ways in which he struggles to reconcile egalitarian ideals and social realities.

That Paul does struggle in this fashion is one of his noblest qualities. His concern is steadily on the formation of a community ethos more than the benefit of individuals, and he constantly urges his readers to move from self-preoccupation to a concern for the whole (1 Cor. 13:1–13; Phil. 2:1–4). His focus is shown by the two major metaphors he uses for the association. The church is a building (*oikos*) whose foundation is Christ (1 Cor. 3:11), and it is built up by the efforts of preachers and prophets (3:12–15; 14:1–12). Indeed, all members of the community, when they act out of love, can "build up" the church (8:1–2; 1 Thess. 5:11).

Because this is a building inhabited by the Holy Spirit, the church is also a temple (*naos*), which is required to be holy (1 Cor 3:16–17).[74] The church is also a body (*sōma*), indeed, the "body of Christ" (*sōma Christou*, Rom. 12:5; 1 Cor. 12:27). It has drunk the one Spirit and become one body (1 Cor. 12:13), all of whose members contribute to the health and growth of the body as a whole (12:12–31). The Holy Spirit is the source both of the unity of the body and the diversity of the gifts exhibited by the members (12:4–11; Eph 4:1–16). The two metaphors coalesce in the complex imagery of Ephesians: through Christ "the whole structure is held together and grows into a temple sacred in the Lord; in him you also are being built together into a dwelling place of God in the Spirit" (Eph. 2:21–22).

---

73. For a survey, see M. Y. MacDonald, "Women in the Pauline Churches," in *The Blackwell Companion to Paul*, 268–84.

74. See L. T. Johnson, "Edification as a Formal Criterion for Discernment in the Church," and "Holiness as a Material Criterion for Discernment in the Church," *Sewanee Review* 39:4 (1996): 362–72, 373–84.

Because Paul seeks the edification ("building up") of the community, he is also consistently anti-elitist, opposed to members of the churches who compete for higher status than others through ritual circumcision (Gal. 5:19–21), knowledge (1 Cor. 8:1–2; 1 Tim. 1:7; Titus 1:14), spiritual gifts (1 Cor. 14:20–22), ascetical practices (2 Cor. 11:22–29; Col. 2:21–23) or mystical experiences (Col. 2:18). He sees such competition as a form of envy that destroys true fellowship (Gal. 5:15–21). Paul exhorts his readers to carry out the pattern of "life for others" exhibited by Christ, seeking unity and reconciliation by means of those powerful and wise and wealthy becoming weak and foolish and poor so that others might become strong and wise and prosperous; this is what he means by having "the mind of Christ" (1 Cor. 2:16; Phil. 2:5).

In his most sustained reflection on the nature and task of the church, Paul proposes that the role of the church is to be the place in the world where the work of Christ in reconciling humans to God should be realized in practice by the reconciliation of Jews and Gentiles (Eph. 2:1–22) and the harmony between male and female (5:32). The task of the church, he suggests, is to be a sacrament of the world's possibility (3:10).[75]

---

75. See now, Te-Li Lau, *The Politics of Peace: Ephesians, Dio Chrysostom, and the Confucian Four Books* (NovTSupp 133; Leiden: Brill, 2010).

RESPONSE TO LUKE TIMOTHY JOHNSON

What strikes me in reading Luke Johnson's essay is the remarkable extent to which I agree with him. If we think historically about the matter, such harmony is not surprising, for the Reformed and Roman Catholics have much in common theologically, despite the differences that remain. Furthermore, the twenty-first century is radically different from the sixteenth, for in a world that is in many respects post-Christian, evangelicals and Catholics have been reminded of what they share in common. In addition, Johnson doesn't emphasize Catholic distinctives in his essay; he reads Paul historically in terms of Paul's own social location.

I must apologize to those who want to see sparks fly, but a balanced assessment needs to identify the many (I don't have space to list all!) places where Johnson and I agree. I remember many years ago reading Johnson's *The Writings of the New Testament*, and the pleasant surprise I experienced when I found that he dissented from critical orthodoxy in seeing all thirteen of the Pauline letters as authentic. Johnson's mind has not changed. He continues to say that we must use the entire Pauline corpus to construct his theology. Such a conclusion, for those of us immersed in New Testament scholarship, is quite astonishing and gratifying. Johnson recognizes that Paul did not write a systematic theology, but his letters were directed to specific situations. Hence, we must pay close attention to the social situation addressed and the rhetorical strategies Paul devised. In other words, the differences between the Pastoral Letters and other Pauline letters are accounted for (in part) by the circumstances addressed in the Pastorals.

The importance of experience and tradition is also sketched in nicely by Johnson. Paul's theology grew out of a powerful experience with Jesus Christ, one that was shared by those in his churches, and Pauline traditions reflect on the significance of that experience. The Holy Spirit was not a theoretical construct but empowered believers to live in a way that was pleasing to God. Believers also celebrated their faith in baptism and the Lord's Supper, which marked them off as a community separate from their society.

I especially resonate with Johnson in his emphasis on the centrality of Jesus Christ. Jesus is the last Adam, the inaugurator of the new creation. The new creation commenced with the resurrection of Jesus from the dead, and he now reigns at God's right hand as the exalted Lord. Paul believed that Jesus was preexistent and that he shared the same identity as God without compromising monotheism. Jesus will be the end-time judge of all, as the Lord of all humanity.

Nor does Jesus' exalted status diminish his humanity. He was the Messiah, and his earthly life was important for Paul. Perhaps Johnson could have emphasized even more the allusions and echoes of Jesus traditions in the Pauline letters, though he does acknowledge the importance of Jesus' sayings. Johnson is no Bultmannian, for the earthly life and obedience of Jesus mattered to Paul. The cross of Jesus Christ plays a foundational role in Pauline thought, for through it human beings find forgiveness, presumably because Jesus' death was sacrificial in nature.

When it comes to Paul's soteriology, I agree that no metaphor takes center stage in Paul's thinking. Johnson rightly sees that Paul describes salvation from a number of different angles: friendship, liberation, forensic, sacrificial, and familial. Salvation, according to Paul, is multifaceted and hence is unpacked with a variety of metaphors. It seems to me that Johnson and I are similar to one another in describing Pauline soteriology in this regard, especially when he says the already but not yet plays a key role in Paul's understanding of salvation.

Johnson rightly sees that churches in Paul are local, and yet the unity of the entire church both creedally and practically is also emphasized. Paul does not conceive of spiritual life as a private mystical experience but as a communal and social experience in which Christians are committed to other believers. The church was conceived of as the new people of God, as the Israel of God.

I hope I have communicated my appreciation for Johnson's essay and for the significant concord between us. Still, we are not carbon copies of each other. There are differences as well. Perhaps it would help to say something about approach. Johnson is a modern scholar, trained in the historical critical method, a shrewd reader of the literary and social dimension of texts. He is keenly and rightly aware of the human dimension of the Pauline writings. Such a standpoint is a helpful corrective to systematic readings of Paul that ignore or minimize the historical context in which the letters were written.

Still, the focus on Paul's social location and history, which is the standpoint Johnson adopts, has some liabilities. In particular, the theological richness and profundity of Paul's thought are not explored in the same depth that we find in the history of the church. Today we particularly study the Scriptures in their historical setting, but we have something to learn from our ancestors who also studied it as the Word of God. It is not that Johnson denies the latter; it just doesn't play much of a role in his exposition of Paul's thought. For instance, Jesus' death is said to be expiatory and sacrificial, and Johnson connects such to human sin, but he doesn't explore deeply what this means and how the two are connected. The two realities (human sin and divine forgiveness) are noted, but they are not explicated in relation to one another, as they are, say, in Cranfield's commentary on Romans 3:21–26. If such a theological reading is pursued, there are good reasons to conclude that Paul doesn't limit himself to expiation but also includes propitiation here.

In the same way (I suppose my Reformed reading of Paul emerges here), Johnson says little about the role the law plays in Paul's thought. In Jewish thought the law was considered to be a pathway to life. Paul's understanding is radically and shockingly different, for the law exacerbates sin (Rom. 5:20; 7:5, 7–25; Gal. 3:19). The quick comment Paul makes on the matter in 1 Corinthians 15:56 reveals that Paul's negative assessment of the law can't be restricted to polemics. The law uncovers the rebellion, the stubbornness, the idolatry, and the self-worship in the human heart. Johnson does write about sin and redemption and forgiveness. It isn't absent. Nevertheless, the stunning grace of God that justifies the ungodly (Rom. 4:5) (the claim that faith rather than works saves) is noticeably absent. Johnson emphasizes that believers live new lives (more on that below), but the foundation of the new life, where human works are radically lacking, receives short shrift. The joy and wonder of forgiveness ascribed to God's grace in Jesus Christ crucified and risen need to receive more attention in Johnson's treatment of Pauline theology.

Perhaps this is the place to bring up another theme. The centrality of faith in Paul's thought is neglected. Perhaps that is not a fair way to put it, for Johnson is a firm believer that *pistis Christou* refers to the faithfulness of Christ rather than faith in Christ.[76] Space is lacking to investigate this matter in detail here.[77] I remain unconvinced. Jesus is described as the obedient one (Rom. 5:19; Phil. 2:8), but there is no unambiguous text in Paul where his obedience is described as his faithfulness. The use of *pistis Christou* with verbal forms does not support a subjective genitive (Rom. 3:22; Gal. 2:16; 3:22), for the verbal and nominal phrases are there for emphasis. What is lost here, then, is the emphasis on faith in Jesus Christ for salvation. In other words, a critical element of Paul's theology is that human beings are saved by faith and not works, that salvation doesn't come fundamentally by doing but by trusting, not by achieving but by receiving.

Still, Johnson rightly says that believers are transformed by the Holy Spirit and do what is pleasing to God. Paul was not an antinomian. He believed the life of the Spirit should be lived out in his congregations. Too often those who grasp that salvation is given by faith instead of works deny this feature in Pauline thought. Johnson rightly spies the importance of good works, but he neglects the importance of faith relative to salvation in Pauline theology.

One of the refreshing characteristics of Johnson's writings is his willingness to contravene critical orthodoxy. He rightly says that personal transformation is the foundation for social change and finds no basis for the notion that the empire was the object of Paul's criticism. As Johnson says, the root problem is with the evil that resides in human hearts. We are all tempted to read Paul so that he fits with our own political and cultural biases, and a regular dose of Johnson helps us see matters more clearly.

I want to pick out a few matters before concluding my response. Johnson says election in Romans 9–11 is corporate, not individual. Before interacting with that claim, it is striking that Johnson says little about election in Paul's theology. Conceptually, it is a major theme (Rom. 8:28–30; 9:6–23; 11:1–7; 1 Cor. 1:23–31; 8:3; 2 Cor. 4:5–6; Gal. 1:6, 15–16; 4:9; Eph. 1:4–5, 11; Col. 3:12; 1 Thess. 1:4; 5:9;

---

76. I am using the form *pistis Christou* for convenience here.
77. See Thomas R. Schreiner, *Galatians* (ZECNT; Grand Rapids: Zondervan, 2011), 163–66.

2 Thess. 2:13–14; 2 Tim. 1:9). It is by no means limited to Romans 9. Indeed, God's election is tied closely to the notion that salvation is by grace, that no one gains it by works (Rom. 11:5–6). Nor is it convincing to say that Romans 9–11 is corporate and not individual. It is a both-and instead of an either-or. Romans 9–11 must be read together as one unit. When Paul indicts Israel because it did not believe (Rom. 9:30–10:21), he is thinking both corporately and individually. Israel as a whole did not believe, and at the same time individuals failed to believe.

When it comes to Israel's belief or unbelief in Romans 10, I have never heard scholars say that it is corporate but not individual. It is evident, after all, that individuals believe or disbelieve. But Romans 10 cannot be split apart from Romans 9 as if Romans 9 is only corporate, while Romans 10 is individual and corporate. After all, both chapters are about the salvation of Israel. Paul is almost willing to be damned because Israel is not experiencing the saving promises (9:3). And when Paul refers to "God's children" (9:8), to election, works, and calling (9:11), and to destruction and mercy and glory (9:23), he uses soteriological terms. I conclude that Paul speaks both corporately and individually in Romans 9 about election and salvation. He is not interested in resolving philosophically the problem of evil. Election is important to him because it grants all the glory to God in salvation (Eph. 1:6, 12), showing that it comes from his grace alone (Rom. 11:5–6).

I have space for a couple of quick comments on matters that are less central in Paul's thought. I am not sure what Johnson means by saying that Romans 11:26 doesn't teach all Jews will go to heaven. I agree if he is saying that there is no promise here of salvation for all Jews of all time. On the other hand, this verse does promise a future eschatological salvation for the Jews at the parousia of Jesus Christ.

I also agree with Johnson that Paul was not a social revolutionary, and he sketches in well the tensions between egalitarianism and hierarchy in Pauline thought. I would simply want to add that such tensions aren't contradictory. Paul wasn't a modern American. He didn't think about equality the same way we do, especially when it comes to the roles of men and women. Now that doesn't mean that he endorses or recommends slavery. He regulates an existing evil institution. Still, Paul's goal wasn't the transformation of society and its structures. He would be happy if such occurred, but it wasn't the fundamental object of his vision.

DOUGLAS A. CAMPBELL

I applaud Johnson's accounts of the Catholic tradition, method, Paul's center, Christ, and salvation, and much that he says about the church. There are brief affirmations of the Melanchthonian model and instances of language insufficiently sensitive to Judaism. But these seem to be occasional regrettable lapses peripheral to his main position. So I will raise here just one slightly different anxiety.

In some of his last paragraphs Johnson runs briefly over "the Household Codes," which appear at several points in the Pauline corpus either explicitly or in the background of the discussion (cf. 1 Cor. 7; 11:2–16; 14:33b–36; Eph. 5:21–6:9; Col. 3:18–4:1; 1 Tim. 5:1–6:2; Titus 2:2–5; also relevant are Rom. 1:14; 13:1–7; Gal. 3:26–28; Col. 3:11; and 1 Tim. 2:1–3, 8–15; 3:1). The issues implicit in Johnson's brief account of Paul's thinking here need to be explored further.

It is important to recall first that these codes were drawn ultimately from Greco-Roman culture. Hence largely the same system as Paul's is discernible in Aristotle's *Politics*. Cutting a long story short—and as Aristotle articulates with matchless clarity—this worldview suggests structuring communities with a series of intercalated binary oppositions. In each opposition one is inferior because less or irrational agents are obedient and ordered under the governance of superior rational agents. When this is done exhaustively—i.e., every binary opposition within an ideal community is named and ordered—the ideal community results: ordered, unified, and rational. The gods or God governs their/"his" people; the government governs its subjects; superior races govern inferior races; owners govern slaves; husbands govern wives; parents govern children; and so on.[78]

Paul's programmatic advice to slaves and to women arises largely out of this way of thinking (see the texts noted above). But, as John-

---

78. A nice overview is Paul Cartledge, *The Greeks: A Portrait of Self and Others* (2nd ed.; Oxford: Oxford Univ. Press, 2002).

son observes, this advice generates a "struggle" that "arise[s] from the internal tensions created by the gap between utopian ideals and social realities"; these ideals—elsewhere called egalitarian—are expressed by different texts, such as Galatians 3:28; 1 Corinthians 12:13; and Colossians 3:10–11. Johnson merely concludes here, however: "That Paul does struggle in this fashion is one of his noblest qualities." And I found this rather unsatisfying, on several counts.

Johnson's earlier decisions about Pauline authorship now seem less convincing. Although the un- and less-disputed letters structure female activity restrictively in terms of the Household Codes, they do not silence women in the church altogether. As Johnson well knows, charismatic speaking is still possible—the utterance of prophecy, prayer, and presumably glossolalia (cf. esp. 1 Cor. 11:5, 13). Moreover, other texts indicate that certain women had power over some men in Paul's communities. Junia is an apostle (Rom 16:4). Phoebe is a patroness (Gk. *prostatis*; Rom. 16:1–2, 7). These women must have spoken to men authoritatively, at least at times. But 1 Timothy simply seems to unilaterally silence women in relation to men in any authoritative sense. Hence it seems likely that 1 Timothy is drawn from a later, more heavily institutionalized layer of texts that through institutionalization moved to curtail the more uncontrolled charismatic activity that was undertaken by women in the earliest days of the church. It is, in short, not genuine Pauline material. Consequently we need not lay responsibility for *completely* silencing women in the church at the feet of Paul. (This is not to deny that he endorsed their subordination in many respects.)

Even more importantly, Johnson's discussions of Paul's treatments of slaves and women fail to articulate a significant textual shortcoming in the Pauline data, which his own discussion then goes on to reproduce— *the absence of any significant conceptual work by either Christology or pneumatology* and, in tandem with this, *the absence of any charismatic account of the church* in these relations. Now Johnson *knows* about these absences but, as noted above, he cryptically characterizes them as a mere "tension" or "struggle" between utopian or egalitarian ideals and social realities. However, these tensions derive from a much more serious source than this. They actually come from all the things that Johnson has been cataloguing through the bulk of his essay about the present realities of Christ and the Spirit as the key constituents of the church—from the activity of *God* in its midst!—which can hardly be dismissed as a mere ideal, a possibility, and one in tension with social reality. God is the definitive reality, and we must seek to structure our social locations, by way of the church, in obedience *to* that divine reality.

Moreover, this reality is named by Galatians 3:28 and its parallel texts, which take us precisely into an ecclesial community characterized by the Spirit, virtue, and a fundamental equality. At this point it seems that we simply have to admit that Paul's admonitions to slaves and women in terms of hierarchical Greco-Roman categories are inconsistent with central Christian truths that he spends much of his time advocating elsewhere. Consequently these texts should be reinterpreted and redeployed (and there are a number of options here, although I would recommend primarily a thoroughly christological approach).

Johnson might appeal at this point, however—although I emphasize the word "might"—to two dynamics he has already identified that could qualify the relevance of Christology to these issues. (a) Earlier on he suggested that the liberation effected by Christian salvation "is not [at least 'primarily'] from social or political oppression, but from forces ... [that lie] in the twisted recesses of the human heart." Personal transformation thus precedes social change. And this might suggest leaving Paul's advice to slaves and women where it is, as a secondary matter concerning social change. But Johnson's account of Pauline ethics here is problematic. Paul's understanding of people is irreducibly *relational*. Hence "personal," "individual," and "internal," and "communal," "external," and "social" considerations *cannot be separated or prioritized*. (They can be distinguished.) Christological and pneumatological transformation affects both, as Johnson's account of the church in Paul as a personal *and* communal phenomenon makes clear. So this potential rejoinder would be invalid.

(b) Johnson also articulates a dynamic affirmed by Schreiner and Nanos at times that Christian reality is constrained by mere eschatological *inauguration* as against its completion or perfection. So he might suggest that Paul's hierarchical advice falls into the space yet to be perfected, and necessarily so, and consequently it can still be endorsed.

This is a widespread interpretative claim and raises complex issues that cannot be discussed in detail here. It must suffice to say, then, that there is something problematic about qualifying the acts of God in Christ in a way that *limits* the effectiveness of that act presently and in a manner that is basically quantitative — so saying, for example, that only 40 or 60 percent of God's salvation has been effected in Christ, or some such. We are probably being betrayed by longstanding but deeply inaccurate Western ontologies if we speak in these terms, that is, conceiving of reality in terms of substances, often static, and hence different overlapping realities in terms of strict zero-sum relationships.[79] But it is unlikely that Christ's impact on our corrupt and sinful reality is a zero-sum game. It is more likely that it is in its deepest and most real sense complete and perfect but that our sinful reality overlies and obscures that completion (and we seem very close to Jewish apocalyptic at this point).

It is then the *simultaneous presence* of *two* opposed realities — although one is hardly worthy of that name — that creates the puzzling situation of both salvation and sin being present that we are currently trying to articulate, and not the partial absence of one, namely, salvation. And this suggests further that it would be unwise to qualify the importance of Christology and pneumatology for our social structures by suggesting that these are merely "inaugurated" dynamics with much still to come. There is a perfection and totality about the work of God in our midst that is directly implicit in the confession Jesus is Lord. We should consequently seek to apply Christology to our social realities as vigorously as we can, which is to say that we should seek to be as obedient as we can be to that reality as it summons us to obedience in our current social realities, many aspects of which resist its lordship and persist in sinful activities and oppressive structures (cf. 2 Cor. 10:1–6).

We must also recall in this relation that the church universal *has* already moved decisively beyond much of the hierarchical advice contained in the Household Codes by abandoning slavery. This was admittedly a long struggle, and sincere exegetes wrote much defending the literal teaching of the Bible against this trajectory. It nevertheless remains true that the church has now judged any construction of social reality in terms of the system of owner and slave as explicitly endorsed by Paul to be deeply sinful, and these texts need to be reread accordingly. But

---

79. It is canvassed nicely by T. F. Torrance, in "Karl Barth and the Latin Heresy" *SJT* 39 (1986): 461–82.

exactly the same considerations apply to these texts' teachings vis-à-vis women, or sound reasons need to be supplied why this is not the case.[80]

We must now add Galatians 3:28 to the conversation, a critical text that suggests not only the christological transcendence of the categories of ethnicity, class, and gender, but the christological transcendence *of those very categories*. That is, not only do Christology and pneumatology suggest the transcendence of class and gender hierarchies, but they call into question the existence of these binary oppositions in the first place because they are accounts of creation (at least in the corrupt reality that we currently occupy) that make no appeal to Christology. Hence they lack final legitimacy.

And this stands to reason. This binary conceptuality preceded Christianity by many centuries and seems to have been developed by Greeks. But Paul now knows that *Christ* is the inner rationale of creation (1 Cor. 1:30; Col. 1:15–20). *He* is the Wisdom of God in relation to whom all other created realities are to be understood. So it needs to be asked if created social realities ought to be structured in terms of binary oppositions *at all*. It is especially encouraging to note as we entertain this thought that Paul himself, when navigating complex social realities, manipulates binary oppositions quite flexibly. In much of 1 Corinthians he reformulates binaries, softens them, multiplies them, and sees movement across their borders running legitimately in both directions. We have a scriptural precedent, then, for questioning the construction of social reality in terms of what is really a neat set of vast oversimplifications, at which point further traditionally excluded groups must at least be welcomed into conversation.[81]

---

80. In this whole relation see Willard M. Swartley, *Slavery, Sabbath, War, and Women: Core Issues in Biblical Interpretation* (Scottdale, PA: Herald, 1983); Wayne A. Meeks, "The Polyphonic Ethics of the Apostle Paul," *Annual of the Society of Christian Ethics* (ed. D. M. Yeager; Washington, DC: Georgetown Univ. Press, 1988), 17–29; and J. Albert Harrill, "The Use of the New Testament in the American Slave Controversy: A Case History in the Hermeneutical Tension between Biblical Criticism and Christian Moral Debate," *Religion and American Culture* 10/2 (2000): 149–86. Also Demetrius Williams, *An End to This Strife: The Politics of Gender in African American Churches* (Minneapolis, MN: Fortress, 2004).

81. That is, LGBT groups, and perhaps also nonmonogamous traditions. David Horrell charts Paul's argumentative dynamics in 1 Corinthians perceptively in *Solidarity and Difference: A Contemporary Reading of Paul's Ethics* (London: T&T Clark [Continuum], 2005). I address the issues raised by Gal. 3:28 briefly in "The Gospel of Reconciliation, according to Gal 3.28," in *The Theology of Reconciliation*, 39–65 (ed. C. G. Gunton; Edinburgh: T&T Clark, 2003), repr. as ch. 5 in *Quest*, 95–111—although Dale Martin offers some salutary warnings about overly enthusiastic liberational uses of even this text in *Sex and the Single Savior: Gender and Sexuality in Biblical Interpretation* (Louisville, KY: Westminster John Knox, 2006), 77–90.

In conclusion, let me state clearly that I do not want to pillory John-son for some brief and late-breaking remarks, and especially when we agree on so much, not to mention when he has spoken so wisely and sensitively in this relation already elsewhere. But I do want to suggest that in an extrapolated form his remarks characterize a great deal of deeply problematic Pauline interpretation. Moreover, what we have grasped in this relation does seem to push us beyond the conceptual boundaries Johnson articulates for Paul's thought at the beginning of his essay—the boundaries of a pastoral theologian speaking to practical issues by drawing on various resources to generate advice that is super-ficially diverse but basically theologically coherent. A more searching examination of Paul's Household Codes suggests the presence of a seri-ous *inconsistency* in Johnson's thinking here. And this inconsistency has had serious consequences for the subsequent life of the church. Two large groups in particular have been affected dramatically by all this: slaves—and in recent centuries also people of color; and women, with the implicit oversimplified binary account of gender going on to mar-ginalize other smaller groups as well.

That Paul's texts contain "tensions" at these points, then, is true. That this tension is addressed "nobly," however, is debatable. Rather, that these tensions should be transcended christologically, pneumato-logically, and eccesially is, it seems to me, a key lesson to learn from Johnson's generally faithful and uplifting account of Paul's thought with which I am in so much agreement—and, indeed, from which I learned so much.

MARK D. NANOS

Luke Timothy Johnson's approach to Paul is commendable on many levels. His methodological sensibilities and confessional awareness, discussion of the role of Acts as well as preference of certain letters in any approach, concern about abstracting systematic thought and theology from evidence that is occasional in nature, and other such careful consideration of the elements involved in trying to understand and discuss Paul from the limited evidence available are refreshing to see articulated. I am not as clear about whether the disputed letters were from Paul or represented the views of a Pauline school with which Paul would concur. I would not think it best to rest major decisions about Paul on them based on the current scholarly consensus. I have not undertaken my own research on them yet or attempted to present a comprehensive portrait of Paul that would require weighing in on this matter (my own research has focused on the topic of Paul and Judaism, which these letters do not explicitly engage as much as some of the undisputed ones). Since the Paul I see in the undisputed letters is in on certain ways so different from the Paul of those who have made the judgments that have shaped the current consensus, it seems likely that my judgments about the disputed letters, and the reasons for making them, might be different too.

Johnson's discussion of the problem of any search for a center of Paul's thought or concern is prudent, and I agree with his judgments about the basic Greco-Roman and Jewish cultural elements that shape who Paul was and what he thought and taught. Helpful too is his discussion of the multiple religious experiences of Paul, of his audiences, and of others who shared their convictions about Jesus.

The overall discussion of Paul's view of Jesus and the implications for those who believe in him as Christ is wide-ranging and balanced. That Paul used the title *kyrios* to attribute to Jesus the name of God expressed in the tetragrammaton seems improbable, although I see how the evidence can be read in that direction. There was plenty of room in Second Temple Judaism for divine mediators, and lots of overlap in how they were identified and discussed. Johnson's own argument emphasizes the lordship or rule associated with the title Christ. I suspect we find this emphasis on Lord in Paul rather than on Messiah, which seems to be more like a title, since the letters are largely, if not entirely, addressed to non-Jews and their concerns. The concept of Messiah is a cross-cultural one for them, while that of Lord and Savior are not. These are part of their native culture; attributing these to Jesus inscribes them in sharp relief to the reality they know: someone else is ostensibly lord and savior of the empire in which they live. That someone and regime does not make claims to be Messiah, that is, to be from the line of David according to the covenant promise of a descendent always ruling on the throne of Israel.

It was interesting to see that defining salvation begins by emphasizing it "is not something accomplished by humans by their own efforts." Who thinks it is? And the second emphasis is on "forces that constrain and distort personal freedom and community integrity," which is further defined as "the twisted recesses of the human heart" and contrasted with the alternative, "liberation is not from social or political oppression," or "the inadequate or even harmful structures and systems of society." This seems anachronistic for Paul's time, and it is inconsistent with many of Johnson's observations leading up to and concluding on pp. 88–89, that Paul's discussions of salvation are not about "the eternal destiny of believers" but "almost entirely social in character": it is about being rescued into a people God is shaping in this "in-between-time" and the social life that entails; in other words, politics.

Johnson's discussion of Paul's assemblies in terms of Greco-Roman associations and synagogues is helpful. So too is his note that Paul's letters address the practical issues that arise therein, rather than being theoretical or systematic in focus. Although I agree in general with his presentation of Paul's views when issues arose regarding his audiences' "pagan" contextual concerns, like idolatry and associated social behavior that entailed in normal life, I do not think that 1 Corinthians 10:1–13 suggests that Paul "puzzles" over the legitimacy of eating of idol meat. Rather, he begins an argument in chapter 8 that theoretically allows for it, but by chapter 10 it becomes clear that he is driving that argument to a very different, very normal Jewish conclusion: he does not permit Christ-followers to eat it if known to be such. But since they are not Israelites and thus not technically under God's Teaching for Israel (= Torah), Paul must fashion various ways to instruct them, including from the examples in Torah, from first principles, from concern for their neighbor, and so on, that they are now to be slaves of righteousness in ways that are not different, usually, from the ways that Jews live according to God's Teaching.[82]

When Johnson discusses the Jewish complex of issues that arise for the non-Jews, which Paul's letters target, I disagree with several statements. Paul does not state that these non-Jews belong to "Israel according to the Spirit" in Galatians 4:21–31 (or anywhere else known to me), and it is unclear that he is speaking of the "Gentile churches as 'the Israel of God'" in Galatians 6:15–16. Many other interpreters who do not otherwise share my views on Galatians also do not find that likely.

Johnson observes the centrality of Torah for understanding Christ and asserts that "Paul has no difficulty with Jewish believers keeping the commandments." That should be altered in my view to communicate that Paul believed it *necessary*: Jewish believers remain Jews and thus must observe the "Teaching" that God has given to Israel (cf. Rom. 3:28–31; 1 Cor. 7:17–19; Gal. 5:3). That is a propositional corollary to Paul's being "adamant that Gentiles not be required to keep the Mosaic law"; indeed, because they are not Jews, not circumcised into membership within Israel, to whom Torah was given as a gift to guide the life of those whom God set apart from the other nations! But it is not the case that "the ritual of circumcision" is "the symbol" of the Torah; rather, circumcision is the symbol of entrance into a people who are governed by Torah. Since these non-Jews do not receive circumcision, they are not under Torah in the technical sense that Jews are.

It is important to keep the role of circumcision as an entrance rite and Torah as that which governs those who are thereby marked as members, thus under its guidance, if we are to follow Paul's articulation of the implications of the gospel for those who are not Israelites, and who

82. See my "The Polytheist Identity of the 'Weak,' and Paul's Strategy to 'Gain' Them: A New Reading of 1 Corinthians 8:1–11:1," in *Paul: Jew, Greek, and Roman* (ed. Stanley E. Porter; Leiden and Boston: Brill, 2008), 179–210.

must not become Israelites but represent the end of the age claim of the gospel that those from the nations are now also being reconciled to the One Creator God of all the nations. It follows, logically, that those from Israel must remain Israelites, or God would be now only the God of all the nations except Israel, which would make no sense to an Israelite who proclaimed Jesus as Messiah.

When Johnson turns to the topic of how conduct at meals would be organized in order to explore the kind of social tensions created by Paul's gospel, the weakness in the way he has set out the issues (in accordance with the prevailing views, in contrast to what I have just argued in the above paragraph) become apparent. Johnson observes that to eat together the "Gentiles give up nothing, but Jews must give up being Jewish in order to eat with Gentiles." His references for this observation are Romans 14; 1 Corinthians 8–10; and Galatians 2:11–14. I have demonstrated why each of these texts suggests precisely the opposite:[83] that the problems for these non-Jews arose because these were Jewish gatherings in which normal Jewish dietary behavior was observed by Paul and the Jews involved as well as any non-Jews present (in Romans and Galatians).

The problem was not whether the non-Jews ate jewishly according to the prevailing norms for non-Jewish guests when at a Jewish meal; it would be natural for them to do so when joining a Jewish subgroup. It arose when they would be treated merely as guests, as less than equals if they did not also become Jews. That ran counter to the proposition of the gospel that Jew and non-Jew in Christ were equal, albeit remaining different as a matter of principle. In 1 Corinthians the issue is different; it arises in the normal idolatrous space of non-Jewish communal life. Yet here too Jewish behavior is prescribed for non-Jews, not on the basis of technical appeal to Torah, as it would be for Jews, but on the basis of the example of Torah, the concern for the best interests of their fellow humans, and their association with God through Jesus Christ.

The net result is the same as that taught by Torah: they cannot eat idol food if it is known to them to be idol food. The social problem that they face, in my view, is how to negotiate their social lives when they

---

83. See my "The Myth of the 'Law-Free' Paul Standing Between Christians and Jews," *Studies in Christian-Jewish Relations* 4 (2009): 1–21. (http://escholarship.bc.edu/scjr/vol4/iss1/4/).

are prevented by Paul's gospel from either becoming Jews or remaining idolaters, yet required to live jewishly, to live according to Jewish communal norms, that is, to become members of Judaism without becoming members of Israel. They are betwixt and between two normative identities and associated norms for behavior, and thus experience problems in both their Jewish and idolatrous social contexts.

In these letters Paul seeks to instruct them how to behave and calls them to endure the marginality that behavior will likely bring for them as a result of the ambiguity of identity the gospel creates for them as non-Jews, and for Jews like Paul, as a result of teaching such views.

CHRIST AND THE CHURCH IN PAUL: A "POST-NEW PERSPECTIVE" ACCOUNT

DOUGLAS A. CAMPBELL

A Starting Point

The phrase "post-new perspective" signals one of the key concerns that drives my account of Paul's understanding of salvation, which from now on we can call his "gospel." Clearly, I share something with the "new perspective," but I also disagree with it. So we need to know first what the new perspective is.

The new perspective on Paul is really a combination of *two* new perspectives: one on Judaism, and one on Paul by way of response.

The first aspect of this—the new perspective on Judaism—is usually associated with the work of E. P. Sanders, especially with his 1977 classic study *Paul and Palestinian Judaism*,[1] although it is not really that new. Since the inception of the modern scholarly period, voices were raised, both Jewish and Christian, suggesting that particular ways of reading Paul were unfair to Jews and to Judaism. But these voices were marginal and faint.[2] By 1977, however, the full horrors of the Holocaust were sinking in, and the Academy had been sensitized to the concerns of hitherto marginalized groups—to the struggles of the poor in Latin America, of women, of African Americans in the United States, and so

---

1. E. P. Sanders, *Paul and Palestinian Judaism* (Philadelphia: Fortress, 1977).
2. See, e.g., the classic study by George Foot Moore, "Christian Writers on Judaism," *HTR* 14 (1921): 197–254.

on. So Sanders was able, in this environment (in tandem with his brilliant articulation of the case), to finally break through with key Jewish questions into widespread acknowledgment by New Testament interpreters. How we read Paul in relation to Jews *matters*, and most interpreters began to face up to this after 1977. They began to consider—to put things at their most simple and painful, borrowing a dictum from Irving Greenberg—whether certain readings of Paul, especially in relation to Judaism, could be uttered in the presence of the burning children.[3]

In all honesty, it seemed that many in fact could not be. That is, Christian interpreters were reading Paul's account of Judaism in a way that was not merely uncharitable; it was untrue and potentially vicious, *thereby corrupting their corresponding accounts of Christian salvation as well.* So clearly a major problem had been unearthed within Paul's interpretation, and I endorse its importance. We must strive to read Paul responsibly in the light of Judaism; the integrity of his gospel is at stake.

The "new perspective on Paul"—the second aspect within the new perspective as whole—is usually associated with J. D. G. Dunn, who made an early and rather interesting attempt to respond to the newly pointed Jewish question.[4] Dunn suggested Paul's phrase "works of law" should *not* be understood to refer to "legalism" but to some problem in relation to Jewish ethnicity in terms of pride and/or exclusiveness. The narrative surrounding this phrase was not an individualistic calculus in relation to future salvation in terms of deeds done or not done, but a communal one informed by important identity-forming practices associated with circumcision, diet, and time—an interpretation more compatible with the "covenantal nomism" that Sanders was urging as a fair description of Judaism in Paul's day. Dunn claimed that this alternative reading solved the post-Holocaust concerns of Sanders as well as those of others troubled in this relation.

I am post-new perspective because, on the one hand, I maintain with the new perspective that the Jewish question is a critical one. I agree,

---

3. Irving Greenberg, "Cloud of Smoke, Pillar of Fire: Judaism, Christianity and Modernity after the Holocaust," in *Auschwitz: Beginning of a New Era?* (ed. E. Fleischner; New York: Ktav, 1977), 7–55.

4. See Dunn's "The New Perspective on Paul," first published in 1983, but now found in its most up-to-date version in *Jesus, Paul, and the Law* (London: SPCK, 1990), 183–206. N. T. Wright is often associated with this approach as well, and really antedated Dunn in its formulation.

further, that certain ways of reading Paul cannot answer this question responsibly; various accounts of Paul's gospel lock the apostle's theology into an indefensible account of Judaism with awful political consequences. There is no way back here. (I am utterly unpersuaded by the various apologetic attempts to deflect or roll back this concern within Pauline studies.)[5]

On the other hand, the new perspective on Paul, with its reinterpretation of "works of law," has not in my view been an adequate response to this pressing question. Its suggested rereading is implausible, it is argumentatively problematic, and it does not actually resolve the underlying problem.[6] So there is a pressing need to articulate Paul's gospel in a way that meets the negative concern of the new perspective with the fair representation of Judaism *and yet* moves beyond the frailties of its positive interpretative suggestion with "works of law" in terms of ethnic boundary markers. We need a *post*-new perspective account of Paul's gospel. But at this moment my reading of Paul moves fairly significantly beyond the views of many new perspective and post-Holocaust interpreters.

I would suggest that the Jewish problem in relation to Paul is a bit like the canary in the coal mine. It is arguably just one aspect of what Krister Stendahl has criticized as a distorting, overly "Lutheran," account of Paul's gospel.[7] Correctly understood, the Jewish question is part of a deeper, broader, and more complex set of problems that entangles many interpreters of Paul. So, like a dying canary, it signals the onset of a wave of crises—and using Stendahl, as well as Sanders, and assisted by various theologians, I have tried to give an account of this wave.[8] As a result of all this, it is apparent then that we do not need a post-new perspective

<hr />

5. See, e.g., *Justification and Variegated Nomism II: The Paradoxes of Paul* (ed. D. A. Carson, Peter T. O'Brien, and Mark A. Seifrid; Tübingen: Mohr Siebeck, 2004).

6. I make this case in ch. 12 of my *The Deliverance of God: An Apocalyptic Rereading of Justification in Paul* (Grand Rapids: Eerdmans, 2009), 440–59.

7. See his collection of important essays, *Paul Among Jews and Gentiles, and Other Essays* (Philadelphia: Fortress, 1976), especially "Paul and the Introspective Conscience of the West," first published in *HTR* 56 (1963): 199–215.

8. See Part One in *Deliverance*, 11–218, which concludes with a chapter entitled "Beyond Old and New Perspectives." Note that the name "Lutheran" is not helpful. I prefer to address the essentially contractual theological model driving this approach as elucidated in a seminal set of essays by Reformed theologian James B. Torrance: "Covenant and Contract, a Study of the Theological Background of Worship in Seventeenth-Century Scotland," *SJT* 23 (1970): 51–76; and "The Contribution of McLeod Campbell to Scottish Theology," *SJT* 26 (1973): 295–311. I articulate the main connections here in "What Is at Stake in Reading Romans 1–3? An Elliptical Response to the Concerns of Gorman and Tilling," *Journal for the Study of Paul and His Letters* 1 (2011): 113–37.

approach to Paul in any minimal or incremental sense; rather, we need a major reappraisal of the apostle's gospel that responds to a massive interpretative crisis within much of his interpretation. The "post" in the title "post-new perspective" is therefore an emphatic one.

I have been working on a solution to these complex interconnected issues for some time now and will simply summarize it in what follows. However, before I do so, it is worth noting that I am not really suggesting anything new within the history of the church. It might be new on the current scholarly scene, but the view of the gospel that I am urging in relation to Paul is one with roots deep in the theological reflections of the church. We are recovering rather than discovering something.

My description emphasizes the importance of revelation as the basis of Paul's thinking about God; the Trinity, as the God who is revealed to him and with whom he is now involved; and mission as the life that Paul is called to, largely by way of participating in the loving mission of God to the world in Christ and through the Spirit. I suggest that this account of Paul's gospel can answer the Jewish question with integrity and can also respond to the other difficulties we run across in this relation as well, which Stendahl began to describe under the rubric of Lutheranism. I suggest further that this account of the gospel is rather old.

We can detect this revealed, triune, missional account of Paul in many of the most important church fathers—most especially in Irenaeus, but also in the great fathers of Orthodoxy like the Gregories, Basil, and Athanasius (and thereby within important parts of subsequent Orthodoxy); within important strands in the Catholic tradition like the Franciscans; within key parts of the Protestant tradition, especially Calvin; within important, modern figures like Reformed theologians Karl Barth, and T. F. and J. B. Torrance; and in many church traditions today, especially those emphasizing the living, energizing work of the Spirit.[9] So a post-new perspective view is clearly an ecumenical account of the gospel in the best sense of that word—a catholic account, as the creeds affirm it ought to be. It is a Pauline gospel both old and new.

But where does this account of Paul's gospel begin in the Pauline data, if we approach that as strictly as we can in historical terms? An

---

9. Miroslav Volf is an excellent example of a theologian positioned here; see his *Exclusion and Embrace* (Nashville, TN: Abingdon, 1996).

important clue is given by the fact that Paul's gospel in its time was clearly controversial.

Paul obviously had high ethical expectations of his converts. He expected outstandingly virtuous behavior in terms of love, generosity, fidelity, and so on (although he didn't always receive it). But somewhat surprisingly it is also clear that he had left a number of key Jewish ethical practices behind in a critical development that profoundly shapes all Christian behavior today. He did not view circumcision and Jewish dietary and temporal practices as incumbent on any of his converts from paganism. This clearly offended many Jews and Jewish Christians at the time; they were shocked by Paul's apparent liberalism, and they were either confused by it or decided to oppose it forcefully (see esp. Gal. 2:1–10, 11–14; Phil. 3:2, 18–19). So Paul was forced to defend this missionary praxis, both within and outside the church, which he proceeded to do with great vigor, and this is one of the main reasons why we have letters from him to peruse today. Moreover, it is almost certain that here we will find Paul's critical theological insights — either this, or his life's work, oriented by his apostleship and special gospel, did not produce his best theology! But where *exactly* do we go to find this rigorous account?

For various reasons Paul seems to have been forced to spell things out with special clarity and fullness in his letter to the Roman Christians, so Romans is the best place for us to concentrate on in this short essay. And the best place to begin in Romans is Paul's second major block of argumentative material: Romans 5–8.

This is actually the longest argument that Paul ever supplies for the view that a Christian ethic transcends the Jewish law. And on closer consideration we find presupposed here a detailed account of Paul's entire gospel — a gospel that reaches others where they are, transforms them in Christ, and opens them up to a glorious life of freedom in the Spirit and of communion with the triune God.[10] It will repay us well, then, to consider this block of text carefully. It is the foundation on which our understanding of everything else in Paul should be built.

---

10. There are lots of good reasons in my view for beginning here rather than with a particular reading of Romans 1–4 and related texts — an approach that I argue distorts Paul's gospel fundamentally; see *Deliverance*, passim.

The Gospel in Romans 5 - 8

As Nils Dahl observed some time ago, the material in Romans 5–8 falls into two principal arguments.[11] The first is initiated in a compact way in 5:1–11 and is resumed and elaborated upon by 8:14–39.[12] This argument consequently brackets a longer discussion extending from 5:12 through 8:13,[13] which discusses ethics and the Jewish *Torah*.[14] We will look briefly at the bracketing argument first.

The Eschatological Argument

Much of Paul's bracketing discussion in Romans 5 and 8 seems aimed at assurance. The discussion names several threats to the present peace of mind of people whom Paul calls "brothers" (an important term that we will define at the end of this section). The brothers seem to face suffering (5:3; 8:17–23, 33, 35–39), whether from more earthly dangers like famine and violence, from some future "wrath" (5:9), or from demonic forces that range from "powers" to death itself. But Paul famously concludes his argument with the claim that *nothing* can separate the brothers from the love of God in Christ Jesus the Lord (8:39), so their hope can be sustained and unshakeable, appearances notwithstanding (8:24–25). He can conclude so confidently because of two powerful arguments.

First, God has delivered up his only Son to die on behalf of people who are his enemies in order to retrieve them (see 5:6–10; 8:31–32). It simply follows from this that God—*who loves so much*—will see the brothers safely through their perils and do anything to save them. Moreover, none of the powers arrayed against the brothers, which seem so strong when viewed from a human perspective, are of any real magnitude when viewed over against God, who *as* God cannot be stopped from saving his people.

---

11. Nils Dahl, *Studies in Paul: Theology of the Early Christian Mission* (Minneapolis: Augsburg, 1977), 88–90 ("Appendix I: A Synopsis of Romans 5:1–11 and 8:1–39").

12. All references are to Romans, unless otherwise indicated. All translations from Romans are my own unless otherwise indicated.

13. 8:14 is not a sharp transition; 8:11 arguably initiates the resumed argument.

14. *Torah* is the best translation equivalent for Paul's Greek word *nomos*, usually rendered "law," so we will use it from now on; see W. D. Davies, "Paul and the Law: Reflections on Pitfalls in Interpretation," in *Jewish and Pauline Studies* (London: SPCK, 1982), 91–122.

Second, the divine Spirit lives within the brothers and assures them directly of this love, going so far as to pray for them when their own words fail (see 5:5; 8:9, 11, 15–16, 26–27). The Spirit also assures the brothers that they are destined like Christ for resurrection (8:11) and for a glorious future inheritance (8:17, 21b). But in this second argument we can detect a further important dimension in Paul's case.

The two arguments actually overlap since the work of Christ and the work of the Spirit interpenetrate one another. The Spirit makes known the love of God the Father that is effected concretely through the sacrifice of his Son (5:5), and the Spirit effects for the brothers the resurrection that has already taken place in Christ, which then leads to a new creation in Christ's image (8:29). And just as the Spirit prays for the brothers when they are pressed beyond the power of speech (8:26–27), Christ intercedes at the right hand of God in the same circumstances and manner (8:34b). We can draw a number of important conclusions from this material, supplementing them with further details from Paul's argument.

We should note first that Paul's thinking about God's activity in Christ is trinitarian. Obviously he lacks the specialized terminology for the Trinity that was developed in the church by the fifth century after much reflection and discussion. But three persons are distinguishable in Romans 5 and 8, acting not only in concert but in an overlapping fashion (what the church later referred to as *perichoresis*—a "standing in one another").[15]

Most scholars today would accept that when Paul speaks of God "the Father" and of the Holy Spirit, he is referring to the divine (although they might disagree over how strongly to distinguish between these two actors as different persons—what the church later spoke of as *hypostasis*). Dispute during the modern period has mainly surrounded Paul's view of Christ. Many scholars have been influenced by an essentially secular, developmental view of theology—in effect, an evolutionary account like Darwin's explanation of the development of humans from primates (etc.) "up" to homo sapiens. If everything in history necessarily evolves from primitive origins through successive levels to higher and

---

15. See Colin Gunton, *The One, the Three and the Many: God, Creation and the Culture of Modernity* (Cambridge: Cambridge Univ. Press, 1993), 155–79, esp. 163–66.

later stages, it is easy to assume that in the New Testament, the "high" view of Christ as divine ought to be late. Paul, however, was one of the earliest writers in the New Testament, and so it follows that he *had* to have operated with a "low" Christology. (And this type of scholarship can, for example, point to the fact that Paul never names or describes Christ as "God" indisputably, the one possible instance of this in the undisputed letters being Rom. 9:5.)[16] However, recently powerful contentions have been mobilized in support of the older, nondevelopmental view that Paul saw Christ as divine; some of the evidence for this is apparent in the material we have just examined.[17]

At the climax of Paul's argument, which refers to the climax of history, the apostle acclaims Christ as "Lord" (Rom. 8:38–39). This title could have a rather mundane meaning—little more than "sir"—but it almost certainly has here the elevated sense of God, the Lord, presiding over the final defeat of all evil and rescue of all that is good—although here it is the figure of Christ! (*Kyrios*, the Greek word for "Lord," was used by Jews to stand for the divine name YHWH in the Greek translation of the Hebrew Scriptures; God's actual Hebrew name was too holy to be used or pronounced.)[18] If Christ is Lord in this strong sense, then he is being acclaimed as God. Christ is also described in these arguments, however, as "son."

The word "son" can take different referents and might mean no more than an obedient follower of God—a good Israelite. However, Paul is alluding in much of chapter 8 to the story of Abraham and Isaac in Genesis 22, from which he is actually quotes in verse 32. He is saying that just as Abraham offered up his only son to God on Mount Moriah, *God* offered up *his* only Son on the cross for a hostile humanity. Now the two figures in Genesis 22, Abraham and Isaac, were clearly equal; they differed only in the roles they played in the story. This suggests that we view Paul's application of this narrative to the divine action in the same way. Indeed, the pathos of Paul's argument and much of its

---

16. The archetypal representative of this approach is Wilhelm Bousset, *Kyrios Christos* (5th German ed.; trans. John E. Steely; Nashville, TN: Abingdon, 1970).

17. See Richard Bauckham, "Paul's Christology of Divine Identity," in *Jesus and the God of Israel* (Grand Rapids: Eerdmans, 2008), 182–232.

18. See C. Kavin Rowe, "Romans 10:13: What Is the Name of the Lord?" *HBT* 22 (2000): 135–73.

consequent validity depend to a large degree on the ontological similarity and intimacy of the two actors involved. Just as a father offered up his beloved son in the original story in a deeply costly act, the Father offers up his beloved Son in Paul's gospel.[19] It is precisely this costly action that demonstrates how much he loves us. The Son is nevertheless "equal" to the Father; both are divine figures.

Furthermore, the divine Spirit whose activity is so apparent in this chapter is also the Spirit "of Christ" (8:9–10); the context makes it fairly clear that this is not a domesticated reference to a *Christlike* spirit, as some scholars have suggested, but an ontological assertion of considerable power. The Spirit is "his" (i.e., Christ's) as it is also "God's," which suggests that "he," Christ, is also "God."[20]

There seems, then, to be an accumulation of strong hints in this material that Paul's understanding of God was what later church tradition would articulate more clearly and technically in terms of the Trinity. So we will assume for the rest of this chapter that Paul operated with "an inchoate trinitarian grammar."[21] This means in turn that Paul's writings witness to the Trinity.[22]

I have spent some time within a short discussion building toward this conclusion because it is so important. We now know who God is in a fundamental sense at the same time as we know the fundamental truth about Christ for Paul.

Christ is God acting in our world, or God incarnate, as the creeds put it. There is, then, no God who lies behind this God—no prior conception of God that is really more important or basic. Christ is intrinsic to the identity of God and vice versa. So to speak of Christ in Paul is to speak of God, and to speak of God we must speak of Christ (although

---

19. See Douglas A. Campbell, "The Story of Jesus in Romans and Galatians," in *Narrative Dynamics in Paul: A Critical Assessment* (ed. B. W. Longenecker; Louisville, KY: Westminster John Knox, 2002), 97–124.

20. See Gordon Fee, *God's Empowering Presence: The Holy Spirit in the Letters of Paul* (Peabody, MA: Hendrickson, 1994), 542–54, esp. 554.

21. To use a description helpfully provided to me by Prof. Christoph Schwöbel in conversation.

22. They also witness to the only way in which the truth of the Trinity can be apprehended, which is not of course by historical analysis—an essentially humanistic methodology—but by revelation, as the Trinity discloses *itself.* See Alan J. Torrance, "Jesus in Christian Doctrine," in *The Cambridge Companion to Jesus* (ed. M. Bockmuehl; Cambridge: Cambridge Univ. Press, 2001), 200–219.

we have already noted that three figures are ultimately in play—the Father, the Son, and the Holy Spirit).[23]

Furthermore, this triune God is known *in an act of redemption* as Christ enters into a hostile world to rescue it. This God is saving the cosmos through Christ—and in a humiliating and costly way. Hence salvation, in this sense, *is part of the being and identity of God*. Moreover, Paul has grasped helpfully that this saving dynamic is rooted in divine love (e.g., 5:8). God's extravagant love led to God's extraordinary and self-sacrificing salvation.

It follows from all this that there is a constant generous extension, giving, and embrace in God, who stoops down to engage with even his enemies, shoulders their burdens, and rescues them. This is God's nature. (The phrase *missio Dei* captures this and illuminates much else in Paul.)[24] I suspect that many of our most deeply rooted assumptions about God and reality need to be reconstructed at a deep level by these realizations.

It should now be emphasized that this divine extension is not logical or necessary (in the sense of causally necessary). Paul is not a logician, a rationalist, or a Newtonian physicist, seeking to understand the divine action in terms of some preconceived scheme about how reality operates. Paul suggests that the relationship between this dramatically benevolent and involved God and the wretched cosmos is a personal one, grounded in God's free act of loving engagement—what he calls God's choice, purpose, foreknowledge, and "preappointment" (*tois kata prothesin klētois ousin. Hoti hous proegnō, kai proōrisen symmorphous tēs eikonos tou huiou autou*, 8:28b–29a). These acts lead in turn to God's deliverance and glorification of the brothers (*hous de proōrisen, toutous kai ekalesen, kai hous ekalesen, toutous kai edikaiōsen, hous de edikaiōsen, toutous kai edoxasen*; 8:30). So here Paul emphasizes that God's love for humanity *precedes* anything that humanity is or does—an insight into God grounded in

---

23. These issues are never put more clearly than by Alisdair Heron, "*Homoousios* with the Father," in *The Incarnation: Ecumenical Studies in the Nicene-Constantinopolitan Creed A. D. 381* (ed. T. F. Torrance; Edinburgh: Handsel, 1981), 58–87.

24. This must be properly understood; see David J. Bosch, *Transforming Mission. Paradigm Shifts in Theology of Mission* (Maryknoll, NY: Orbis, 1991), 389–93. See also John G. Flett, *The Witness of God: The Trinity, Missio Dei, Karl Barth, and the Nature of Christian Community* (Grand Rapids: Eerdmans, 2010).

his "revelation"[25] of himself through Christ, and, in particular, through Christ's sacrifice for us.[26] And it has to, given the human condition.

Even as we learn that God has come unconditionally into the human condition to rescue humanity, we learn that humanity could contribute nothing to this process; people are redeemed by grace, unconditionally, and are shown at the same moment to be utterly depraved and corrupted (an insight that will be elaborated further in relation to Rom. 7). Hence, in this discussion Paul specifically connects election with the practice of hope in the face of suffering, and this makes perfect sense.

Humanity could not and cannot rescue itself. But it can rely on the God of love who initiated his salvation of humanity freely before humanity could do anything to generate this. God's love for humanity is not grounded in any human fulfillment of conditions, so it can be relied on to carry humanity through any apparent dangers and obstacles. Election suggests quite simply that God "is on our side." He always was and he always will be. (Any difficulties in humanity's relationship with this God will be contributed entirely from the human side.)

We should turn now to briefly consider some of the dramatic implications of these basic theological truths for some other important questions in Paul—his understandings of the person, of the church, and so on.

We learn first from these truths that a person is a fundamentally relational being. We learn this initially, and by analogy, from the nature of the God who has been revealed, and then see it instantiated more dimly in the community that has been called into existence through this revelation.

Critical distinguishing features of Christ are that he is, on the one hand, the Son of the Father, and, on the other, the one bound up with the Spirit. To remove either of these two links would disrupt his identity and nature decisively; these relationships are *constitutive* of his being and personhood. And we learn from this that Christ's *personhood* is *relational*. Christ is who he is because of whom he is in relationship to. It

---

25. Greek *apokalyptō*, hence the importance of an "apocalyptic" approach to Paul; see esp. Gal. 1:15–16; 2 Cor. 4:4–6; and Phil. 3:3–11. The leading apocalyptic interpreter of Paul is J. Louis Martyn.

26. This set of insights is grasped most fully and clearly by Karl Barth in his *Church Dogmatics*, II/2.

follows from this that all human persons, made in the image of God, are fundamentally relational as well; this is the secret of their imaging of God.

This may well challenge our customary ways of thinking about persons. Do we think of people as self-contained individuals—as entities distinct from and bounded off from other individuals? Or do we think of humanity in terms of larger groups that absorb individuals within them—of tribes, classes, genders, or nations? Both these conceptions are mistaken. People are extrinsic, relational, networking phenomena.[27] This realization leads directly to a further important feature of Paul's position that we are especially interested in here.

God's gift of himself to humanity in Christ calls a community into existence, and the nature of this community simply follows from the nature of the God who has created it. God *is* a communion and delights to share himself with others. (The Eastern tradition tends to develop this further as *theosis*; Pauline scholars tend to speak of this as "participation.")[28] We tend to speak of this as "the church," although this is not the language Paul tends to use. Paul prefers to speak of this community as the "brothers." And in 8:29 we have the only explicitly theological account in his writings of this term.

The people we call "Christians" are usually called "brothers" by Paul because they all bear the image of the resurrected and glorified Christ, who is the Son. He is the firstborn, Paul explains, and the brothers are those stamped with his image who are therefore his siblings. They are also then, by means of this, children of his Father. Consequently, this community of brothers has a number of important features. It is (of course) communal, but it is also ethical through and through. It is eschatological and embodied (although in a special sense). As we explore these features in more detail, we will find answers to some of our key questions for this chapter—concerning salvation and the church.

There are "many brothers." Paul never speaks of "brother" except when addressing someone specific for a particular reason. Hence, to focus on a single brother theologically is, for reasons that we have just

---

27. See esp. John Zizioulas, *Being as Communion* (New York, NY: SVS Press, 1985).

28. Michael J. Gorman has recently emphasized this dimension to Paul's thought: see *Inhabiting the Cruciform God: Kenosis, Justification, and Theosis in Paul's Narrative Theology* (Grand Rapids: Eerdmans, 2009).

discussed, an absurdity. This community is necessarily a networked entity in which the participants can only be what they are as the other participants are what they are. They inform one another, and their name tells us this. To call someone a brother is immediately to suggest that this person is defined by a relationship with someone else — in this case, primarily by a relationship with the Son, Christ, and with his Father, who is now (miraculously!) also ours, but through them secondarily by all the relationships that exist with the other brothers.[29]

The nature of this existence together now entails directly that the question concerning how to behave — in other words, the ethical dimension of Christianity — is inseparable from what the brothers are. To speak of people in relationship with one another is automatically to speak of certain sorts of relationships and of their constituent activities and broader narratives. So ethics is part of the warp and woof of communal Christian reality. Moreover, this ethic will be captured best for much of the time by the language of the virtues.[30]

This brotherhood is also eschatological; that is, it exists primarily in the new creation established in Christ. This is real and dependable. But it is not located in the "here and now" in the sense of the reality that people can see all around them and struggle with so often. As Paul puts it, the brothers do not live by what they see but by hope and perseverance (8:24–25).

The new reality is nevertheless concrete and embodied. The brothers' present bodies are flawed and corruptible, but they will be transformed (8:23). Their inheritance is a new creation. However, it seems that many distinctions in the old creation will be left behind when this redemption takes place.

Paul is particularly concerned with the transcendence by this new reality of the distinction between Jews and Greeks; *ethnicity* will be superseded (see 1:15–16). However, Paul states in a famous set of claims made in another letter that the distinctions between slaves and

---

29. Paul's notion of adoption clearly fits in well here; see Rom. 8:15, 23; 9:4; Gal. 4:5; Eph. 1:5. Robert Jewett surveys it in *Romans* (Hermeneia; Minneapolis: Fortress, 2007), 497–500.

30. The classic initial recovery of this ancient ethical tradition is Alasdair MacIntyre, *After Virtue* (3rd ed.; Notre Dame, IN: Univ. of Notre Dame Press, 2007). It should be pursued in both his further work and the work of Stanley Hauerwas (from whom I have learned much of the foregoing); see, among others writings, *A Community of Character: Toward a Constructive Christian Social Ethic* (Notre Dame, IN: Univ. of Notre Dame Press, 1981).

freedmen will be transcended as well—distinctions in status, class, and occupation. Most dramatically of all, the very distinction between men and women will be superseded (Gal. 3:28; see Gen. 1:27), although this stands to reason. The body that is thrown off and left behind is a body that sins, gets sick, and dies, and Christ gifts a new, literally incorruptible, bodily existence to humanity. While it is difficult to conceive of living in bodies that cannot die, Paul insists that this is the destiny of the brothers because this is what has happened to Christ.

It seems to follow, then, from this remarkably dramatic transformation, that Paul's use of the term "brothers" is not gendered. It does not suggest that the brothers will be biologically male, but rather that they will bear the image of the Son, Jesus, who is being called the Son in Romans 8 primarily because he is fulfilling the *role* played by Isaac in the story of Abraham and Isaac that is now playing out within God. The brothers are consequently related to one another personally and even narratively, *and in bodily terms*, but *not* biologically or ethnically.[31] The community is constituted in some sense beyond gender and race.

Much more could still be said,[32] but it is time to move on to the material in Romans 5:12–8:13, which is longer but in certain respects more straightforward.

The Ethical Argument

In the extended argument of Romans 5:12–8:13, God's loving action for humanity in Christ is given more precise shape, so we learn more here about salvation in Paul and about its "framework." It becomes apparent that God has not merely benevolently come all the way down to humanity in Christ, living as a person, but that he has done this for a reason. He has done what humanity could not do—dealt decisively and powerfully with the evil that surrounds it and lives within it. And in doing so he has lifted humanity back up to himself.[33] His grace is therefore a "yes" provided to a "yes."[34]

---

31. See my *The Quest for Paul's Gospel: A Suggested Strategy* (London: T&T Clark [Continuum], 2005), esp. 69–131.

32. Space constraints forbid addressing issues of death and temporality here as would be appropriate; but see Barth, *Church Dogmatics*, III/2, § 47, 437–640.

33. Few have grasped this aspect of Paul more clearly than Calvin. His position is elegantly summarized by James B. Torrance, "The Vicarious Humanity of Christ," in *The Incarnation*, 127–47.

34. A favorite saying of Alan J. Torrance.

This ongoing living in Christ by the brothers is a critical feature of Paul's thought. It explains his basic approach to ethics and his flexibility toward aspects of the Jewish *Torah*—the specific issues that structure his argument in the central part of Romans 5–8. Once we have grasped these dynamics in a little more detail, the basic elements of Paul's thought will be in place and the specific questions that we are exploring in this volume will have been answered in a powerful, provisional fashion.

Paul's argument in this section is constructed out of four main blocks of material—5:12–21, 6:1–23, 7:7–25, and 8:1–13—along with a short illustration (7:1–4), and an even shorter transitional summary statement, which is nevertheless quite revealing (7:5–6). Each block supplies new insights so we will address each briefly in turn.

Romans 5:12–21: The Scope of the Problem and the Solution

In this section Paul suddenly and dramatically frames his ensuing discussion by juxtaposing narratives of Christ and Adam. However, Paul's main point here is significantly qualified.

Before Paul makes certain programmatic claims concerning the parallelism between Christ and Adam in vv. 18–21, he takes pains to emphasize in vv. 15–17 that the second kingdom (of Christ) is vastly superior to the first one associated with Adam; these kingdoms are *not* parallel in any simple sense. His argument is not crystal clear, but he seems to suggest that the "quantities" involved in the situation are dominated by Christ.

Adam committed one transgression and the result was his death (v. 15). Unfortunately, everyone following him proceeded to sin (v. 16; see v. 12), leading to further deathly consequences for all. Christ, however, completely resolved the issue of death for the many through his life of obedience and resurrection, which was effective for all. Hence his *single* act of life overwhelmed the *multiple* grievous acts of Adam and his descendants, thereby indicating Christ's almost immeasurably greater power. As Paul puts it, the gift of life in Christ, in stark contrast to Adam, is characterized by "abundance" or "overflowing" (v. 17).

Having introduced this qualification, Paul goes on to his main point in verse 18 (which was probably initiated and left unfinished in v. 12): an articulation of "the problem" facing humanity in terms of an entire kingdom—a regime—of transgression, condemnation, and death, inaugurated in the garden of Eden and affecting everyone. Over against this Paul sets a kingdom gifted to humanity in Christ, a regime that has effected liberation rather than a death sentence and now rules in life and not death. These are the parameters for all that follows — the overarching stories of Christ and Adam, of life and death.

Paul uses the word "all" eight times through this short text, and in critical positions. ("Many" and "all/every," *polloi* and *pantes*, were interchangeable at times in Koine Greek and seem necessarily so here.) That is, his discussion is never qualified or filled with conditions. And this seems reasonable. God's decisive act on behalf of humanity in Christ is not likely to be qualified, limited, or inadequate. As the act of God it is necessarily perfect, complete, and sufficient. It is both premeditated and victorious. Paul has grasped this universal dimension in Christ's activity and expressed it directly in 5:12–21, using the universal story of Adam as a counterpoint. *Christ's being and narrative are determinative for all humanity* — and for the entire cosmos — *dominating* the being and narrative of Adam. The latter is a pale shadow that brings the dazzling illumination and significance of the former into still sharper clarity.[35]

Of course, this leaves some obvious questions hanging unanswered concerning present difficulties like sin and suffering, ultimate destiny, and so on. Christ's story is not obviously dominant all around humanity or even in it. But Paul is well aware of these phenomena and addresses them at length — and with some sophistication — in what follows in the letter. The crucial point to grasp here in relation to 5:12–21 is that Paul will consistently treat these as *secondary* phenomena and understand them on the basis of the *primary* reality, which is God acting in Christ. God's act comes first — the truth to which the community is called to witness.

Unfortunately, Paul's interpreters often seem to proceed in the other direction, taking "realities" like sin and suffering as primary and qualifying them partially in terms of the Christ event, *which has thereby in turn been deeply qualified.* God's act here becomes secondary, inadequate, and/or only partially applicable. Paul's exposition in 5:12–21 is a permanent rebuke to such distorted conceptualizations of God and his saving activity. Christ's significance for Paul tends to exceed what many of his interpreters can even imagine (so Eph. 3:20). But the way in which

---

35. Again, this point is made well by Barth, esp. in *Church Dogmatics*, IV/1, passim. A more accessible account of this is Jeff McSwain, *Movements of Grace: The Dynamic Christo-realism of Barth, Bonhoeffer, and the Torrances* (Eugene, OR: Wipf & Stock, 2010).

Paul justifies these narratives is as crucial as an appreciation of their universal dimensions and applications.

Paul sets up his extended qualification concerning the superiority of Christ with a telltale comment in 5:14b—that Adam "is a type [*typos*] of the coming one." This passing remark states that Christ is the original image and Adam a pale anticipation of Christ, much as a single seal in a blob of wax on a letter is a secondary and somewhat less clear imprint of an original signet ring.[36] And this remark indicates that Paul is "thinking backward"[37] when he crafts this comparison of narratives; he is working out his account of "the problem" in the light of the information that he has received about it from "the solution." The justification for Paul's claims concerning Adam lies in Christ's revelation of the solution, not vice versa. Certain clues in context support this judgment.

When Jews in Paul's day looked at the basic problem confronting both them and humanity more widely, they tended to be optimistic in some sense about the way that the *Torah* could help them out. In line with this, they tended to view the situation for humanity in Adam as dire, but never utterly without hope.[38] Human nature had things to offer. Paul, however, sees the *Torah* as offering *no* hope, and unassisted human nature as being utterly lost. So it looks very much as though he has decided at some point that the only way out of this entire situation is through the saving act of God in Christ. Everything else is then excluded by definition, which is why his account of humanity and the assistance of the *Torah* are so much more pessimistic than those of his contemporaries. He is, in short, "thinking backward." In the light of the solution that he already knows, he has gone on to set up an account of the problem—one that matches it. We can see this pattern in the way Paul's argument fits together as well.

Paul emphasizes Christ's grace, liberation of humanity, and life in 5:12–21—all benefits that flow from Christ's resurrection. Consequently, it seems plausible to suppose that Christ's resurrection to eternal

---

36. Barth was (of course) alert to the importance of this text: see *Christ and Adam: Man and Humanity in Romans 5* (trans. T. Smail; New York: Collier, 1962).

37. E. P. Sanders's important phrase and insight concerning Paul in much of *Paul and Palestinian Judaism*; see esp. 434–35, 438–40, 442, 474–85.

38. Brendan Byrne makes this point nicely; see *Romans* (SP 6; Collegeville, MN: Liturgical, 1996), 174–75, 181–82.

life *suggested* the narrative counterpart of Adam, where death originated. The liberation from death provided by Christ could then generate a further counterpart in the sentence of death pronounced in the garden of Eden. And so on. Moreover, if we read Paul this way—backward—he is able to make his assertions about human incoherence in a way that is ultimately coherent as well. (A tricky conundrum is lurking here.)

The situation is a bit like a recovering drug addict who is able to give a more accurate account of his or her previous life looking back on a severely addicted period, rather than while he or she is actually in it. Events are simply viewed more accurately with a clearing mind in retrospect rather than from within their unfolding when an addicted mind is probably engaged in deceptive rationalizations and other distorted mental games. Similarly, Paul wishes to emphasize the sinfulness of humanity, and he is well aware that this sinfulness extends through the human mind (see esp. 8:5–8, 13; 12:2). Such claims, however, cannot really be made before the arrival of the solution, which clarifies the mind to the point where it can grasp the truth. To make them *from within the addicted and sinful state would be to make claims that are true with a mind that is addicted and sinful.* Such claims can only be made plausibly in retrospect, looking back on a previous state with a clear mind.

Now Paul could be making incoherent claims. But we have already seen some indications that he is in fact thinking backward, as he ought to, so we should probably extend to him the argumentative benefit of the doubt (i.e., that he is coherent until proved otherwise).[39]

In short, 5:14b, a comparison with contemporary Jewish accounts, the "fit" in the argument, and an initial presumption that Paul is making sense, all combine to suggest that the view in 5:12–21 is backward or retrospective; hence, it is based on revelation rather than on unassisted human reason or reflection.

Romans 6: The Transition, and Its Freedoms

Paul turns after 5:21 to address an obvious rejoinder to his universal claims—in terms of sin. Is his declaration of the universal reality of Christ for humanity not something that allows people to sin freely

---

39. And our later consideration of Romans 7—a text that raises many of the same issues—will confirm this decision.

(6:1)? Is it just a pious rhetorical façade masking dirtier realities? Paul responds to this challenge—which was probably a real one, as indicated by 3:8b—with horror, and then with an argued set of counterclaims. These are developed through an interpretation of Christian baptism in terms of participation in the death and resurrection of Christ (6:3–4a, 5–6).

In essence, Paul claims that Christ has been set free from a condition of mortality, sin, and death, by dying and being resurrected (vv. 7, 9–10). Obviously once he has died, he does not need to die again.[40] He lives now in glory (v. 4b). But Paul insists that Christians have been immersed into this trajectory as well, although their movement into glory is not as overt as Christ's. Nevertheless the execution of their sin is emphatic. And it is this identification with Christ's death and resurrection that baptism, understood as a single act of immersion under water and reemergence, communicates so resonantly for Paul (the Greek *baptizō* meaning "immersion" or "dipping").

Paul turns in 6:13 to exhort the brothers to live righteously since they have now been made righteous, beginning an argument that can puzzle his modern readers. Having made such strong declarations about the reality of the new being of the brothers in Christ—which implies some causal account of their state—it seems odd to suddenly appeal to the brothers as if they freely engage with this reality, and yet this is just what Paul does. The brothers are to present themselves to God for righteous activity (v. 13b), partly because they stand in a reality marked by two basic "options"—a kingdom of obedience, righteousness, and life, and one of disobedience, sin, and death. But existence is also apparently a slavery, although the nature of the slavery in question differs dramatically (vv. 15–23). The brothers should respond to the slavery characterized by freedom, holiness, and life and shun the servitude that is degrading, disgusting, and deathly.

It can seem strange that Paul appeals to the brothers to freely participate in a reality that has already been established for them, and even worse that he then weaves these appeals into a discourse of slavery. These claims all seem to be at cross-purposes with one another. But any

40. Paul's argument is clearer if Robin Scroggs's important contention is grasped that Christ is the subject of 6:7; see "ὁ γὰρ ἀποθανὼν δεδικαίωται ἀπὸ τῆς ἁμαρτίας," *NTS* 10 (1963): 104–8.

confusion here may well be caused by the assumptions that contemporary readers bring to this discussion.

Modern readers tend to operate with a post-Enlightenment worldview that understands causality in strongly determinative, if not entirely mechanical, terms. The "natural" world, in particular, is held to be governed by fixed causal processes that operate remorselessly. By way of contrast, people are held to possess "freedom," which tends to be analogized in essentially spatial terms and so understood in terms of free will and choice.[41] People supposedly make decisions between different options, thereby exercising their freedom and "moving" in one of several different possible directions from a fixed point, much as one might choose to dribble a ball north, south, east, or west across a basketball court (by oneself of course!). It follows from these basic images that any encroachment by the necessary or causal, or by other people or structures, onto the "zone" in which human freedom operates is a direct infringement on freedom per se in something of a tyranny. Causality and/or slavery, and human freedom, exist in zero-sum relationships.[42]

Paul, however, is not operating with modern notions of causality and freedom. He is almost certainly informed distantly by the ancient virtue tradition developed especially by Greek-speaking philosophers, which is much closer to the rather different conceptions of causality and freedom suggested by Christian orthodoxy.[43] So we should try to read Paul's argument in Romans 6 more in these terms.

In an embodied, complex, and relational situation, freedom is not a matter of sheer choice—the latter being something of a chimera—but of an incremental creation of new possibilities for bodily action that must be learned and internalized. All action is initially the gift of new possible actions from someone else, to which humans can freely and appropriately respond. Freedom is therefore complex, communally mediated, and embodied. Above all, it is *learned* and hence *taught*, much as someone is only free to play a violin beautifully after years of practice

41. Just how causally determined bodies and free minds join together to make one person is a matter of ongoing debate.

42. This is an important but large discussion. A useful entry point is Richard Bauckham, *God and the Crisis of Freedom: Biblical and Contemporary Perspectives* (Louisville KY: Westminster John Knox, 2002).

43. See again MacIntyre, *After Virtue*. A similar account is provided from a very different direction by Barth in *Church Dogmatics*, III/1.

and instruction, ideally by a maestro. Freedom is an accumulation of smaller freedoms in the sense of growth in possible concrete actions learned from one who has mastered them beforehand.[44]

This pedagogy can consequently be described accurately as a slavery in the sense that people must respond obediently to the possibilities set before them in order to grow into further specific freedoms. But freedom denotes a critical aspect of this response as well; it is precisely *not* mechanical or necessary. Each human response is free and facilitates further concrete actions that one is then free to make.

Hence, Paul's discussion in Romans 6 really assumes that an embodied existence, freedom, and slavery all belong together. The brothers ought to continue to respond freely to the set of concrete righteous actions being set before them in Christ. (This is also the reasonable or rational thing to do; see Rom. 12:2.) As they learn these actions, they will then be free to do them again, and in this way they will realize true freedom and an effective ethic — something that can also be spoken of as a certain sort of slavery.[45]

In view of all this, it makes little sense for the brothers to turn to any alternative ethical system. They are already on the pathway of life, established by God, and should continue, freely, to walk on it. That is, to be ethical in this way is to be saved and to enjoy life rather than death. Paul now has a lot to say about the deceptiveness of any alternative ethic that would lure the brothers from this path — especially one that appeals in a certain way to Scripture.

Romans 7: The Horrifying View Backward

Paul spends most of his time in this chapter articulating a problematic set of dynamics caused by the *Torah* in the fleshly and sinful state (see vv. 7–25). But two short discussions precede the main analysis.

In 7:1–4 Paul draws an analogy between the post-*Torah* existence of the brothers and a Jewish marriage. Fortunately, we do not need to untangle all the details of this analogy. We just need to appreciate Paul's

---

44. It is consequently critical to try to make a transition from ocular and spatial metaphors to sonic and even musical ones in this relation. On this general dynamic see Jeremy Begbie, *Theology, Music, and Time* (Cambridge: Cambridge Univ. Press, 2000).

45. These are not Paul's actual emphases in context. He presupposes most of what we have just discussed. But we do not need to dwell on his specific exhortations here.

basic claim that the brothers now live in a situation legitimately beyond the Mosaic *Torah*: "you died to the *Torah* so that you might belong to another" (v. 4).

A pregnant summary statement follows in 7:5–6. The brothers used to live in a state characterized by "the lusts of sin that ... were working in our members and bore fruit ultimately in death" (v. 5). But the brothers have now died to this situation of constraint and so been released from it (as Paul has emphasized especially in ch. 6), leading to a new slavery in terms of the Spirit (v. 6b). Moreover, the *Torah* apparently further troubled this initial lustful situation, being present there in some sense as "the letter," but it has been left behind after the decisive transition has taken place (v. 6). After these comments Paul turns to a longer discussion that has two stages.

In 7:7–13 Paul tells the story of someone's attempt to obey one of the Ten Commandments (see Ex. 20:17; Deut. 5:21)—specifically, the prohibition against coveting (and this resumes the language of desire introduced in Rom. 7:5). But into this story he weaves a modified version of the fall in the garden of Eden. When the specific, written commandment "arrives" (here against desire) in all its glory, promising life, sin slithers in and deceptively arouses all sorts of false desires in the poor person trying to obey. The result is a dastardly reversal. Instead of facilitating obedience and eliciting life, the written commandment, manipulated by the snakelike sin, instead produces transgression and death.

Paul goes on to point out that the *Torah* is technically blameless in all this; it is and remains good. But given the other elements present within the broader situation—notably the seductive activities of sin—the results of the *Torah's* presence turn out to be sin and death. The person at least knows just how sinful he or she is (so v. 13). But clearly this is a dead end in and of itself. The story of Adam and Eve seems to overwhelm the famous gift given through Moses.

Paul now goes on to speak in the second main phase of his argument (vv. 14–24) of a person who seems to be in a still more difficult situation. He might even be alluding here to the story of Medea as developed by playwrights and philosophers in his day.

Medea famously sought revenge on her unfaithful husband by killing their children, although as a mother at least part of her naturally did not want to do this. In the play written by Euripides, she struggles on stage with these clashing desires, but, tragically, her vengeful passions overcome her nobler instincts. In just this way, the person depicted in verses 14–25 is no longer merely deceived by sin but cannot do what she wants to do; sin is too powerful. Instead, she does what she does not want to do. Hence she is a divided and even tortured self. Some *Torah* in her members is "waging war" on her more elevated mind, where God's *Torah* lives, and "imprisoning and enslaving" her (vv. 14, 23). At the climax of this depiction Paul cries out, "What a wretched person I am!" and begs for "rescue" (v. 24).

Scholars have struggled in the past to locate these interlinked stories biographically. They have wondered whether Paul is describing his life before he became an apostle or after his call to Christ, although there are problems with both these positions.[46] More recently, many have been persuaded by W. G. Kümmel's suggestion that a more general view of humanity is in view. This reading's plausibility is reinforced if stereotypical comedic or philosophical conventions from Paul's day are detectable in Paul's text, as some of the church fathers thought—the sense that a speech is being made in the dramatic, exaggerated voice of a character that is not Paul himself. Certainly "the foolish person" who cries out in verse 24a was a stock character in much ancient drama and philosophy.[47]

A final decision here will be helped if we can show once more that Paul is thinking "backward." To this end we should note that Paul has placed his extended account of a struggle with *Torah* and sin after two accounts of Christian transformation, when the brothers have moved from a state of death through to one of life decisively—one extended (6:1–23) and one pithy and analogical (7:1–4). His important summary in 7:5–6 also locates the letter's viewpoint in the state beyond *Torah*, operating in the "new way of the Spirit" (7:6b). So the context suggests in three successive discussions that 7:7–25 is composed from

---

46. R. N. Longenecker canvasses many of the key issues in this text insightfully in *Paul, Apostle of Liberty* (New York, NY: Harper & Row, 1964), 86–97, 109–16.

47. A good introduction to the complex issues involved is Stanley Stowers, *A Rereading of Romans: Justice, Jews, and Gentiles* (New Haven, CT: Yale Univ. Press, 1994), 258–81. If so, this would be an instance of play-acting by Paul—Greek *prosōpopoiia*—where he makes a speech in a voice and role not his own. Kümmel's views can be found in his *Man in the New Testament* (trans. John J. Vincent; London: Epworth, 1963).

the Christian point of view and looks *back* on the state from which the brothers have been rescued (7:24b–25). And certainly Paul never tells us explicitly that he has changed his point of view from 7:7 onward and moved back to a consideration of his pre-Christian life as it felt then. (Indeed, it is hard to know why he would want to supply this sort of biographical description at this point in his argument.)

In view of all this, it seems that Kümmel is right and Paul is not speaking biographically in 7:7–25—except in a rather general sense. Most likely he is supplying a warning to his Roman Christian listeners not to lapse back into a *Torah*-governed ethic and thereby necessarily fall back at the same time into a life in the flesh that recapitulates the twisted and tragic story of Adam. This is a deceptively appealing ethical option—to resort to the *Torah* to deal with sin and the lusts of the flesh, and to try ultimately in this way to avoid death. But Paul dramatizes the view that only agonies—and perhaps even the agonies of Medea— await such a person. Any person turning back from the gospel in this way will be torn and wretched, and will be assailed by sin! They will need to be rescued again! God's solution to this awful plight has *already* been supplied in Christ, a solution that is simply different from the *Torah* (although, Paul would say, it is anticipated in *Torah*; see 3:21). It is victorious and perfect, so there is no need to supplement or displace it.

Certain critical consequences follow from all this for our understandings of salvation and the church in Paul, but it will be clearest to address 8:1–13 before these are highlighted.

Romans 8:1 - 13: The Solution

Paul begins chapter 8 by stating resonantly, "there is no death sentence for those in Christ Jesus." So clearly a massive transition has taken place— between no less than death and life. Liberation has been established, and the ability to do the good willingly has arrived with the Spirit.[48] In the next few verses Paul goes on to supply perhaps his clearest account of the atonement (see v. 3a)—although it remains compact—stating that a trinitarian dynamic has liberated humanity (vv. 2, 4, 10b;[49] see 7:24b).

---

48. This fulfils a series of important promises for Paul; see esp. Deut. 30:6; Jer. 31:31–34; Ezek. 36:26–27.

49. Supplying a "forensic-liberative" account of Paul's *dikaio-* terminology in vv. 4 and 10b. This approach is justified in *Deliverance*, esp. 656–65.

God's own Son has been sent into the flesh, taking on the precise or exact likeness of flesh, and has died, thereby *executing* sin and the flesh (v. 3). These evils have now been terminated precisely in and by this death.[50]

But Christ has been raised from the dead into a new inheritance (v. 11), of necessity leaving the old state behind (see ch. 6). As a result, his Spirit can introduce a new mind for the brothers of peace, obedience, and life (vv. 2, 6–8)—and this seems to be Paul's main emphasis in context. This spiritual mind operates beyond and against the fleshly conditions that are hostile to God, disobedient, and destined for death. So the brothers can now recapitulate Christ's execution of the death-dealing practices of the flesh, being led by the Spirit of God (vv. 5b, 6b, 12–14) as they await the re-creation of their corrupt bodies (v. 11). They can behave!

Paul uses the terminology of what we might call indwelling repeatedly through this discussion (see vv. 2, 4, 8, 9 [3x], 10, 11). It becomes apparent that to be "in" someone or something is Paul's chosen language for speaking of ontology; it denotes fundamentally determinative being—here either flesh, or Christ and the Spirit.[51] This realization explains in turn the interchangeability of the language of location or "in-ness" with Paul's language of possession and belonging in verse 9b. If people are "in Christ" and he is "in" them, they also "have" him, he "has" them, and they "belong" to him.

Paul is talking in all these places about what people are made of in a real and deep way, and of their connection with Christ—something we noted earlier that is spoken of frequently by scholars in terms of "participation." But this is also clearly indistinguishable for Paul from how people act. In Christ and the Spirit it seems that the conventional distinctions that we often make between being and acting do not hold. God *is* how God *acts*. So being *itself* is dynamic and active.[52] We need to push past any being-act dichotomy in our thinking about God and/or humanity.

---

50. The significance of Christ's death and burial are emphasized especially insightfully by Alan Lewis, "The Burial of God: Rupture and Redemption as the Story of Salvation," *SJT* 40 (1987): 335–62.

51. See 1 Cor. 15:22, 45–49. The classic treatment of "in Christ" terminology in Paul is G. Adolf Deissmann, *St. Paul: A Study in Social and Religious History* (2nd ed.; trans. L. R. M. Strachan; London: Hodder & Stoughton, 1912).

52. See esp. Eberhard Jüngel, *God's Being Is in Becoming: The Trinitarian Being of God in the Theology of Karl Barth: A Paraphrase* (4th German ed.; trans. J. Webster; Grand Rapids: Eerdmans, 2001).

We noted earlier, in relation to 8:14–39, how a communal reality has been created by God in Christ. There is no single subject in Paul's discussion of Christian existence; the "I" of chapter 7 has been truly left behind. Moreover, we have just noted how the new constructive ethical capacity within this situation comes from the creation in the brothers of "the mind of the Spirit" (v. 6b). To possess the Spirit of both God and Christ, and to be possessed by the Spirit, is both to live and to live rightly. We need now to combine these realizations together.

Paul has articulated in this text a basis for Christian ethics that is rather direct and personal. The brothers need merely to walk in accordance with the mind of the Spirit—which is to say, the mind of God. They have direct access to this; they live "in" it. However, because such thinking is oriented by a loving personal communion—by a community—it follows that the activities suggested by this mind will tend to have a certain shape, although presumably specifics may vary. A "virtue ethic" will consequently point helpfully to the essentially relational dynamics in play. The actions of the brothers will be characterized by "love, joy, peace, forebearance, kindness, goodness, faithfulness, gentleness, and self-control" (Gal. 5:22b–23a—virtues arguably writ large across Rom. 12:1–15:6 as well). Moreover, the spiritual minds of the brothers will clearly need to be habituated into these virtuous relational dynamics. New concrete possibilities for the right sort of relationality will need to be given to them from Christ and the Spirit, to which they can then respond. Four aspects of this community are now becoming increasingly apparent.

1. We learned from 5:12–21 that the Christ narrative is actually determinative for the reality of the cosmos and hence inclusive of all humanity, over against the Adamic narrative, which also determines all of humanity although in an immeasurably reduced sense. Certainly the community of brothers is responding to this christological reality in a way that reflects it more accurately than those people still responding to the inferior Adamic reality; the latter are living in a situation and a manner that is fundamentally untruthful. However, it follows from this that the community is not fundamentally different from the rest of humanity but rather *represents its true nature*. It

therefore fulfills priestly, anticipatory, and representative roles, rather than occupying an explicitly different location.[53] It is more clearly what all of humanity is—the firstfruits of the full harvest.[54]

2. We also learn here that the community is beyond Scripture in ethical terms—if Scripture is used in a simple "written," instructional sense. Indeed, Paul would probably disparage any such use, saying, "The letter kills" (see 2 Cor. 3:6). Certainly Scripture witnesses to Christ (Rom. 3:21; 2 Cor. 1:20a), and texts can mediate ethics (see, e.g., Rom. 15:1–13; 1 Cor. 10:1–22); but Christ, through the Spirit, directs the righteous activity of the community personally (Rom. 12:2–8; 1 Cor. 2; Gal. 5:16–18, 22–25). The brothers have not died to sin and then been raised to new life in the Scriptures. They have done so in Christ and now live in him. He is, therefore, their concrete possibility for righteousness—their ethical as well as their cosmic Lord.

   Hence any appeal to the letter of Scripture to direct the community that is not folded into the direct command of Christ and the virtuous relationships that characterize the divine and human communion risks being hijacked by fleshly lusts and sin, and being used to cripple, condemn, and kill. Such an approach will, in short, lapse back precisely into the horrific situation articulated by Romans 7. Christians are meant, rather, to live in the church—a community of brothers—which is described in Romans 8. This community, indwelled richly by the Spirit, is characterized by virtue and freedom. Its guidance comes from the Spirit's mediation of the mind of Christ.

3. It seems to follow distantly from this that the community is rather free and flexible in specific terms. Indeed, Paul, mediating the mind of Christ, can address the brothers in numerous other letters in strikingly diverse ways. In these letters we see

---

53. And we link hands here with the priestly role of Christ that has already been emphasized; see n. 33.

54. Indeed, Paul's language of "firstfruits" is especially indicative in this relation; see Rom. 8:23; 11:16; 16:5; 1 Cor. 15:20, 23; 16:15; 2 Thess. 2:13; see also Jas. 1:18; Rev. 14:4.

specific groups of brothers engaging those alongside them in quite distinctive ways, while the right behavior by the brothers in each of these situations seems to be subtly different.[55] The demands of diverse locations, of consequently contextualized missions, and of a presiding commander-in-chief sensitive to these[56] seem to combine here into a flexible approach to community-creation and building.[57]

As a result of this, we can probably learn much concerning the ethical situation of the brothers from a "command" as well as from a virtue ethic. A command ethic speaks of the quite specific instructions that God can issue to the brothers in different locations.[58] Indeed, one aspect of the freedom of the brothers will be captured by this approach, a freedom that we have already seen operating to a degree as the brothers live beyond direct instructions from the *Torah.*

4. Finally, it seems that the brothers always stand on the brink of an abyss. While their reality is determined by Christ, it seems that the inferior reality of Adam "crouches at the door." At any moment the brothers can turn again to the flesh and lapse back into the divided and agonized situation of Romans 7. Romans 7 consequently trails Romans 8 as a misshapen shadow trails behind a person. It is a false reality, an untruthful and distorting story, and yet one that continually threatens to rise unhappily from the dead. The brothers are to stay resolutely turned away from it! Its ways *are* death (8:6, 10).

---

55. Diversity is a key feature of the Pauline data. An important methodological statement of and response to this—in terms of "contingency" and "coherence"—is J.-Christiaan Beker, *Paul the Apostle: The Triumph of God in Life and Thought* (Philadelphia: Fortress, 1980).

56. The function of Christ for Paul as a ruler who issues commands that are, in classic Hellenistic mode, automatically thereby "law," is expounded by Bruno Blumenfeld in *The Political Paul: Justice, Democracy and Kingship in a Hellenistic Framework* (Sheffield: Sheffield Academic, 2001). (And this *might* be the most helpful way to understand "the law of Christ"; see 1 Cor. 9:21; Gal. 6:2).

57. A classic account of the theological as well as "practical" importance of mission to the church is Bosch, *Transforming Mission*; see also Flett, *The Witness of God.*

58. I am referring to a christological account of a command ethic, as we find, e.g., in Barth; it is usefully introduced by Eberhard Busch, "Exacting Exhortation—Gospel and Law, Ethics," in *The Great Passion: An Introduction to Karl Barth's Theology* (trans. Geoffrey Bromiley; Grand Rapids: Eerdmans, 2004), 152–75.

With these final insights gleaned from Romans 8 concerning salvation and the church, it is time to draw our discussion together.

The Resulting System: Our Questions Answered

Paul is specifically concerned in Romans 5–8 with eschatological assurance and ethics. In making extended responses to these concerns, however, he provisionally articulates a systematic theology. All the key theological topics are addressed, including the important questions occupying us in this book concerning salvation, the significance of Christ, the right framework for understanding his gospel, and the church.

Paul's consistently retrospective purview suggests the priority of Christ over all other contentions. Christ's disclosure of God — inseparable from the acts of the Father and the Spirit — is basic to Paul in every way. But God's act in Christ is, of course, a saving act, and the nature of this salvation reveals a great deal about God. God is unconditional and elective, gracious and giving, and utterly and fundamentally benevolent. Christ's revelation of God is clearly therefore also the "framework" that we need in order to understand everything else in Paul.

But we can say all these things about God only because this saving act in Christ has called a community of brothers into existence — and in fact to participation in the divine communion where Christ is the firstborn Son of the Father. So the brothers are constituted as brothers as they participate in this reality and receive Christ's image; in doing so they become sons of the Father. Much more can be said about the "church" in Paul, but this set of insights, flowing from his central insights into God's acting in Christ, seems fundamental. We need now to make one further claim as this essay concludes — concerning "centrality."

We need to ask if the system we have detected in Romans 5–8 is effectively transferable elsewhere in Paul. Does it represent Paul's thinking as a whole?

Clearly I would not have treated it in such detail if I did not think it gave us definitive insights into the thinking underlying all his letters. As it turns out, we link hands here with a long-standing debate within modern Pauline studies.[59]

---

59. It is represented now most clearly in Sanders's work (who looks back specifically to Albert Schweitzer); see esp. *Paul and Palestinian Judaism*. I supply a brief summary in *Deliverance*, 1–2, and short elaboration of the issues (leaning on William Wrede) in 176–88.

Since deep in the nineteenth century, scholars have frequently suggested that participatory arguments do most of the work in Paul's texts, which is to say that for most of the time, and in relation to the most important apparent issues, the apostle's contentions are couched in fundamentally participatory terms — in relation to the notions explicated more fully in Romans 5–8 in terms of life "in Christ." Moreover, this system does not just underlie most of Paul's overt articulations of the theological grounds why particular brothers should behave in certain ways as Christians — the texts where Paul seems to be speaking in a way that we recognize now as explicitly theological. It seems to underlie many of his more emotional appeals, his ethics, and most of his particular actions as a missionary and pastor.

Another way of grasping this is to observe that Paul's most common phrase, occurring frequently in all his letters, is "in Christ" or its close equivalent, the formula that summarizes the soteriology set forth by Romans 5–8.[60] We might say, then, that this system is the hub in Paul's cartwheel, *and* it seems to provide most of the spokes as well — a provisional judgment with which our discussion here will have to conclude.

Conclusion

I have suggested here, in essence, that Paul's answers to the four questions programmatically informing this book flow from a clear understanding of the gospel as grounded in revelation, revealing of the triune God, and consequently missional; and that the clearest account of this gospel is found in Romans 5–8. That is, Christ's disclosure of God is at the heart of his significance for Paul in a way that can be distinguished but not separated from his saving disclosure. Christ reveals God definitively, and he specifically reveals a God who loves so much that he saves by giving of himself and drawing humanity back to himself — a missional God!

This is then also the "framework" that comprehends the gospel properly in Paul.[61] So the answers to our first three programmatic ques-

---

60. A. Deissmann found upward of 160 occurrences in his *St. Paul*.

61. It follows from this, moreover, that all other frameworks must be rejected — especially when couched in prospective or "forward-looking" rather than retrospective terms. Such frameworks tend to override the centrality and significance of Christ for Paul, and consequently to come up with essentially different understandings of salvation.

tions all flow from the same point and around the same truths. And we may be confident of our answers because only they allow us to give a responsible answer to Paul's transcendence of a *Torah*-informed ethic in a way that is sufficiently sensitive to the nature and ongoing reality of Judaism.

While exploring Paul's answers to questions concerning Christ and salvation, however, we have also repeatedly encountered the apostle's basic understanding of the church—the answer to our fourth and final overarching question. The apostle everywhere presupposes but also seeks to shape a community of "brothers." This community has been established by a revealing and extravagantly benevolent God, so it is called to mediate this reality to others *and* to correspond to it, thereby becoming a missional church! Indeed, Paul clearly expects to see a community that relates in a particular way: an ethical community, facilitating both a liberating virtue and a virtuous freedom, and responding to the loving commands of its crucified and enthroned Lord to seek and save the lost (or, failing this, simply to befriend them).[62] This dynamic explains almost all the endorsements of and exhortations to community found in Paul's writings, as well as those specifically enacted in his journeys, friendships, visits, letters, and prayers, with and on behalf of specific people in particular places and situations.

It is a definitive understanding of what God in Christ is doing in our world—an understanding both new and old. We would be wise to pay it careful attention.

---

62. In this relation see esp. Christopher L. Heuertz and Christine D. Pohl, *Friendship at the Margins: Discovering Mutuality in Service and Mission* (Downers Grove, IL: InterVarsity Press, 2010).

THOMAS R. SCHREINER

Doug Campbell has written a fascinating essay, and his work is certainly provocative and tantalizing. If my view is Reformed, perhaps his can be labeled über-Reformed, or even hyper-Calvinist. For someone who is Reformed, however, there are many themes that strike a chord. Campbell rightly trumpets the electing grace of God that saves sinners. The influence of Calvin and Barth is evident. God's gracious election displays his astonishing and wonderful love for those who are undeserving. Sinners do not prepare themselves to receive this grace. They do not receive it because they have lived in a way that is ethically praiseworthy. God's love rescues and delivers those who were heading toward destruction.

Campbell also rightly highlights the trinitarian character of Paul's thought. Salvation is the work of the Father, the Son, and the Spirit. Nor does Campbell conceive of the Trinity exclusively in functional terms. The ontological equality of the Son and the Spirit with the Father is taught as well. Campbell especially brings out well the relational nature of this salvation. Believers experience the love of the Father, the Son, and the Spirit when they are delivered from sin and death. And this love, this grace, has ethical and communal consequences. Believers live virtuously and righteously. The Spirit empowers them to live in a new way as brothers and sisters, and they are motivated to share the love of God with the world. At the same time, this new life is not automatic. Freedom is like learning to play a musical instrument. One experiences "more freedom" as one pursues and practices righteousness. The danger of succumbing to sin and to life in Adam continues to threaten believers, and thus they must continue to pursue righteousness.

Campbell's work resonates insofar as he exalts the grace and love of God, and his work is God-centered, featuring the Father, the Son, and the Spirit. The radical love of God pulsates through his thought. If I understand Campbell rightly, there are problems with his construal as well, though I am happy to withdraw my critique if he says otherwise as the conversation continues. He strikes some of the right chords, but some chords are missing and even the chords that are struck are off key.

Campbell takes Romans 5–8 as having a special clarity, using it to exposit Pauline thought. Certainly Romans 5–8 plays an important role in Paul's thought, and explaining his theology through the lens of these chapters is useful. But the limitations of such an approach should be acknowledged more clearly and directly. The window into Paul's world is much larger, and hence it is inherently distorting if one privileges these chapters at the expense of the remainder of his writings. In fact, Campbell does bring in what Paul says elsewhere into his essay but only to a limited extent. Campbell doesn't defend well why Romans 5–8 becomes the lens for reading Paul, especially given the size of the Pauline corpus. We need a fuller explanation and defense of why these chapters are the proper framework for interpreting Paul.

Perhaps a specific example will illustrate the problem relative to Paul's ecclesiology. Since Campbell restricts himself to Romans 5–8, he investigates the significance of the term "brothers" for Pauline ecclesiology. His remarks are illuminating and helpful, but a much wider canvas is needed to explore Paul's view of the church. The significance of the word "church" and the notion that the church is a temple and a body receive little or no discussion. I conclude that the framework of Romans 5–8, therefore, is not wide enough or broad enough to exposit Pauline theology, for it doesn't include enough of Paul in the picture.

I think it is misleading when Campbell says that his view is not distinctively new, for he finds its roots in Irenaeus, Athanasius, the Gregories, Basil, and Calvin. Yes and no. There are certainly bits and pieces of his view that can traced to these early writers. I would suggest, however, that when we consider the theological whole of these illustrious ancestors, they would find more common ground with the view I propose than with Campbell. Let me be specific. I am thinking particularly of the theme of judgment in Paul, for if I understand him correctly, this is the major difference between Campbell and me. Campbell appears to argue that the Adam-Christ parallel in Romans 5 is all-inclusive. There are no limitations or qualifications. All human beings are in Adam, and all human beings are also in Christ. This seems to fit with my reading of his previous work where he rejects the idea that God's justice is retributive.

Now this is a stunning reading of the love of God in Christ, reminding us of what Barth wrote. Of course, Campbell's thought cannot be equated with Barth's in every respect. One can also see how this fits broadly with a Reformed reading of Paul. Paul reads retrospectively, says Campbell, for just as everyone was swept into the orbit of Adam's sin, so everyone is caught up in the powerful and overwhelming grace of Jesus Christ.

I contend that Irenaeus, Athanasius, Gregory of Nazianzus, Basil the Great, and Calvin would find Campbell's theology problematic, because they confessed that unbelievers would be judged and suffer eternally.[63] Of course, the key question isn't what the church fathers believed, but what Paul himself taught, and there is ample evidence that he believed in a future judgment in which the wicked would be destroyed. Indeed, the theme is pervasive in Paul's thought (cf. Rom. 2:5, 16).[64] A fundamental datum of Paul's gospel is that God will judge the world (3:5–6). Indeed, even in Romans 5–8 there is recognition of a final judgment: on the last day wrath will be poured out on those not justified (5:9); "the wages of sin is death" (6:23); all those who are not liberated from sin and the law will die (7:5, 9–11, 13); those who practice sin will die (8:6, 13).

Many more texts could be adduced to demonstrate the reality of the final judgment and the notion that some will suffer everlasting punishment, but one is particularly clear. Paul teaches in 2 Thessalonians 1 that the eschatological judgment of the wicked is "just" (*dikaion*, v. 6). A flaming fire awaits those who don't know God or who disobey the gospel (v. 8). The penalty (*dikēn*) will be "eternal punishment" (v. 9). Some object that 2 Thessalonians was not written by Paul. I disagree with such a conclusion; but even if it were true, we would have here the writing of a Pauline disciple who thought he was faithful to the Pauline teaching. Indeed, the church accepted the writing as part of the Pauline corpus, finding it to be in harmony with what Paul wrote elsewhere.

---

63. Gregory of Nyssa is an exception here, for he follows Origen. But Origen's view of universalism was judged to be unorthodox. Hence, the mainstream teaching of the church flies against Campbell's view.

64. I realize that Campbell offers another interpretation of these texts, but space is lacking here to enter into a fuller discussion.

Even in the Adam-Christ parallel in Romans 5:12–19 we have evidence that the salvation achieved by Jesus Christ does not include all without exception. Reigning in life is restricted to those who "*receive* ... the gift of righteousness*" (Rom. 5:17). A parallel text in 1 Corinthians 15:21–22 confirms this reading of Romans 5:12–19, but before discussing those verses, I want to point to a few places in 1 Corinthians that anticipate a final judgment, for they support the notion that what Paul says about Adam and Christ does not eliminate a future judgment. Paul makes it clear that those who do not continue in the faith until the end have believed in vain (1 Cor. 15:2; cf. 1:18); that is, they will face final judgment. Those who destroy the church will face eschatological destruction (3:17). If the man committing incest does not repent, he will not be saved on the last day (5:5; cf. 5:13). The unrighteous who practice evil will not inherit the kingdom (6:9–11). Similarly, if the Corinthians follow the example of the wilderness generation, they will perish as that generation did (10:1–12).

This brings us to 1 Corinthians 15:21–22, which at first glance seems to support Campbell's reading of Romans 5:12–19: all die in Adam and all enjoy life in Christ. But texts must be read in context both near and far. Verse 23 provides a crucial qualification, for life is restricted to "those who belong to [Christ]" (*hoi tou Christou*). Space precludes further discussion, but there are far too many texts about the final judgment in Paul to accept the notion that Christ's grace spares everyone from retributive judgment.

A question also arises regarding Campbell's view of ethics. He rightly emphasizes the power of the Spirit and the importance of virtue. But what role do the moral norms disseminated in the Pauline letters actually play in Campbell's understanding? If I read him correctly, he seems to suggest, given the situational and Spirit-shaped nature of Pauline ethics, that norms written in the Pauline letters are not necessarily normative. Whatever Campbell is saying, life in the Spirit and ethical norms harmonize in Pauline thought. Those who walk in the Spirit and are led by the Spirit serve others in love (Gal. 5:13–18), and those who love refrain from adultery, stealing, or murder (Rom. 13:8–10). Life in the Spirit is not congruent with sexual immorality (1 Cor. 6:12–20; cf. 1 Thess. 4:3–8), or with fits of anger, strife, hatred, dissension, jealousy, and the like (Gal. 5:20). Paul's specific directives prohibiting divorce

(1 Cor. 7:10–16) and homosexuality (Rom. 1:26–27; 1 Cor. 6:9; 1 Tim. 1:10) do not contradict but harmonize with life in the Spirit. Perhaps there is no disagreement here, but the way Campbell framed the issue left me wondering.

Campbell also makes some comments about the new perspective. He praises it because the older view of Judaism could not be defended in the presence of burning children. The old perspective potentially had terrible consequences, promulgating a defective view of Judaism. What can be said by way of response? Certainly, Christian history is littered with examples of believers sinning against Jews and others. Luther wrote some terrible things about the Jews. Nor is there any claim here that the old perspective necessarily captured well Jewish soteriology. There were caricatures that needed to be corrected. Still, Campbell paints with a broad brush. We must be careful, however, about implying that old perspective theology in and of itself led to the Holocaust or to persecution of the Jews. Historical causality is a complex matter, and it needs to be demonstrated much more carefully that Lutheran theology inspired the Holocaust or discrimination against the Jews. Dietrich Bonhoeffer certainly espoused Lutheran soteriology but fiercely resisted Hitler's regime, and Nazi ideology wasn't exactly Christian.

Nor can I join Campbell in his post-new perspective view, for I am convinced that Sanders's own reading of the Jewish sources was flawed. The work of Friedrich Avemarie, Mark Elliott, Simon Gathercole, Andrew Das, and volume 1 on *Justification and Variegated Nomism* indicate significant shortcomings in Sanders's construal. Stephen Westerholm and others have demonstrated that the old perspective, the reading of Paul articulated by Luther and Calvin, is substantially on target.

To sum up, Campbell's emphasis on the grace of God and his sovereign love are thrilling. Still, he is shaped fundamentally by his own social location, for he seems to be saying that God's love finally reaches everyone. Though Campbell says his view has roots in history, his construal matches well the sentiments of our culture. I believe, then, that Campbell's Paul replicates what we have seen in historical Jesus research. Campbell investigates Paul, but the Paul he discovers ends up looking a lot like Douglas Campbell.

LUKE TIMOTHY JOHNSON

Professor Douglas Campbell's essay is at once highly idiosyncratic and thoroughly conventional. Rather than attempt to characterize Paul on the basis of all the letters, he chooses to make his argument on the basis of Romans alone, not Romans as a whole (which is, as I have argued, conventional), but solely on Romans 5 – 8, with no attention to the argument preceding or following those four chapters (which is idiosyncratic, as well as wrong-headed). His apparent rationale for such a truncated target is that the subject of a "vision" of Paul must be Paul's "theology," and in all the other letters, Paul is in a defensive battle on opponents' turf, so that in them we don't get his full "theology." By contrast, Romans is written above the fray and at leisure, and in it we get what Paul really thought all the time but could not say because of the shape of his controversies. Or something like that.

This is an unassailable even if erroneous position. If one objects that such a small selection of text cannot represent all of Paul, Campbell can respond, "Oh yes, it does," and if pressed to demonstrate why one should think that these four chapters represent what Paul really thought, he can respond, "Because I say they do." Since his position has been adopted without benefit of analysis of the letters as a whole, it resists any objection raised from analysis of the letters as a whole.

The same sort of deductive logic attaches to his opening remarks about a "post-new perspective." On his account, the "old perspective" was based on an erroneous and harmful reading of Judaism, which the "new perspective" corrected; but the new perspective on "works as ethnic boundary markers" turned out to be theologically inadequate and needs to be replaced with "a major reappraisal of the apostle's gospel that responds to a massive interpretive crisis within much of his interpretation."

Although Campbell states that the "post" in his title is emphatic, however, the tautologous character of the sentence just cited does not give great confidence that the emphasis in "post" is accompanied by much clarity. A "major reappraisal," for example, might have meant questioning the premises that have distorted the earlier visions of Paul, namely, that his theology is shaped primarily in terms of opposition to the law (or in contrast to Judaism), and the place where the essential Paul is to be found is in Galatians and Romans. It might have even sought another textual starting point for thinking through Paul's theology, such as 1 Corinthians 15. But in Douglas's essay, the post-new perspective seems to amount to a doctrinal reading of Romans 5–8 from the perspective of the Nicene Creed that ignores Judaism altogether—and this, in the letter where (together with Galatians) the issues of Judaism most forcefully appear.

Even if it were legitimate to pick Romans as the place where Paul's theology is best to be found, Campbell's assumption that this letter is distinctive because of its nonoccasional character can be sustained only by completely ignoring the long and sustained "Romans debate" among scholars. Even if one adopts the position, as I do, that Romans is not generated by disputes within the Roman churches but by the circumstances of Paul's ministry, Romans retains its occasional character; at the very least, it is a fund-raising letter intended to persuade the Roman congregations to support his ministry to Spain.

Similarly, Campbell's decision to eliminate from consideration—and with no real argument for doing so—the first four and the last eight chapters of Romans, goes beyond the idiosyncratic to the irresponsible. Campbell approaches the middle section of Romans as though it were a free-standing treatise rather than part of a longer theological argument. He ignores the substantial work on Romans that has demonstrated the rhetorical character of the composition, as well as the way in which its argument, from the thesis in 1:16–17 to the final recapitulation of God's work among Jews and Gentiles in 15:1–21, follows the conventional stages of the Greco-Roman scholastic diatribe.

As a result, readers of Campbell's essay can have little idea that Romans 5 as a whole culminates Paul's positive argument concerning how God establishes righteousness that began with the thesis in 1:16–17, was restated in 3:21–26, and was illustrated from Torah by the example of Abraham in 4:1–25. Note how chapter 5 begins: "Therefore, since we have been justified through faith, we have peace with God through our Lord Jesus Christ" (5:1). Campbell's readers are not told how in 6:1, 15 and 7:7, Paul poses questions that have arisen precisely from the positive demonstration of God's grace in 5:1–21. Nor do they learn that it is his triumphant declaration that nothing can separate believers from the love of God that comes to us in Christ Jesus our Lord (8:39) that sets up the anguished reinterpretation of Torah in chapters 9–11, which seeks to answer the question whether God's word to Israel had failed (9:6). Nor would they ever learn that Paul's moral instruction in chapters 12–15, based on the renewal of mind with the capacity to discern God's will (12:1–2), represents a reversal of his portrayal of the "darkened mind" that led humans to idolatry and its attendant vices (1:20–23).

Campbell's essay has the form of a close reading of Romans 5–8, but it falls short of an adequate exegesis even of these chapters in several respects. First, by his own admission, Campbell spends a considerable amount of space within a short essay to demonstrate that Paul "operated with 'an inchoate trinitarian grammar,'" which he takes to mean that Paul's writings "witness to the Trinity." Well, no, an inchoate logic does not constitute a witness to the Trinity, especially not with a capital T; more problematic in this statement is Campbell's use of the term "writings," for he has not looked at, much less demonstrated an inchoate trinitarian logic in the other letters—at best, he has shown its presence in these four chapters of Romans.

He says that he has spent so much effort on this point "because it is so important," but it is not at all clear wherein its importance lies for Campbell. Establishing an inchoate trinitarian logic is surely not important for grasping Paul's thought in these chapters, for Campbell wanders far from anything Paul was capable of thinking when he speaks of "incarnation" and "*perichoresis*." Importance, then, must mean that Paul's language can serve to support an explicitly Nicene theology. But has any student of the history of theology ever been in doubt on this point, or in further need of its demonstration?

The amount of space Campbell spends on a point of dubious importance for Paul's theological argument apparently prevents him from attending to elements in these chapters that are of clear significance to Paul himself and deserve some attention. In Romans 6:1–11, Paul builds his case for the new identity of believers on their experience of baptism, elaborating the manner in which their ritual immersion was also "a burial with him in his death" (6:4), and an "emplanting into the likeness of his death" (6:5) and a "co-crucifixion of the old person" (6:6), and a "dying together with Christ" (6:7) — as well as an opening to the new life of resurrection because of Christ's exaltation.

Paul's stress on baptism is emphatic and difficult. Here is where the sense of sacrament and mystery and participation in the divine action invites close reflection. Here is where Paul sees the gift of God ("God's love has been poured into our hearts through the Holy Spirit," 5:5) made actual in the lives of his readers, the essential moment in their "incorporation" into the Son — and therefore, the life of the Trinity! Campbell gives it one line: "And it is this identification with Christ's death and resurrection that baptism, understood as a single act of immersion under water and reemergence, communicates so resonantly for Paul (the Greek *baptizô* meaning 'immersion' or 'dipping')."

Even more striking, in his discussion of Paul's rhetorical comparison of Christ and Adam in Romans 5:12–21, Campbell fails in exegetical attentiveness. He speaks of Christ's "life of obedience and resurrection" as the positive pole of the comparison. But what he fails to observe is Paul's insistence on the obedient action of the "human being" (*anthrôpos*) Jesus Christ, in contrast to the human Adam. It is Jesus' response to God precisely as human that Paul argues here as the inner reality of the gift of salvation. Once more, the argument of Romans as a whole is critical: this obedience of Christ is Paul's way of defining (compare Phil. 2:5–11) the *pistis* ("faith") of Jesus that he three times emphasizes in the restatement of his thesis in 3:21–26. In the comparison of 5:12–21, precisely the human response of the two primordial humans is the point: "For just as through the disobedience of the one man [*henos anthrôpou*] the many were made sinners, so also through the obedience of the one man [*henos*] the many will be made righteous [*dikaioi*]," Romans 5:19).

Even in terms of its own narrow self-selection, Professor Campbell's version of Paul fails to meet the standards of adequate exegesis, and because of its severely truncated target text, it falls even shorter of providing a genuine vision of the Paul we encounter in all his letters.

MARK D. NANOS

I could not agree more with the need for a "*Post*-New Perspective" approach to Paul. Since it is equally important to both of us, it is a good place to focus my evaluation of Campbell's argument.

Campbell begins his approach with the assertion that Paul "left a number of key Jewish *ethical practices* behind in a critical development that shapes all Christian behavior today," which he defines in the next sentence: "he did not view *circumcision* and *Jewish dietary* and *temporal* practices as incumbent on any of his converts from paganism" (emphasis added). There is much here to discuss.

The second sentence about Paul's view for non-Jews (which is itself suspect) categorically does not lead to the foundational decision about Paul that Campbell reached in the first sentence. In the second sentence Campbell refers to three specific Jewish ritual practices (marking of bodies, social functions, and time — precisely the same ones that the "New Perspective" advocates name, calling them boundary marking and nationalistic practices; cf. J. D. G. Dunn; N. T. Wright), which he claims were not "incumbent on" *non-Jews* who turned to God through Paul's gospel proclamation.

Although I believe Campbell, and the "New Perspective," are mistaken about Paul's view of those ritual practices for non-Jews when grouped together as he and the "New Perspective" do (to which I will return below), if he was or they were correct, that would not indicate that *Paul* abandoned *these* Jewish *ritual* practices or, as he states the case, *a number of key* (or, I would add, *any*) Jewish *ethical* practices! Campbell's decision about Paul's ethical disposition is fundamental to Campbell's arguments throughout (and no less importantly, to what Campbell's interpretations suppose that Paul's audiences know about Paul when they receive a letter, which would shape their interpretation just as it does his), but it is based on a logical deduction that would only apply to Paul if he were a non-Jew!

That (universalizing) category failure leads him into the same problematic logic that ineluctably arises in the discourses about Paul conducted by traditional or "New Perspective" interpreters, posing the meaning of Christ for Paul in antithesis with the meaning of Torah. That problem is further compounded by the failure to maintain the distinction Paul retains between what represents faithfulness for an Israelite (which, importantly, includes Paul) versus faithfulness for a non-Israelite when discussing Christ, Torah, or both. The terms need to be defined more carefully.

1. *Jews/non-Jews.* As an Israelite bringing the good news to his fellow Israelites and from Israel to those from the rest of the nations, Paul sees the world divided along this particularistic ethnic line (just as he sees a difference between men and women, slave and free). Otherwise Paul would not make these distinctions central to the messages in his letters, and the qualifying of these differences — that they should not produce discrimination of the kind usually associated with such distinctions — a matter central to his call for unity (but not sameness) in passages such as Galatians 3:21 and Romans 3:31 (see my essay). When Paul writes about a topic, especially the topics of Jewish identity and Torah-defined behavior (leaving aside the topic of Christ for the moment; see my essay), he does so with respect to how it applies to Israelites (members of the nation/people [Gk. *ethnos*] Israel; Jews) or non-Israelites (members from the other nations/peoples [Gk. *ethne⁻*]; Gentiles; non-Jews) now that the end of the ages has arrived. If there are any exceptions, those too should be considered carefully and may be revealing.

One useful example arises when Paul specifies that he is addressing his rebuke in Romans 11 to non-Israelite Christ-followers (cf. v. 13), wherein he develops the allegory of the olive tree in verses 17–24. He identifies the non-Israelites as a wild shoot grafted onto a tree alongside of natural branches (Israelites), some bent temporarily (others not, such as he sees himself), in order to warn the non-Israelites of their precarious place and enormous danger, all the more, compared to the natural branches. He explains therein that what God is doing with each is not precisely the same: even if being worked together to an endpoint that is for the common good of all according to God's plan for each, the distinction between them remains salient and forms the basis for how Paul's rebuke of the wild branch proceeds from a fortiori inferences.[65]

As explained in my essay, toward keeping that distinction in view any statement regarding what Paul upheld ought to be accompanied by a qualifying phrase. For example, Paul's view on circumcision is insufficient unless followed by one of the following four qualifiers: *for Christ-following non-Jews*; *for Christ-following Jews*; *for non-Jews who do not follow Christ*; *for Jews who do not follow Christ*. If Campbell practiced this simple, albeit cumbersome distinction, he might have avoided the error of making a statement about Paul's view of certain Jewish ritual identity and behavioral (ethical) practices for himself and other Jews who follow Christ, from what Campbell decides that Paul's view of those practices are for non-Jews who follow Christ.

2. *Circumcision.* Like the "New Perspective" (and the traditional Christian view too), Campbell conflates circumcision with Torah observance, specifically running it together with dietary and calendrical practices. I cannot emphasize enough how important that (mis)step is to any interpretive trajectory, and how common it is to encounter in any discussion of Paul. Thus, although I have discussed this in my essay, I trust that the reader will appreciate the need to emphasize this matter in direct response to how Campbell proceeds.

When Paul is instructing non-Jews about the topic of circumcision, which is usually the case, circumcision signifies the completion of the rite of proselyte conversion for males who undertake to have their *identity* transformed from being non-Israelites to being Israelites, and thereby counted among the people of God, the children of Abraham, the righteous ones, and so on. Campbell, like "New Perspective" interpreters, is (mis)led by his interpretation of Paul's phrase "works of law" (as usually translated, see my essay for discussion) into supposing that it signifies more than just completing the rite of proselyte conversion but also includes other "works."

---

65. See my *The Mystery of Romans: The Jewish Context of Paul's Letter* (Minneapolis: Fortress, 1996), 239–88; idem, "'Broken Branches': A Pauline Metaphor Gone Awry? (Romans 11:11–36)," in *Between Gospel and Election: Explorations in the Interpretation of Romans 9–11* (ed. Florian Wilk and J. Ross Wagner; Tübingen: Mohr Siebeck, 2010), 339–76; idem, "Romans 11 and Christian-Jewish Relations: Exegetical Options for Revisiting the Translation and Interpretation of This Central Text," *Criswell Theological Review* (forthcoming, 2012).

But circumcision and the other ritual practices named are categorically different. No matter how often one eats or observes time according to Torah-defined norms, that will not make one an Israelite, but completing the rites (works) of proselyte conversion can (according to many Israelites, anyway), which is symbolized by circumcision (of males at the completion of this rite). As discussed in my essay, it is only the rites of identity transformation, signified by circumcision at completion, that Paul has in view in his usage of the phrase "works [rites] of law [of the convention for proselyte conversion])."

If one is born into a non-Israelite family but later decides to complete the rite of conversion to become an Israelite, one would be thereafter under Torah, which is God's "Teaching" (lit. meaning of Torah) for Israelites. This Teaching is the gift by which God instructs the people how to live rightly; in other words, how to properly show loyalty to God and to one another (i.e., how to love, which as Paul notes [Jesus too], is a summary signifier of God's "Teaching").[66] *After* a non-Israelite (male) is circumcised and becomes an Israelite, *then* the other two elements that Campbell (just like "New Perspective" interpreters) lumps together with circumcision, namely dietary and calendrical practices, become relevant for the "convert." The identity transformation completed, they are then *under* Torah, obliged to observe the whole of God's Teaching for Israel (Paul makes this same case in Galatians 5:3).

What Paul teaches about Torah-observing behavior, at least technically, will depend on who is in view, Israelites or non-Israelites, and whether they are Christ-followers or not. Since Paul is a circumcised Israelite who teaches that an Israelite is to remain an Israelite when becoming a follower of Jesus (1 Cor. 7:17–20, and that a non-Israelite is to remain a non-Israelite), and he argues that anyone who is or becomes an Israelite is obliged to observe all of Torah (Gal. 5:3), it follows that Christ-following Israelites are under Torah, and Christ-following non-Israelites are not (this is also how the author of Acts interpreted Paul; cf. Acts 15; 21).

3. *Ethics*: Campbell understands Paul to have had "high ethical expectations of his converts." Of course he did. But stating the mat-

---

66. Abraham Joshua Heschel, from within an Orthodox rabbinic perspective, states the matter similarly: "all observance is training in the art of love" (*Between God and Man: An Interpretation of Judaism* [New York: Harper, 1959], 162).

ter apart from what that means in Jewish communal terms (in Judaism) misses the relevant contextual point. And it is troubling when this supposedly *Post*-New Perspective view is presented in supersessionistic terms to introduce the way that he will approach Romans in the remainder of the essay: "This is actually the longest argument that Paul ever supplies for the view that a Christian ethic *transcends* the *Jewish* law" (p. 117; emphasis added).

In sharp contrast, I believe that Paul had *normal* ethical expectations of the non-Jews who were his disciples — precisely because his expectations were *Jewish*! That would represent inappropriately high expectations for non-Jews who were not Christ-followers, but normal ones for non-Jews who had abandoned other gods and turned to the God of Israel as the One Creator God of all humankind. It is because these non-Jews are being enculturated by Paul into Judaism, into the Jewish communal way of life, while at the same time remaining non-Jews, that many of the most significant issues arose that led him to write the letters we now investigate, such as Romans.

If Paul expected ethical behavior from these non-Jews that is fully Jewish (i.e., within Judaism), albeit as applied to non-Jews who became members of Jewish subgroups within the larger Jewish communities (and thus within norms guided by those who were under Torah), that significantly alters the interpretive landscape. Then Paul, like any teacher of non-Jews, would need to explain how to behave appropriately in Jewish communal terms; but in his case, he must tread carefully because they are being taught that they are neither proselytes (so not technically under Torah) nor non-Jews who remain merely guests and thus expected to still practice non-Jewish cult as part of their "other" lives. As members of a (Jewish subgroup) community in full standing with Jews (according to the gospel proposition), their lives are shaped by the norms of Torah, or as Paul puts in Romans 6, they have now become "slaves of righteousness."

Now we can briefly discuss the other two elements that Campbell (and the "New Perspective") strings together as if of the same kind. First, why would Campbell (and the "New Perspective" interpreters) conclude that Paul teaches non-Jews (or upholds for Jews) that they are not to observe Jewish dietary norms? They have joined Jewish subgroups, and eating according to Torah-based norms would be the cultural convention into which they are now socialized. The rub is that these non-Jews expect to be treated as if full members; that is what they have been taught by Paul and other Christ-following Jews to expect. That could imply that the practice of Jewish norms is not enough for them to receive equal treatment as if proselytes. Indeed, it is not enough to make one a Jew according to anyone, including Paul; and no one supposes that it is! But the logical disconnect is raised by the gospel's new proposition on their status; apart from that contextual element, construing the issue in universal faith versus behavioral terms misses the point. Since their subgroup table is Jewish, of course they eat jewishly, for they have joined a Jewish group. They have faith and appropriate behavior, but have not become Jews; proselyte conversion is the "work/ rite" at issue and thus what Paul must address. The gospel teaches that they must remain non-Jews although behave jewishly and be treated as equals at their subgroup's Jewish table!

Second, the issue of calendar, which I also dealt with briefly in my essay, is (like the issue of dietary norms) simply a function of the new socio-cultural orientation of these non-Jews because of their turn to God taking place within Jewish subgroups that believe Jesus is Christ. Paul regularly assumes that they understand and live according to Jewish time-keeping norms, and that they naturally know that he continues to do so (1 Cor. 5:7–8; 16:8; cf. Acts 20:16). See my essay for why Galatians 4:10, to which most interpreters point, instead indicates a calendar of idols and lords governing non-Jewish communal life to which he fears these former idolaters will feel compelled to return if they do not become proselytes and thus remain treated as if mere guests. It is not a Jewish calendar at all.

I believe that Campbell sees limitations in the prevailing views, and I hope he, and the reader, will perceive in this response my shared concern to find a way forward that does not begin from the same faulty premises and thus limit the possibilities for creating new (including *post*) perspectives that evaluate Paul, and Judaism, in more helpful as well as probable terms.

MARK D. NANOS

Traitor." "Apostate." "Convert." "Deceiver." These are the common characterizations of the apostle Paul in popular Jewish imagination, even if not from the perspective of all Jewish scholars and, as will be explained, certainly not from mine. But first it will be useful to discuss why a negative view of Paul is so widely held among Jews.

Why Jews View Paul Negatively

Christians generally celebrate Paul as the champion of faith and of God's Word, of adaptability to win everyone (Jew and Greek) to the gospel of Christ, and perhaps most famously, as the advocate of freedom "from slavery to the law." As Christians see it, Paul declared the "law-free gospel," which magnified heartfelt love of God and neighbor in a way that the law could never enable, offering freedom from Judaism's mistaken focus on external rituals, on legalism and seeking to earn God's favor, on spirit instead of letter, on grace and faith instead of works, ethnocentricism, exclusivism, arrogance, presumption—and so on. This gospel offers forgiveness from sins once and for all. It offers eternal life instead of the curse of the law.

All of these statements are predicated on Paul's view of Christ as the fulfillment of the law; thus, the law has been terminated so that it can no longer enslave or separate Jew and Gentile. All can now live in harmony under God's grace. Circumcision will no longer limit the inclusion of all nations into God's family by an external rite; rather, circumcised hearts are what matters. The gospel offers salvation to everyone; if not for Paul, Christianity may have offered salvation only within Judaism. Why would anyone negatively value or characterize the messenger of such sublimely good news?

Comparative denunciation of Judaism's supposed ideals is built into the very language used to describe Paul's unique contribution to the foundations of Christianity. The concepts it represents are referred to as Paulinism, which is a traditional construction of these Christian ideals supposedly championed by Paul and then faithfully reiterated and adapted in later generations by his disciples. As a result, to question the interpretive portrait of Paul and the consequent foundations of Paulinism, especially as he and this tradition stand in relationship to Jewish identity and values, then and since, puts at risk the content of the historical and theological fabric from which Christian ideology has been woven.

But have you ever thought about how this presentation sounds to Jews? Every strength attributed to Christianity is compared to a negative one attributed to Judaism. The language choices describe Judaism in value-laden judgments that would have been as unrecognizable to Jews of Paul's time as they have been ever since. Jewish motives are maligned as well in a catch-22, wherein the motives for Jews doing good deeds are judged to be self-righteous and legalistic at the same time that Jews are condemned for failing to do enough good deeds to escape judgment as unrighteous.

In addition to celebrating more virtuous motives and overall religious superiority, Christianity claims to be the replacement of Judaism. Its gains are even described as if Judaism no longer exists as a legitimate expression of faith in the God of Israel—sometimes as if it never did, and as if the other celebrated values were never central to Judaism and its Scriptures and covenants, even though they were enjoined therein before Christianity emerged. Were they not the very ideals in Judaism to which Paul appealed, as did Jesus?

If one simply looks at what has been traditionally valued positively when Christians portray Paul, and at how that thinking is inextricably bound up with the way Judaism is negatively characterized in making these comparisons, one can readily see why Jews have traditionally understood Paul as an enemy and a danger to their communal interests. In fact, comparative superiority often appears to be essential to describing the ideals of Christianity and its reason for being, so that loving Christianity includes demeaning Judaism, whether this is intended or not.

Imagine if a religious group presented the values of your group in negative comparative terms while simultaneously claiming to exemplify the ideal values you actually perceive your group to uphold, thereafter not only stereotyping your group with values you do not hold, but at the same time claiming to be the "true" version of what your group should be. If that group legitimated this viewpoint by appealing to texts that were not part of your canon and written by someone you did not really read, how would you feel about that person, and how likely is it that you would concern yourself with reading those texts or, as an outsider, challenge their interpretations of them? That is the role Paul and his letters play for Jews.

The general negative valuation of Paul's worth among Jews can thus be seen as a direct response to the way that Christianity, by the way it interprets and applies Paul's voice, conceptualizes its own identity in comparative triumph over Judaism. In addition to Jews perceiving that Judaism has been misrepresented in this Christian discourse, it also becomes evident that this is the direct result of Christian interpretations of Paul's polemical statements independent of an objective effort to study Judaism's self-presentation on its own terms.

It cannot be stressed enough that this portrayal of Judaism by way of how Paul's polemical statements have been interpreted misrepresents and misjudges the impulses, motives, policies, and behavior of Jews—from the viewpoint of those who practice Judaism as a way of life. Recently, it is becoming more common to find interpreters who express their own personal distance from the views they attribute to Paul about Judaism, which are perceived to be mistaken or motivated by his competitive context. Christian scholars are beginning to evaluate Judaism on its own terms as well as in comparative terms framed by Christian theological and cultural perspectives.

This trend is characteristic of the "New Perspective on Paul," which recognizes that Judaism upholds values other than those Paul appears to attack in traditional interpretations. However, by and large its leading advocates still approach Paul as if he stands outside Judaism and finds fault with it as inferior to his new religion, however described and labeled. Although the problems of legalism and works-righteousness have been rightly recognized as failing to describe Judaism, the fault that Paul is now imagined to find with Judaism—it appears to be a given that he must find fault—is generally transferred by the New Perspective interpreters to Jewish ethnocentric exclusivism and particularism. The first charge is for upholding proselyte conversion (circumcision); the second one is for maintaining Torah-based norms such as Sabbath days and diets, which by definition create and retain identity differentiation from non-Jews.[1]

Thus the way the discourse on Paul and Christian origins continues to develop, even in most New Perspective approaches, has not quite shaken the notion that a contrast to Judaism is essential to interpreting Paul, even if what he is understood to find wrong has shifted.[2] While Sanders works back from Paul's solution discovered in Christ to search for a necessary prior problem in Judaism that Paul had not yet realized (rather than working in the traditional direction, which imagines Paul had a problem in Judaism to which a solution was offered only outside of Judaism, in Christ), the idea that there must be a problem in Judaism as the source for understanding Paul remains unchanged. So too does the quest to legitimate Paul's perspective regardless of the hoops that must be jumped through to do so, including the perpetuation of judgments on Jewish motives by Paul.

Although many Jews holding negative views of Paul have never actually read Paul's letters, it is not unusual for Jews to have been exposed to certain portions of those texts most commonly cited by Christians to support their judgments of Judaism. As a result, few Jews investigating Paul are open to respecting his ideas in the same way that the

---

1. Yet proselyte conversion is actually inclusivistic, creating a way to cross a religio-ethnic boundary and become a full member, while Torah-based identity is predicated on a covenantal relationship involving commandments from God to behave toward God and neighbor in certain specific ways that would involve breaking that covenant not to perform. In comparative terms, these features of Judaism are no less universalistic, ethnocentric, exclusivistic, particularistic, and so on, than are similar Christian norms, which define a religious community by faith and baptism for admission to full membership and uphold the performance of certain special moral and ritual behavior to remain in good standing, in addition to enculturating children from birth (thus expressing an ethno-religious identity) and believing that this is based on divine injunctions defined by a covenant relationship.

2. Cf. Mark D. Nanos, "Paul and Judaism: Why Not Paul's Judaism?" in *Paul Unbound: Other Perspectives on the Apostle* (ed. Mark Douglas Given; Peabody, MA: Hendrickson, 2010), 117–60.

texts of most other historical figures are approached. Most Jews would not expect to uncover positive valuations of Torah, Jewish identity, or Judaism in Paul, which would complicate if not mitigate the often-cited negative valuations, because the affirmations and adulations have played such a minor role in Christian constructions of Paul's theology. It is his ostensibly negative and negating statements that get noticed; his positive comments about Torah and Jewish identity tend to remain unknown or get qualified as less significant—although I propose that these less recognized elements more likely represent what Paul upheld, rather than the other way around.

Nevertheless, some new approaches to understanding Paul as well as his views of Judaism are beginning to emerge. Since the mid-nineteenth century, following the rise of historical criticism and the reevaluation of Jesus as a first-century Jew within Judaism who did not seek to create a new religion, a few Jews have deeply engaged Paul's texts and his interpreters.[3] These scholars recognize, and share with a growing number of Christian scholars, the view that Paul can be read differently, that to varying degrees and in various ways he can be understood in Jewish terms, even if they do not agree with him, and that some of the popular perceptions of Paul derive from misunderstanding the contexts of his writings.[4]

In summary, Jews have for the most part simply accepted and responded negatively to Christian portrayals of Judaism through Paul as misrepresenting and devaluing their own teachings. Jews assess these value judgments from a point of view that undermines them, both by challenging them to be mistaken and rejoining that those values that Christians champion in supposed contrast to Judaism via Paul are instead inferior to the values Jews actually uphold. For example, the idea that faith is to be contrasted with good deeds (i.e., the proposition of faith *alone*) involves a binary approach to these values that misrepresents

---

3. Cf. Daniel R. Langton, *The Apostle Paul in the Jewish Imagination: A Study in Modern Jewish-Christian Relations* (New York: Cambridge Univ. Press, 2010).

4. Cf. Pamela M. Eisenbaum, *Paul Was Not a Christian: The Real Message of a Misunderstood Apostle* (New York: HarperOne, 2009); Paula Fredriksen, "Judaizing the Nations: The Ritual Demands of Paul's Gospel," *NTS* 56 (2010): 232–52; David J. Rudolph, "Paul's 'Rule in All the Churches' (1 Cor 7:17–24) and Torah-Defined Ecclesiological Variegation," *Studies in Christian-Jewish Relations* 5/1 (2010): 1–24 (http://escholarship.bc.edu/scjr/vol5/iss1/2/).

what Judaism teaches in order to create a foil; moreover, for Judaism, faith that is separated from faithfulness is undesirable as a value anyway.

Judaism does not teach that good deeds are motivated by an effort to be saved (as it is presented in the traditional view), or are undertaken to express particularism or exclusivism (as it is presented in many New Perspective views), even if it will differentiate the people who do what is right from those who do not do so—not unlike how Christians prize being differentiated. The motive is not to be seen as different per se, but that is an unavoidable consequence of being devoted to God and neighbor and thus living differently. In Judaism, good deeds are motivated by the conviction that Jews are in a covenant relationship initiated by God (i.e., akin to the Christian claim of grace-based faith), in which God instructs them to do what is right, shows them what that has meant in the past, and enables them to do so in the present. Who would want to do anything but what God calls good?

Let us consider this comparison in a little more detail. If Judaism expressed itself in a Christian-based conceptualization of the issues, there would be little contrast with the basic ideas that are usually attributed to Paul—apart from Jesus Christ. To be part of God's called (read "saved") people means committing yourself to doing what God calls you to do, but it begins with God's calling (read "grace"), to which Jews respond faithfully, that is, with faith and proper actions (read "good works") as legitimate (read "justified") members of the family. You are now in a partnership (read "covenant") with the One who does what is right and just and loving, to whom you are grateful and thus committed to being faithful, which involves living rightly, justly, and lovingly, enabled in this effort by God's Spirit.[5] Within this context, Jews hold that faith without good deeds is meaningless, and this is in line with what James says in James 1:22–27; 2:14–26, and what (see, e.g., Rom. 2:1–16; 6:1–23; Gal. 5:13–26, and throughout the instructions that fill all his letters) Paul upholds as well!

If there must be an either/or choice, Jews would respond to Christians claiming to exemplify faith over works that good deeds surpass faith if faith is not accompanied by doing what is right. Moreover, the

---

5. E.g., see Abraham Joshua Heschel, *God in Search of Man: A Philosophy of Judaism* (New York: Jewish Publication Society of America, 1955).

contrast represents a false binary (this *or* that), for good actions generally bear witness to faith; indeed, they are usually the expression of faithfulness (this *and* that), of loyalty and trust within a relationship, for proper actions should manifest faith at work and strengthen faith. Moreover, they are right and good for the other. They are thus desirable on their own terms apart from one's own self-interest. I believe Paul upheld the same view.

Is this a view with which Christians should disagree? Or are both sides now rather caught up in a game of "you say, I say," which then results in both camps staking out positions that are no longer balanced in this *and* that terms? Do both sides instead project positions in this *or* that binary terms that do not reflect the nuanced and much broader actual values that both traditions teach and practice (although perhaps representing what each declares at the level of slogans of comparison)?

The perception of an ostensibly impassable divide existing between these faith traditions and their supposed ways of interacting with God and each other is perpetually fueled by appeal to citations from Paul. In fact, however, they are more similar than different on most matters of significance, except about the meaning of Jesus Christ—where most of the difference should actually be recognized. What is at stake here is the way that views of Paul continue to play a central role in this process of othering.

Paul's Practice of Judaism and Development of Jewish Subgroups

By this point it should come as no surprise to learn that I think Paul is generally misunderstood and misrepresented by Jews *and* Christians. Chutzpah? Perhaps. But before deciding that I am overreaching, let me explain why I have come to this decision, as a historian, as a Christian-Jewish relations critic, and as a Jew.[6]

As a historian, I uphold the view that we should strive to get our history as correct as we possibly can regardless of our opinion of the figures and events. Paul's influence—or better, the way that interpretations of Paul have influenced the development of Christianity and Western civilization as well as relations with Jews and Judaism—is undeniably

---

6. Given the constraints of space here, the reader might like to know that many papers and lectures are available for downloading at my website, marknanos.com.

important. Although I may not share Paul's convictions about the meaning of Jesus, my goal is to understand and explain them. At the same time, it is only fair to expect Christians to listen to how Jews represent their beliefs and values, and all the more so when Jews object to the way that Paul has been used to (mis)interpret Judaism. Ideally, both faith communities should be able to express their own values without invoking a negative contrast to those of the other.

I recognize that my views on Paul pose challenges to long-held views among Christians, which can be disconcerting. But my views also challenge long-held views of Paul among Jews, which can be similarly troubling, for I maintain that Paul should be taken seriously as a first-century Jew rather than an apostate. Thus, he cannot be ignored when mapping out the breadth of ideas and practices within first-century Judaism.

I sincerely hope that the views I propose will be beneficial to those who look to Paul's voice for guidance. I believe that the way I have come to understand him and his teachings in historical terms offers a platform for Christians to understand Judaism more respectfully, and likewise for Jews to understand Christian origins more respectfully; thus, my approach offers promise for better Christian-Jewish relations in the future. I also cannot help but wonder if this way of interpreting Paul might have, for Christians, helpful implications for other matters of theological and spiritual importance. Whether one agrees with all of my interpretations or assessments of historical probabilities — and who could suppose that they have achieved an incontestable interpretation of any historical figure — I assume that few would object to the pursuit of the historical and ideological goals at the heart of my effort to revisit the interpretation of Paul.

Paul's Judaism

I find Paul's arguments and his assumptions about how his audiences will receive them make most sense if he remains a Torah-observant Jew — and they know this to be the case. In other words, after his Damascus Road experience, Paul remains committed to Jewish communal behavior as enjoined in the Mosaic covenant. He keeps Torah fully as a matter of fidelity, that is, as an expression of faithfulness, since he is a Jew. In his role as an apostle of Christ, I believe it is correct to speak of Paul's continued practice and teaching of Judaism, and of his communities as founded within the larger Jewish communities as Jewish subgroups. He is involved in the spread of first-century Judaism from the perspective of a Jewish "coalition" ("a temporary group committed to a specific task" within and on behalf of the larger Jewish community). This subgroup understands the end of the ages to have begun with the resurrection of Jesus.

In keeping with Paul's understanding from Scripture, Israel's special trust is to receive and declare God's Word among the nations (Rom. 3:1–2; 10:14–15, 18). Paul understands himself to be undertaking this responsibility to announce the news of the beginning of the restoration of Israel, and through Israelites, like himself, to announce this news also to the rest of the nations. He believes this mission will result in the reconciliation of humankind to the One Creator God (Rom. 1:1–6, 14–6; 3:21–22; 15:8–19). How he presents the "gospel" (good news) about Christ is therefore adapted to the premises of his various audiences, but this does not involve him compromising his fidelity to Torah, as is usually supposed.[7]

Paul believed in Jesus as the Christ, that is, as the Messiah and Savior/Lord. However, it is important to qualify what that meant, and did not mean, in contrast to what that came to mean later, after the development of Christianity. To refer to Paul or his communities as Christian is not only anachronistic, but it also masks the real issues that arise when his language is approached from within Judaism. Moreover, Paul taught non-Jews who turned to God in Christ that they were to remain non-Jews — thus that they were not technically "under Torah." At the same time, I believe that this means something very different from what it is usually understood to mean and that does not extend to Christ-following Jews, including himself. Explaining why can get at many issues central to my view of Paul.

The careful reader will recognize that the way I state this proposition about the relationship of non-Jews to Torah already contains several

---

7. Mark D. Nanos, "Paul's Relationship to Torah in Light of His Strategy 'to Become Everything to Everyone' (1 Corinthians 9:19–23)," in *Paul and Judaism: Crosscurrents in Pauline Exegesis and the Study of Jewish-Christian Relations* (ed. Reimund Bieringer and Didier Pollefeyt; London: T&T Clark, and New York: Continuum, 2012), 106–40; see also www.marknanos.com/1Cor9-Leuven–9–4–09.pdf.

qualifications to the traditional wording; the differences are not merely on the surface. First of all, I do not refer to the term "Law" but to "Torah" when denoting the Mosaic covenant, the Tanakh (Old Testament), or Jewish teaching in general, which I will continue to do when it seems to me the distinction should be upheld. This is not least because Torah, which signifies "teaching" in Hebrew, is a much more dynamic concept than simply "law," or legal matters. In addition to being reductionist, the emphasis that "law" puts on commandments alone is misleading. It plays into a common Christian value-judgment of Judaism, that it is legalistic and enslaved to obligations and restrictions, to outward behavior, to emphasizing the letter over the spirit, and that it is preoccupied with exploiting loopholes in the law.

The traditional emphasis on "law" supports the notion of the superiority of Christian values associated with "freedom from slavery to the law," an ideological statement that functions conceptually as if Christianity did not also observe instructions (read "laws") as central, and at the same time as if freedom is not a central value of Judaism as well — in addition to the central values of faith, grace, and love. After all, Christianity upholds moral obligations for its members (for the most part exactly the same ones upheld by Judaism), as well as its own rituals (from Sunday services and Eucharist/Lord's Supper to baptism).

In spite of New Perspective interpreters' claims to the contrary, Paul's communities of faith in Christ are no less identifiable by social boundary markers (in ethnocentric, particularistic, nationalistic, exclusivistic, and similar terms, to use the negatively valenced language the New Perspective as well as traditional perspectives use to describe Judaism). These boundary markers are beliefs and behaviors that set off their groups from others, such as profession of faith in Christ, baptism in Christ's name, and celebrating certain rites such as Eucharist/ Lord's Supper; to be a group involves bounded identity by definition. In the case of Paul's communities, as in the case of Judaism, these signify identity that can be gained and thus religio-ethnic identity that can be regarded as inclusivistic — if one is willing to adopt the identity requirements to which the particular group subscribes.

Pertinent to a discussion of Paul is his instruction to non-Jews who follow Christ, for example, to be enslaved to righteousness (Rom. 6:15–19), to the commandments of God (1 Cor. 7:19), and to doing good works

(Gal. 6:9–10). In fact, the majority of time in Paul's letters is focused on instructions about what to do and not do, including severe warnings for failure to comply, which could be labeled "laws," if fair play is observed. Paul summarizes keeping the commandments of God as loving God and neighbor — but the point is nevertheless to observe God's commandments (Rom. 13:8–10; Gal. 5:13–14). He does not write of love working through faith, as one might expect if upholding faith "alone," but rather of "faith expressing itself through love" (Gal. 5:6).

Paul's letters are filled with many specific details about which behaviors to adopt and which to avoid, which is akin to halakhic elaborations of Torah in rabbinic Judaism, where principles as well as specific behaviors are set out to help Jews to walk in love of God and neighbor throughout the specific circumstances they encounter in everyday life. Paul expresses that everyone will be judged by their actions according to the standards of justice, and that the intentions of the heart as known only to oneself and to God will be judged, regardless of how just and loving they may seem to be to one's peers. In other words, according to Paul, truly good deeds will be rewarded (Rom. 2:1–16; 1 Cor. 4:1–5).

Paul says he makes his own choices based on which behaviors will gain him the right to boast of the good works he does, that he will receive his just reward from God (1 Cor. 4:5; 9:8–18). He enjoins his addressees to persevere in faithfulness and good deeds: "as you have always obeyed — not only in my presence, but now much more in my absence — continue to work out your salvation with fear and trembling, for it is God who works in you to will and to act in order to fulfill his good purpose" (Phil. 2:12–13). A balanced approach to Paul's theology requires, just as it does for Judaism, attending to all of the evidence that might run contrary to prevailing views.

Although many declare that for Paul Christ fulfilled "the Law," and thus that Torah has ended for Christ-followers, would anyone uphold that Christ fulfilled "love of God and neighbor" and thus that love is made obsolete thereafter for his followers? It is interesting to wonder what might be recognized differently if every time "Law" would have traditionally been used when discussing Paul's texts, instead "God's Teaching (for Israel)," "God's Teaching of How to Rightly Love God and One's Neighbor," or something similar, was substituted. In any case for this essay, whenever Paul's use of *nomos* appears to refer to Jewish teaching rather than to other norms, conventions, rules, customs, and so on, whether Greek or Roman, or even in the sense of general or specific principles — Paul also uses *nomos* for these terms — I will refer to Torah, or Teaching, or Love, rather than Law.

Second, as I understand Paul, the dissociation from Torah fidelity described in Paul's position on Torah for non-Jews does not extend to all of humankind as if it applied equally to Jews, including Christ-following Jews. In other words, it does *not* apply to "*everyone*," unlike the way that this proposition is usually universalized. So-called freedom from Torah *only* applies specifically to "*non-Jews* who are *Christ-followers*." They alone, Paul maintains, are not *under* Torah, the Teachings of God for how *Israelites* are to love God and neighbor — although they are under *the Teachings of God* for how the righteous from the rest of the nations are to do so (e.g., the "Torah [*nomos*] of Christ"; Gal. 6:2 with 5:13–14).

Paul reasons that these non-Jews (non-Israelites) are not "under Torah" because they are not Jews, not members of Israel, and thus not participants in the covenant made with Israel at Sinai; hence, they are not *under* Torah — and never have been. Likewise, logically, they are not being *freed* from Torah, as is so commonly claimed. For these Christ-following non-Jews had not undertaken proselyte conversion, which, for males, means they had not been *circumcised* to signify *Israelite* identity. To be under Torah one must first become identified as a person of Torah (i.e., an Israelite) and thus under the Mosaic covenant. Logically, identity as Israelites precedes the behavioral obligations outlined in Torah for Israelites.

Paul's letters address specific concerns he has for the non-Jews in these communities. They are the encoded/implied reader, the target reader of Paul's instructions, regardless of the fact that there are (probably) Jewish Christ-followers in the assemblies receiving the letters, and that non-Christ-followers also might read them. In order to keep this distinction front and center when interpreting what Paul means and does not mean with regard to Jews such as himself (i.e., with respect to Torah, circumcision, dietary commandments, etc.), virtually every statement Paul makes in his letters should be accompanied by the implied phrase, "*for non-Jews who are Christ-followers*." Many of the suppositions of Paul against Jewish identity and practice would be altered by this simple and yet historically responsible adjustment. This brings us to the real heart of the issue.

The Role of the Shema[c] in Paul's Theology

Paul maintains emphatically as a matter of principle associated with the truth of the gospel itself that Christ-following non-Jews *are not now to become (place themselves) under Torah by becoming proselytes.* That is, they are not to be "circumcised," a decisive act in the rite of proselyte conversion for males that Paul uses as shorthand (i.e., as a metonymy) for the entire identity transformation that is involved in this rite of passage, even though literally the act of circumcision does not apply to females who become Jews. If non-Jews *do not become* Israelites by undertaking proselyte conversion, then they *are not under* the behavioral guidelines of Torah given specifically to Israelites in the Mosaic covenant. Why? Because according to Paul's gospel proclamation (and that of his fellow apostles too), non-Israelites do not become Israelites when they turn to God in Christ—and they must not do so afterwards.[8] Why not? Because, as the logic at work in Romans 3:29–31 and elsewhere indicates, these non-Israelites represent the awaited incorporation of *members from all of the other nations* turning to the worship of the One God of all humankind—alongside of Israelites!

At the center of Paul's theological opposition to the proselyte conversion of non-Jews is the central Jewish theology of the One God as declared in the *Shema[c] Israel* (this prayer begins "Hear [*Shema[c]*], O Israel: the LORD [is] our God, the LORD is one [or: only]"; Deut. 6:4).[9] Paul thus argues that the One God of Jews, of Israel ("the LORD is *our* God") is also the One God of the members of all the other nations when

---

8. Many suppose that Paul asserts non-Jews are "grafted" into Israel in Rom. 11, but that is not the most likely meaning of his expression or argument. See Mark D. Nanos, "'Broken Branches': A Pauline Metaphor Gone Awry? (Romans 11:11–36)," in *Between Gospel and Election: Explorations in the Interpretation of Romans 9–11* (ed. Florian Wilk and J. Ross Wagner; Tübingen: Mohr Siebeck, 2010), 339–76; see also www.marknanos.com/Broken-Branches–8–1–08.pdf.

9. I explain how Paul develops this theology throughout Romans in Mark D. Nanos, *The Mystery of Romans: The Jewish Context of Paul's Letter* (Minneapolis: Fortress, 1996), 179–201; and more broadly in "Paul and the Jewish Tradition: The Ideology of the Shema," in *Celebrating Paul: Festschrift in Honor of Jerome Murphy-O'Connor, O.P., and Joseph A. Fitzmyer, S.J.* (ed. Peter Spitaler; Washington, D.C.: Catholic Biblical Association of America, 2012), 62–80; see also www.marknanos.com/Paul-Shema–10–27–08.pdf.

they turn to God by way of faithfulness to Christ ("the LORD is one [or: only]"), in keeping with the expectations from Torah for the end of the ages (Rom. 3:29–31).

In this present age the Lord may be only known by Israel to be our God, to be the God of a particular people called in grace, the God to whom a people has committed itself ("the LORD is our God"). It is thus logical that anyone turning to that God must become a member of this people by way of proselyte conversion. But the situation changes when the age to come arrives. Then the One God of Israel will also be known by those from all of the other nations to be the only God ("the LORD is one" or "the LORD only"). According to Paul's logic, the declaration that this age has arrived with the resurrection of Christ would be undermined if those from the other nations were now to become Israelites, for then God would only be the God of Israelites, implying that God is not the only God of all the nations.

For Paul, the times have indeed changed with the resurrection of Jesus, and with this change the most fundamental matter of identity has arisen as the major platform in his proclamation of the good news to Israel and the nations. Israelites must remain Israelites and thus remain faithful to their covenant obligations (i.e., Torah observance), while members-of-the-other-nations must remain members-of-the-other-nations and thus faithful to the ideals and teachings of Torah righteousness for all humankind, having become members of the Jewish communities and their way of life. They are adherents of Judaism, but they are not under Torah on the same terms as those who are Israelites.

Is this difficult to achieve successfully? Sure, utopian notions always are. That is precisely why Paul appeals at critical points to the need to look to God's Spirit to enable the life of righteousness rather than sinfulness, to which these non-Jews are now called. The Spirit working among non-Jews as well as Jews represents the arrival of the age to come in the midst of the present age, and thus is needed to help negotiate the paradoxes that naturally arise in early dawn, before the full light of day shines for all to see.

Paul's propositional logic leads to a very different relationship to Torah for non-Jews who become Christ-followers from that incumbent on Jews who become Christ-followers. That is the other side of the Shema᷄ Israel logic to which Paul appeals for non-Jews remaining non-

Jews. *Jews must remain Jews* who turn to Christ; they represent the *members of Israel* demonstrating this worship alongside of these non-Jews/non-Israelites. Otherwise, God would only be the God of the nations other than Israel! In that role Jews remain those who represent Christ *by way of observing the Mosaic covenant.* Christ-following Jews/Israelites are, according to Paul's theological system, still *under* Torah (cf. 1 Cor. 7:17–20). That includes Paul. But it does not include the non-Jews whom he addresses in the extant letters. This is the most central contextual factor for discussing Paul's theology in terms of Judaism, yet one that is downplayed in the interpretive tradition, when not entirely overlooked.

This essay explains what I mean in more detail, and why this kind of detailed definition of terms, often (relentlessly) maintaining a difference between Jews (Israelites) and non-Jews (non-Israelites, members of the other nations) at every turn (although making for cumbersome as well as complex sentences, to be sure, as witnessed herein!), is so central, in my view, to getting Paul right—who was and remained a Jew practicing Judaism—regardless of whether one is reading him from one's own later perspective as a Christian (Jew or non-Jew), or as a non-Christian (Jew or non-Jew).[10] That was a distinction that remained salient for his first readers as well, but they did not yet have to bridge the gap, conceptual and verbal, that later readers must overcome because of the eventual development of Christian identity as different from and opposed to Jewish identity and practice (i.e., Judaism).

The early Christ-followers had other issues to overcome. They had to figure out how to fashion and express the conviction that the end of the ages had begun and thus that non-Jews could join the Jewish communities (synagogues) and Judaism (the Jewish way of life) without becoming Jews, which had enormous ramifications both for the

---

10. In order to avoid continuously making this double reference, from here on I will refer to Jews or Israelites synonymously, and non-Jews and non-Israelites, members of the other nations, Gentiles, also synonymously, following what I understand to be Paul's perspective on these terms. I do not mean to signify that Jew and Israelite refer to different people or groups. When Israel/non-Israel is used, this tends to highlight the historical, biblical dimension of this people and its separation from the other nations, or the eschatological dimension when reflecting on the hope for all the nations to be reconciled to the One God. Jew/Jewish/Judaism arose later than Israel, but became prevalent with the people known to dwell in Judea, their convictions and way of life, and designated those who lived elsewhere in the Roman empire or beyond (the Diaspora), i.e., in other nations.

Jews who proclaimed this proposition and for the non-Jews who were convinced by it. The tensions for them arose from a Jewish perspective when confronted with this new development, not from the later Gentile perspective of Christianity. Originally, it was the problems that arose from their inclusion of non-Jews as full members rather than as mere guests (however welcome guests might be in other Jewish groups) or potential proselyte candidates (if making such claims in other Jewish groups). This "Gentile question" gave rise to many of Paul's letters, which is especially evident in Romans and Galatians.

Paul's Calling "to the Nations"

What do most people who have not studied Paul, including Christians, know about Paul? If nothing else, that he was *converted* from Judaism to Christianity on the road to *Damascus*, when he was *blinded* and *fell off of a horse*.[11] Although he may have been on a horse, it is well-known by those who study Paul that this image is unsupported by the original documents we possess; rather, it is familiar because of paintings by Renaissance artists Michelangelo and Caravaggio. That something happened on his way to or arrival in Damascus is more probable, although we do not know this from Paul but from a later account in Acts 9. Likewise, Paul never mentions he was blinded, but that is also a feature in Acts 9. Those two details, like so many features that figure in most portrayals of Paul — for example, that he was from Tarsus, that he was trained under Gamaliel (grandson of Hillel), that he was a Roman citizen, that he was present at and instrumental in the stoning of Stephen — cannot be confirmed from his own writings (and some seem out of step with what is implied therein), but arise only from the narrative details in the later text known as the Acts of the Apostles.

At the same time, Acts does not mention that Paul wrote letters or that his collection among the non-Jews for the Judeans was a central feature of his travels, and it does not develop justification by faith. Acts emphasizes that Paul remained a Pharisee and practiced Torah and temple sacrifices (cf. Acts 21:23–26), and that Paul advocated

---

11. I have confirmed this time and again by asking private-religious as well as public university students beginning a class on Paul to briefly write down what they know about Paul, which ranges from nothing to elements of this basic description, and it is also the response when I ask a similar question to just about anyone, Christian or Jew.

observance of appropriate Jewish ritual behavior for non-Jews joining his communities in agreement with the views of the other apostles (i.e., the Apostolic Decree of Acts 15–16), because, notably, his subgroups were part of the larger Jewish communities into which these non-Jews were being included.

Such features bring into question the nature of what we know when elements from these two sources of information are selected or ignored when creating a portrait of Paul. My own reading of Paul's letters independent of Acts in effect brings Acts closer to the portrait of Paul in his letters than do many traditional approaches, because, ironically, on my reading of his letters Paul continued to practice and promote Judaism, just as in Acts. Be that as it may, the significant issue at this point is whether the idea that Paul was a *convert* is accurate, or, more precisely, whether he in any way converted *from Judaism* or *to Christianity*. Let us begin by looking closely at Paul's account in Galatians 1:11–17.

The only case where Paul explicitly sets out to describe his change of course following a revelation from Jesus Christ is in his writing to a non-Jewish audience in Galatia (those who formerly worshiped other gods; 4:8–9). In 1:13–16, Paul writes:

> For you have heard of my previous way of life in Judaism, how intensely I persecuted the church of God and tried to destroy it. I was advancing in Judaism beyond many of my own age among my people and was extremely zealous for the traditions of my fathers. But when God, who set me apart from my mother's womb and called me by his grace, was pleased to reveal his Son in me so that I might preach him among the Gentiles....

There are several elements to discuss.

First, note that the NIV translation implies that Paul previously lived in Judaism but no longer does so. The Greek can be translated that way, but it also can be translated to communicate that Paul remained within Judaism but now lived out his practice of Judaism differently: "you have heard of my previous way of living in Judaism." Similarly, a Christian today who has changed the way he or she understands and thus lives out his or her faith might describe, for example, a move from a more liberal to a more conservative position, or vice versa, or other changes of view on a specific topic or in general. Such a person might use the phrase, "my former way of living (or the way I formerly lived) as a Catholic," which would imply a contrast to "the way I live as a Catholic now" (or, similarly, "my former way of living as a Southern Baptist, versus the way I live as an American Baptist now"). The possible variations are endless between, among, and even within the same Christian group or groups. The choice of translation is thus a function of what one believes beforehand that Paul is most likely seeking to communicate, and that has to do in this case with whether one assumes that Paul left Judaism or stayed within it. I assume he stayed within it, and there are other elements in the context and elsewhere in the way Paul argues that lead me to take this course.

Second, what has changed for Paul is that he no longer seeks to destroy this movement but instead promotes it "to the nations [*ethnē*]." When *ethnē* is translated "Gentiles," it obscures the idea carried in the Greek that Paul understands his new role to be to declare this message about Christ to the nations, to the people of the world, which may well include proclaiming it to his fellow Jews. Israel is also a nation for whom he understands Christ to have meaning; indeed, it is the first nation, many of whose members live among the other nations (cf. Acts 9:15; 22:14–15, 21; 26:6–18).

Third, note that Paul does not describe himself moving away from the Torah or anything along that line. It is unlikely that Paul is dissatisfied with his practice of Judaism, being zealously engaged, or that he has some burden of guilt or sense of failure, since he elsewhere mentions his "blamelessness" in terms of righteousness under the Torah in the same sentence that he also notes his persecution of these groups (Phil. 3:5–6).[12] This need not mean that Paul has never failed to do what is right—after all, he calls his persecution of these groups a grave sin that he regrets (1 Cor. 15:9)—but the Torah also makes available God's forgiveness through repentance and sacrifice when that might occur. Paul practices Torah fully.

Fourth, Paul describes his former way of life as a Pharisee here by way of referring to their unique commitment to the so-called Oral Tradition in the well-recognized phrase, "the traditions of my fathers." This

---

12. Krister Stendahl, *Paul among Jews and Gentiles, and other Esays* (Philadelphia: Fortress, 1976), 8–9, 12–13.

refers to a specific way of living in a Jewish manner, one that he claims to have been the most zealous to live according to, and also that his life was notably different from other Pharisees in that he sought to destroy this Christ-movement; most Pharisees presumably did not. Note that Paul's identity remains tied to his Pharisaic perception of reality some seventeen years after the events he is describing, which he betrays by referring not simply to the traditions of *the* fathers, but of "*my* fathers." Paul still directly refers to himself as a Pharisee also in Philippians 3:5, and Acts presents Paul as continuing to refer to himself as a Pharisee (Acts 23:6; 26:5).

When these four factors are combined with the historical probability that there was not yet a new religious institution of Christianity to which Paul could move (which is widely recognized even by those who may favor and perpetuate the traditional view that Paul left Judaism), it becomes reasonable to speak of Paul remaining within Judaism, even within Pharisaism. Pharisaism was a movement characterized by encouraging a highly devoted lifestyle of holiness among Jews (who were not priests) in ways that were technically only specified in Torah for priests. This may help explain Paul's preoccupation with holiness (sanctification, set-apartness to God) among these non-Jews, even his addressing them as "holy ones" (commonly translated "saints"). It is probable that Paul means to communicate that he moved to a different Jewish group, perhaps a subgroup of Pharisees,[13] to a different way of living Judaism among a relatively small group of people who held certain views of the meaning of Jesus that were not shared by most other adherents of Judaism (or other first-century Judaisms, if you prefer), including other Pharisaic subgroups.

Consider too why Paul would choose to make this point here, in Galatians 1:13–16, to those who have known him already to be a Christ-following Jew rather than as a Pharisee opposed to their movement. His larger rhetorical aim is to convince the non-Jews addressed to remain non-Jews claiming full membership identity apart from undertaking the

---

13. That some Christ-followers remained Pharisees is attested in Acts 15; for evidence in Matthew, see Anders Runesson, "From Where? To What? Common Judaism, Pharisees, and the Changing Socioreligious Location of the Matthean Community," in *Common Judaism: Explorations in Second-Temple Judaism* (ed. Wayne O. McCready and Adele Reinhartz; Minneapolis: Fortress, 2008), 97–113.

traditional path to full inclusion as proselytes, even if that involves continued marginalization within the larger Jewish community as well as outside of it. His experience similarly includes taking the road less traveled, the one that may presently involve opposition from some Jews as well as non-Jews. But this lonely course is the only way to proceed if one has experienced a revelation from Christ, as has he, and has experienced God's Spirit on this course, as have they. Paul's argument makes sense as a discussion taking place within Judaism about how to live jewishly (i.e., halakhically justified by faithfulness to Christ apart from becoming a Jew) when a non-Jew is convinced that Jesus is Christ and is thereby rescued (read "saved") *from* worshiping false gods and from the "slavery to sin" associated with that, *into* fellowship with the Jewish members of the family of God (i.e., into Judaism), where one is free to practice righteousness.

One might call such a change of course a "conversion" without meaning that it involves a change from one religion to another, of course,[14] but language being what it is, the implications today for describing Paul as a convert lead away from clarity about the probable first-century meaning of Paul's language and life. In recent years, the alternative of "calling," and even more specifically of "prophetic calling," has gained ground. This alternative is helpful, especially since it keeps in view the vocational nature of the event.[15] It is similar to the calling of Isaiah or Jeremiah to go to their fellow Israelites or Judahites with a new message, but not with a new religion; even Paul's language choices are similar (Isa. 49:1, 6; Jer. 1:5, 7).

Another approach to explore within the calling paradigm derives from the model of benefaction within Greco-Roman society. On this model, which is common to philosophical groups (a relevant comparison for Paul's groups), one who turns to a certain philosopher and becomes their student gains a benefit (favor/grace) from the teacher that cannot be paid back in kind, but rather repaid with their gratitude, loyalty, good will, and the proclamation of their wisdom and ideas to others.[16] That certainly fits Paul's reaction to Christ, mutatis mutandis.

---

14. Alan F. Segal, *Paul the Convert: The Apostolate and Apostasy of Saul the Pharisee* (New Haven, CT: Yale Univ. Press, 1990).

15. Stendahl, *Paul*, 7–23.

16. Zeba A. Crook, *Reconceptualising Conversion: Patronage, Loyalty, and Conversion in the Religions of the Ancient Mediterranean* (BZNW 130; Berlin and New York: De Gruyter, 2004).

These alternative models offer perspectives wherein the assumptions and interpretations of Paul's relationship to Judaism need no longer involve (mis)understandings of Judaism or its inferiority in order for the interpreter to make sense of Paul and his teachings. Instead, Paul practices Judaism. We can even speak of Paul's Judaism, or Pauline Judaism, and the Judaism of his communities. There is nothing wrong with Judaism that he must escape, but simply something within Judaism to which he is devoted, and even more specifically—because of his revelation and new Jewish subgroup affiliation—something he understands in a new way that leads him to undertake a new direction. At the same time, this development is one he believes was expected within Judaism, even if some of his fellow Jews, like himself formerly, do not share his new point of view that the end of the ages has arrived and that some adjustments must be made in light of God's new work in and through Israel for the nations.

In other words, there is a disagreement about where Israel and the nations are on God's timetable taking place among Jews (and affiliated non-Jews). The issue is not ethnocentric exclusivism any more than it is works-righteousness; it is *chronometrical*: the conflict revolves around assessing *what is appropriate now*, at this time, and thus how to properly interpret "God's Teaching" for how to incorporate those from the nations into God's people in view of the dawning of the awaited age. We can read Paul in intra- and inter-Jewish terms, wherein a variety of views are in tension and where even heated disagreements are taking place, but without suggesting that his positions represent anti-Judaism or a post-Judaism point of view. Rather, they represent an alternative within the wider parameters of first-century Second Temple Judaism. That alternative turns around the meaning attributed to Jesus, whether he is the Messiah (Christ/ruler) of Israel and thus the anticipated Savior of the rest of the world.

Paul's Views on Circumcision

Another matter that surfaces in Galatians 1:13–16 naturally leads us into the subject of how the gospel message Paul proclaims relates to the topic of circumcision. That is, what is it about certain groups of Christ-followers that provokes Paul to oppose them before his experience of Christ? Paul does not make it clear here or anywhere else, nor does Acts.

It is commonly held that these Christ-following Jewish groups were not observing Torah in significant ways—for example, that they had stopped circumcising or eating according to dietary commandments. But the Christ-followers we know about from Paul and Acts as well as other New Testament texts all suggest that the Jews who followed Christ, from the apostles to those whom they led, were zealous for the Torah within their Christ-based Jewish groups and participated in temple sacrifices. They did not see Torah and Christ in binary terms or as incompatible; that way of thinking is usually attributed to Paul after his change of course.

I think the most probable meaning arises from consulting a statement Paul makes in Galatians 5:11: "If I am still preaching circumcision, why am I still being persecuted? In that case the offense of the cross has been abolished."

We must clarify Paul's use of language here. As already noted, circumcision functions here and often in Paul as a metonymy for proselyte conversion, and that is not precisely the same thing as Torah-observance. The distinction is commonly neglected in discussions of Paul and circumcision, which conflate circumcision with Torah-observant behavior, such as stringing together circumcision, dietary laws, and observance of Sabbath and other festivals. But identity transformation rites and observance of the rules for those who have completed the process and thus gained the new identity are not categorically the same thing. While it is the case that Jewish parents are observing Torah when having their baby boy circumcised, this is neither the child's decision nor the topic to which Paul is referring when discussing the entrance rite of proselyte conversion for non-Jewish males (and by extension, signifying all non-Jews who wish to convert to Jewish identity). For non-Jews, "circumcision" is an identity transformation rite, which is not the same as the Torah-observing behavior enjoined thereafter.

After completing this rite, a non-Jew is no longer a non-Jew but a Jew, and he is thus under the covenantal obligation to walk rightly according to the Torah commandments God enjoined on Jews/Israelites. Presumably the proselyte candidate has already begun to observe Torah to some degree, and will increasingly do so as he is involved in the process of completing this rite—that is, observing Torah by undertaking circumcision at the completion of this rite. But I hope the distinction I am trying to make is nevertheless clear. For example, in Galatians Paul opposes the circumcision of non-Jews who are already Christ-followers, and at the same time he does *not* oppose Torah-observance for those who are circumcised already. He instructs these non-Jews that they have not been accurately taught by those (Jews) who were influencing them to undertake proselyte conversion, for after the completion of that rite, they will be obliged thereafter to observe Torah fully (Gal. 5:3: "Again I declare to every man who lets himself be circumcised that he is obligated to obey the whole law"). It seems that the interests of those influencing them as well as those of his non-Jewish audience are focused on the completion of the transformation rite, which is inappropriate from Paul's point of view, and I would expect (Paul's polemical accusation notwithstanding) that it is also not right from the point of view of those influencing them.

Paul builds his case on the fact that the rite of proselyte conversion is but an introduction to a new identity with many responsibilities, not just a solution that will resolve their present plight as non-Jews seeking full, indisputable membership within Jewish subgroups (Gal. 5:2–6; 6:12–13).[17] It is this ostensible lack of concern for their welfare by those influencing them to become proselytes to which Paul appeals, not because Paul is against the obligations of Torah, as many suppose. It is instead because his aim is to undermine his addressees' trust in those who appear to be helpful guides, when guides with their true interests in mind, like Paul, would warn them to calculate the costs that result.

This is, in fact, a custom practiced in rabbinic Judaism, wherein the proselyte candidate must declare awareness of the afflictions suffered by Israelites and the responsibility to uphold Torah upon completion of the rite (*b. Yebamot* 47a-b). The rabbis are not against Torah observance, to be sure, and do not consider it an undesirable slavery for the people of the covenant under which God offers blessings. Neither does this rhetorical effort to undermine the authority of these "influencers" (those whose influence on his addressees Paul seeks to prevent) suggest that Paul is against Torah observance, or that he considers it a burden to be

---

17. For a detailed discussion of the context of Galatians, including the identity of his addressees and those influencing them, see Mark D. Nanos, *The Irony of Galatians: Paul's Letter in First-Century Context* (Minneapolis: Fortress, 2002).

avoided. However, it is not the spirit of Torah to encourage proselyte conversion without spelling out the weight of this decision.

Paul separates the issue of circumcision/proselyte conversion (the matter of "identity") from Torah observance (the "behavior" incumbent on those with Jewish/Israelite "identity"). Moreover, often overlooked, Paul builds his case on the assumption that his non-Jewish audience would be startled to learn that those influencing them toward proselyte conversion might be doing so from self-interest rather than the best interests of themselves (whether such a polemical accusation is true or not cannot be deduced, but Paul must suppose that it is a reasonable inference to draw to their attention). Paul thereby hopes that they will heed his warning not to follow the course being proposed, regardless of how traditional it may be.

It is important to note that Paul's approach only makes sense if he believes that the influencers in Galatia have not been instructing these non-Jews to observe Torah, or even that it will be required after proselyte conversion. It thus makes little sense to suppose that Paul is opposing Torah observance for them in this letter, as is so commonly claimed to be Paul's purpose and message: *proselyte conversion is what is at stake for these non-Jews in Galatians, not Torah-observance!* No one in Galatia is proposing Torah observance even *after* their proposed conversion to proselytes, and that is just Paul's point: proper guides should be instructing these non-Jews about the concomitant obligation to observe Torah, according to Paul, and presumably this would be the viewpoint of any responsible guide involved in such matters.

Another important topic arises here about Paul's own relationship to Torah. Paul's argument implies that his audience knows him to observe Torah fully. They know that Paul is circumcised, that he identifies himself as a Jew, and at the same time that he is also a Christ-follower. *Thus Paul must observe Torah fully* to make such a claim about the responsibility that would follow for them if they become Jews!

On the usual reading of Paul, they, like Paul, would not be obliged to observe Torah because it is no longer applicable to Christ-followers, circumcised or not. How then can they be supposed to find Paul's argument persuasive? Why should they not seek to gain the social identity that proselyte conversion offers without the obligation to observe Torah that Paul says would logically accompany that choice of reidentification, since that standard does not even apply to Paul? If Torah observance and Christ-faith are binaries, they would instead be expected to answer him thus: "Paul, we just want what you have, undisputed identity within the Jewish communities as Jews, without the obligation to observe Torah since we are Christ-followers, like you."

In short, if his audience knows that Paul does not observe Torah as a matter of covenant faithfulness, then Paul's argument would have no force, and one would expect Paul to recognize that he is not making a reasonable case against them becoming proselytes to gain the social acceptance they seek. But that Paul argues in this manner suggests that he realizes that his audience knows him to be faithful to Torah because he is a Jew. They are not Jews, and thus not under Torah on the same terms as is he. Maintaining this difference between Jews and non-Jews in Christ is just how Paul believes it must remain in order to demonstrate the chronometrical truth of the gospel proposition that the end of the ages has begun in Christ.

Paul's Opposition to Proselyte Conversion

Paul connects any continued policy of proselyte conversion among Christ-following non-Jews to undermining "the offense of Christ's cross," that is, to subverting the meaning of Christ's execution. Jesus was executed for being perceived to represent a threat to Roman order, likely because of fears of an uprising in the making. There are several issues here. Among the most important is how the policy of not converting non-Jews into proselytes represented a threat ("offense") to the Roman ordering of proper social behavior.

Paul's argument plays off the idea that the Roman society will perceive the policy of including non-Jews within Jewish subgroups as full members apart from their becoming proselytes to be a threat to its interests in a way that is parallel to the threat Jesus posed. In Galatians, the cross signifies the claim by which non-Jewish Christ-followers are instructed to remain non-Jews and yet to understand themselves as being equal members with Jews in the community of the children promised to Abraham, regardless of whether other Jews or non-Jews accept this propositional claim to such ambiguous identity as legitimate (i.e., as justified on the basis of their faithfulness to Christ apart from proselyte conversion). That is just the point: this policy and behavior is based on an appeal to the "true" meaning of the cross of Christ for non-Jew as well as Jew.

The cross (and by inference the resurrection that subverts that cross's intended outcome) is a central symbol for anyone who becomes a Christ-follower, signifying the claim that something has changed in the course of history—namely, that the awaited end of the ages, when all of the nations will turn to Israel's God as the One God of all humankind, of all creation, has begun. They too can now be children of faithful Abraham, the one who was promised that in his seed all of the faithful from the nations were to be blessed (Gen. 12:1–3; 17:4; Rom. 4:16; Gal. 3:8–9; cf. Acts 3:25). Non-Israelites can be rescued from this present evil age alongside of Israelites, who had been awaiting this day promised in God's covenant with Israel. It is no longer appropriate to bring Christ-following non-Israelites into Israelite identity, even if all other Jewish groups still uphold that it is necessary to do so because they do not share the conviction that Christ, as represented by his death at the hand of the leaders of the present age, was raised by God and thus that the new age has been initiated.

Jewish groups not sharing this conviction about the meaning of Jesus would logically seek to protect themselves from Roman interference in response to some of their (sub)group members subverting existing proselyte conventions for defining who was a member of the Jewish community. Why was this so important to Roman as well as Jewish civic leaders? Because members of the Jewish community had the right to refrain from civic cult without thereby signifying disrespect for Roman rule and conventions. They were also allowed to practice their ancient traditions, along with several other exceptional rights for subjects of the Roman empire.[18] For example, Jews made a twice daily offering at the Jerusalem temple "on behalf of Caesar" that was paid for by Jews from all over the Roman empire, perhaps supplemented by provincial taxes, which permitted Jews to abstain from many expressions of local civic cult without being unpatriotic.[19]

---

18. Josephus, *Ant.* 14.185–267; 16.27–65, 160–78; 19.278–316; *Ag. Ap.* 2.65–78; Philo, *Embassy* 152–61; Claudius, *Pap. Lond.* 1912.73–105; *CPJ* II, no. 153, col. V, lines 86–88; Tacitus, *Hist.* 5.4–5; Juvenal, *Sat.* 14.96–106; full discussion in Miriam Pucci Ben Zeev, *Jewish Rights in the Roman World: The Greek and Roman Documents Quoted by Josephus Flavius* (TSAJ 74; Tübingen: Mohr Siebeck, 1998).

19. Josephus, *Ant.* 14.110–13; 16.160–73; *J.W.* 2.195–98, 409–10; *Ag. Ap.* 2.65–78, 193–98; Philo, *Embassy* 133, 156–57, 315–18; Tacitus, *Hist.* 5.4–5; Cicero, *Flac.* 66–69.

Now, however, if some non-Jews are refraining from civic cult without having become proselytes and have no intention of undertaking this identity, this fact is a breach of policy and represents a threat. The danger is not only lack of loyalty to the rulers on earth, but also to the gods who look after their interests. It is necessary to bring these non-Jews and the Jews who are convincing them of such policies into conformity with prevailing conventions. That is what Paul seeks to resist, and that is why he calls this the offense of the cross of Christ. For Paul, the propositional truth of the gospel cannot be compromised by undertaking proselyte conversion to avoid the offense it causes, or even punishment (read "persecution," which highlights a victim's perspective that the punishment does not represent legitimate discipline).

The difference between Christ-following Jews such as Paul and other Jews does not turn around faith versus not-faith per se, for the other Jews have faith in a different interpretation of events concerning where Israel and the nations are on God's timetable. Rather, the difference turns specifically around different responses to the propositional claims made about the meaning of Christ and thus about what is appropriate now—whether it still is the present age (and thus that policies remain as they were) or whether it is a new day, or at least the dawning of one within the midst of the present age. It is this *chronometrical* issue around which the significance of Jesus turns. Has that day arrived? That is, is he the awaited one (i.e., Messiah/Christ/Savior), by whom the Creator God restores Israel and who by way of Israel's faithful proclamation of this awaited event (through servants such as Paul) brings restoration (salvation) to those from the other nations who turn to God through Christ?

What does it mean to be faithful to that propositional truth claim for Jews? Christ-following Jews must remain Jews and raise Jewish families, but they cannot advocate proselyte conversion for non-Jews who are Christ-followers. These Christ-following Jews must be willing to suffer whatever marginalization results from the reaction of their fellow Jews within the larger Jewish communities, wherein the majority of its members do not share this conviction or accept the terms by which this change of behavior toward non-Jews is legitimated ("justified on the basis of faithfulness [to Jesus Christ]") within their subgroups. In addition to not sharing these Christ-followers' convictions, they themselves do not want to be punished by Roman and other local authorities for failure to bring about compliance within subgroups of their communities. That is the basis for Paul's accusation that the influencers advocate proselyte conversion in Galatia "to avoid being persecuted for the cross of Christ" (6:12). It is a proposition about the cross of Christ in which they do not believe.

Magistrates of Rome were responsible for the proper ordering of society, including overseeing that proper worship of the gods in society and in the home was carried out according to tradition, to ensure that the welfare of the Roman people continued under the care of the gods and did not provoke their wrath (Cicero, *Leg.* 2.30; 5.7). It is not hard to comprehend that Jewish communal leaders under pressure of Roman authorities who did not share the Christ-followers' convictions would dismiss their claims for the legitimacy of their policies in Christ. Why would they be willing to suffer at the hands of the Romans for allowing such deviance to go unchallenged within their communities? So these Jewish leaders presented the alternatives: remain non-Jews and thus obliged as mere guests to return home to family and civic cult, as expected (see Gal. 4:8–10, where Paul fears a return to the civic calendar is just what is under consideration), or undertake the process of proselyte conversion and legitimately avoid participation in the wider culture's idolatrous practices.[20]

The issue is not whether non-Jews were welcome as guests, for many groups of Jews were embracing such policies, for any number of reasons. The issue is whether these non-Jews should be treated not as guests but as full members of the Jewish community, as if they had completed — at least begun the process — of proselyte conversion. For the Jews, such as Paul, who now uphold that non-Jews "must" remain non-Jews, this also involved the need to develop new policies for interaction, and just

---

20. See my *Irony of Galatians*, 257–77, which explains why the calendar to which Paul refers in v. 10 is specifically not a Jewish calendar, for it is missing the unique marker of a Jewish calendar of the time, "weeks"; thus Paul is not analogizing a turn toward a Jewish calendar with a turn toward idolatry, but quite the contrary. Paul is referring here to turning to idols, including the participation in cultic events to those gods, which the Galatian non-Jews are tempted to return to since the road to proselyte conversion is being denied to them by Paul's teaching. They are thus not free without suffering to desist from idolatrous cultic participation on the prevailing social norms, although Paul taught them to turn away from such behavior. This is what led to this crisis and their conclusion that they must choose either proselyte conversion or else return to practicing idolatrous cult.

as importantly, to stand up for these non-Jews. They would be facing enormous pressure to either become proselytes or to continue to practice familial and civic cult, since they remained non-Jews and had to continue to function in the larger polytheistic society in ways that Jewish proselytes were categorically more free to avoid. It is just this kind of advocacy of the rights of these non-Jews that arose in the so-called Antioch Incident, also found in Galatians (Gal. 2:11–14).[21]

This brings us back to the topic of the centrality of circumcision for Paul and his fellow Christ-followers. Their position does not signify that Jews should not continue to practice circumcision of their sons; rather, it is specifically about *the standing of the non-Jews who turned to Christ and joined their Jewish subgroups.* Paul had earlier severely opposed the groups making such a stand, in no uncertain terms; now, just as determinedly, he advocates this policy, for it signifies the change of eons that is central to the propositional truth that is at the heart of why anyone, Jew or non-Jews, follows Christ.

As you can see, the matter of Paul's position on circumcision is a many-faceted topic and cannot be accurately represented by asking in nonspecific terms: "Why was Paul against circumcision?" It also should not be answered as if "he was only against it if undertaken for the wrong reasons," or phrased so that "it is allowed but not necessary." Paul was adamantly against it, *but only for a specific group*: non-Jews who followed Christ. He was just as adamantly committed to its continuation among Jews who followed Christ, as part and parcel of the same principle as his opposition: Jews must remain Jews (or better, Israelites must remain Israelites), non-Jews must remain non-Jews (or better, members of the other nations must remain members of the other nations). The truth of the gospel that the end of the ages has arrived in Christ, as promised—bringing about the reconciliation of *all* the nations under the rule of God—must be symbolized by the policies and lifestyles of the community of those who confess Christ. They must together practice Judaism as equals within these Jewish subgroups, yet remain different,

---

21. For full discussion, see Mark D. Nanos, "What Was at Stake in Peter's 'Eating with Gentiles' at Antioch?" in *The Galatians Debate: Contemporary Issues in Rhetorical and Historical Interpretation* (ed. Mark D. Nanos; Peabody, MA: Hendrickson, 2002), 282–318. See also discussions in Mark D. Nanos, "The Myth of the 'Law-Free' Paul Standing between Christians and Jews," *Studies in Christian-Jewish Relations* 4 (2009): 1–21 (http://escholarship. bc.edu/scjr/vol4/iss1/4/).

just as is the case for difference without discrimination that is enjoined for males and females, and for masters and slaves (Gal. 3:28).

That is "the truth of the gospel" for Paul (Gal. 2:14), regardless of how many problems this utopian notion might pose for his communities, which were arising already in his time, as the matters addressed in his few letters bear witness. That is why, in Paul's teaching, the role of God's Spirit to guide communal behavior according to the norms of the age to come, not those of the present age, was so central. To keep in view this dynamic social principle of maintaining difference without allowing discrimination when reading Paul, care should be taken not to universalize his language about circumcision or Torah observance. Failure to do so causes the confusion and suggests that Paul was against and trivialized central Jewish practices — indeed, central elements of the covenants with Abraham and Moses, matters for which many Jews suffered the loss of their lives. Instead, the topic to discuss is specifically: "Why was Paul against non-Jews following Christ undertaking the rites involved in proselyte conversion (i.e., 'the works of law,' the actions symbolized by circumcision for males upon completion)"?[22]

Paul's Opposition to "Works of Law"

The topic of proselyte conversion is also central to understanding Paul's contrast between justification "by faith" and "works of law," which has been such a decisive topic for declaring Paul to be against the continued role of Torah for Christ-followers, including Jews like himself. It is common to find this interpreted to mean that Paul signals a contrast between faith and action (or good deeds/human effort); it is also interpreted to mean that Paul is against observing Torah per se, or specific Jewish ritual or boundary-marking behavior. But this contrast is built around the specific action that the non-Jews in Rome or Galatia had already taken to follow Christ *as non-Jews, as members of*

---

22. It may help the reader to think about this matter from a different angle. Consider coming across a statement that "Jews do not circumcise" without context, so that it seems to signal a universal, and one that is wholly mistaken. Then, upon further examination of this seemingly uninformed perspective, one finds out that it was stated in a specific context in answer to the question whether Jews circumcised infant girls, or women, as does a specific African culture in which the question arose. Then it makes sense that this is not a universal statement; as a result, it must be restated for those who are seeking to understand it apart from that original context in order to avoid misunderstanding; e.g., "Jews do not circumcise (*females*)."

the other nations, versus the option of undertaking in addition the *rites* ("works") involved in proselyte conversion. Proselyte conversion was the convention that had traditionally accompanied non-Jews/non-Israelites turning from other gods to the One God of Israel. The phrase usually translated "works of law" would communicate the contrast better if it were to signify proselyte conversion — for example, "actions of proselyte conversion," "rites of proselyte conversion," "actions involved in proselyte conversion," or, consistent with Paul's use of circumcision as a metonymy for proselyte conversion, as the "actions involved in undertaking circumcision."

Proselyte conversion is the contextual contrast to "justification by faithfulness to Christ" in every case in Paul's letters where the phrase arises, rather than doing good deeds, or obeying Torah, or legalism, ethnocentrism, exclusivism, works-righteousness, human effort, and so on. The question is: Are non-Jews legitimately included (i.e., justified) in the family while remaining non-Jews? Paul's answer is "Yes," just as Jews are legitimately included while remaining Jews. All, regardless of prior ethnicity, are equally legitimated by faithfulness to the gospel declaration of the faithfulness of Christ. Thus it is wrong to change ethnicity in order to seek to gain that which is already gained, for that would involve a denial of having already gained it apart from such maneuvers. Paul's argument in Galatians 3:2, 5 offers the clearest example that the contrast is about identity transformation to proselyte standing for non-Jews who have already turned to Christ, not to Torah-based behavior for Jews including proselytes.

Keeping the focus on circumcision resolves the contextual ambiguity without requiring Paul, and those who look to him for guidance, to suppose that there is something fundamentally wrong with Torah observance, or even with specific aspects of Torah observance. At issue is the identity transformation of proselyte conversion for Christ-following non-Jews. That has ended for non-Jews who have faith in Christ and are faithful to the truth of the gospel, for they must remain members who represent the other nations turning to the One God of all the nations, not simply the One God of Israel. In addition, more generally (and I hope the reader will forgive me for speaking from outside), this also obviates the conundrum posed for Christian theology when supposing that Paul taught that good deeds were somehow by definition inherently oppositional to faith (and thus the need to fill in the blanks with wrong motives), in addition to finding fault per se with Torah and its observance or rituals, laws, and so on. The context is very specific.

This is also a good place to note that I find that in each place Paul mentions "faith," he is really talking about an active kind of conviction, better rendered "faithfulness," "loyalty," or "trust," for the point is to be faithful to the truth claim that is professed. By definition *faithful deeds* are not in contrast to faith but integral to what it means to have and express faith. Doing good deeds in faithfulness is implicit in what it means to become a member of the Christ-followers, of those who trust in and are faithful to Christ.

Faithfulness means something slightly different for Jews and non-Jews, but it is nevertheless the case that most of Paul's letters are not preoccupied with an effort to persuade people to faith as in believing a truth claim; rather, Paul's arguments proceed on the assumption that his audiences share his conviction in the truth claims about Christ. His letters are preoccupied with explaining how to live faithfully in view of that fact. Because they have completed the rite of conversion by turning from other gods to the One God, the one who does right (however, not the rite of proselyte conversion that would make them Israelites/Jews), they have become members of the family of the righteous ones from the other nation now obliged to observe fully the truth about how to live rightly ("righteously")—that is, by doing good works.

Final Thoughts

I hope the reader has been challenged to reconsider Paul's arguments, to consider a new way to think about how to approach Paul not only as one who remained a Jew, but as one who continued to practice Judaism according to faithfulness to the Mosaic covenant and to develop communal subgroups practicing Judaism. This extends to reconsidering the context of the non-Jewish audiences he addressed as knowing that he was in no way critical of Judaism, but rather was engaged in helping them negotiate their new identity as non-Jewish participants in the Jewish communal way of life. In that effort he did criticize some of his fellow Jews and their way of practicing Judaism, especially where it impacted the way that he believed things should be done.

The identity of his non-Jewish audiences was contested by Jews who did not share their convictions about Jesus. Most Jews were not persuaded of the chronometric-based claims on which Christ-followers legitimated their expectations and behavior, including the claim that these non-Jews should be regarded as if they had equal standing with Jews while maintaining that it was important that they did not actually become Jews. It was equally — perhaps even more so — contested in their local Greco-Roman contexts, in the responses of their families, friends, neighbors, and civic leaders, to the degree that this behavior included neglect of family and civic cult and thus threatened the well-being of everyone. The rest of humankind was not similarly convinced that the end of the ages had dawned around events attributed to a Judean executed by the Romans, and thus that this change of communal status and accompanying behavior was legitimate ("justified") in the present age.

It is in such contexts that I suggest Paul's arguments should be measured. He sought to identify with his non-Jewish disciples in the marginal situations that this message about Christ created and perpetuated for them; thus, he appealed to his own marginality among his fellow Jews for upholding this position. He qualified his own privileged standing in order to make clear that the identity they shared in Christ was paramount (Phil. 3:3–9).[23] But this qualification was based on his continued Jewish identity and behavior, not its dissolution, or else the relative comparison would have held no persuasive force. The value of the Torah and Jewish identity was a given, but at times he had to qualify for them that this did not put them at the disadvantage, for in the end of the day it is faithfulness to the One God of Jews and non-Jews according to their own calling and the responsibilities that God will measure them by.

The prevailing interpretations understand Paul's qualifications of Jewish identity and behavior to be dismissals by reading them as

---

23. I understand Paul's comments about the value of his Jewish identity and behavior are highly contextualized for their "pagan" situation, which gave rise to his concerns about his audience. They are no more dismissive of Jewishness than of "everything," for nothing is worth more to him than knowing Christ (and it should be the same for them, if such a binary choice had to be made); see Mark D. Nanos, "Paul's Reversal of Jews Calling Gentiles 'Dogs' (Philippians 3:2): 1600 Years of an Ideological Tale Wagging an Exegetical Dog?" *BibInt* 17 (2009): 448–82.

universals — that is, as equally applicable to everyone, Jew as well as non-Jew. I propose that they were instead based on the understanding of their everlasting value shared by his audiences, but at the same time he had to make clear that these were gifts to Israel in order to walk rightly and in order to bring the words of God to all the rest of the nations at the proper time. That did not involve bringing non-Jews into standing as Israelites and thus to being equally under the Mosaic covenant made with Israelites. The gospel sought to reconcile them to the One God of all of the nations and thus to living rightly according to standards that were overall not that different.

Because these non-Jews entered into Jewish communal life and its culture (i.e., Judaism), they would learn to live rightly as non-Jews within that culture, but that is not the same thing as becoming Jews. And that mixing of multiethnic peoples within a specific ethnic cultural system is a messy proposition. No one was to regard oneself to be superior among those in Christ, even if some were actually inferior in terms of the majority, present-age way of assessing cultural standing and associated dynamics such as honor and access to goods. They must assess relative standing differently. They must learn to live according to God's Spirit, which would empower them to live according to the age-to-come ideals of equality and concern for the other that the gospel proclaimed to have arrived among themselves when they gathered.

Paul believed that fellow Jews who did not share his convictions about these matters were mistaken or not "yet" adequately informed. They were still within the covenant, unlike those from the other nations who had not yet turned to Christ, but they were missing out on the promised day of glory for Israelites, when they would declare God's message of reconciliation to all of the nations. He came to the conclusion that many would not be convinced until those from the nations who turned to Christ from idols lived out the righteousness that would stop his fellow Jews in their tracks and make them reconsider whether Paul and the Jews who were proclaiming Christ were perhaps right, and that they were themselves missing out on this honor (Rom. 11). Then he would appeal not only to the Scriptures, but also to the proof that those from the nations were turning from idols and from lives of sinfulness to the One God and to lives of righteousness, just as would be expected at the dawn of the awaited age.

For Paul, that day had arrived, even if it was only early in the morning. For most Jews then and since, it has not appeared to be so. I like to think Paul would recognize that, apart from his fellow Jews experiencing a revelation such as he claims to have experienced, they are also being faithful to what God has so far revealed to them. It is, after all, Paul who claims that God is bigger, and God's plans more complicated, than any human can fully grasp (Rom. 11:33–36), and moreover, that "all Israel will be [rescued]" (11:26). I, for one, really appreciate his utopian ideals and the vision of a day when differences among us can be respected without discrimination, and I believe also, albeit for different reasons, that we should do everything we can to foster such ideals in our own time, (i.e., *tikkun olam*).

THOMAS R. SCHREINER

Sadly, Christians have discriminated against and persecuted Jews in the preceding centuries. Believers in Jesus the Christ must acknowledge and express sorrow for what has been done by those who called on the name of Jesus. Mutual understanding is always gained by talking to one another, and Mark Nanos helps us understand how Paul is typically viewed in Jewish circles. Even though I have some significant disagreements with Nanos, it is always good to converse with one another, so that we come to a better understanding. It is hoped that we can have significant disagreements and still love one another. True tolerance doesn't mean that we accept the other person's point of view as legitimate and right, but that we try to understand what others are saying and continue to love them even when we believe they are mistaken.

I am not saying I disagree with everything Nanos writes. Jesus fulfills what is written in the Law and the Prophets (Rom. 3:21). Paul regularly appeals to the Old Testament as authoritative, arguing that the gospel he preaches is the fulfillment of its promises (Rom. 1:2; 16:26). Nanos also rightly emphasizes that Paul was not against Jewish believers following the Torah. It is likely the case, especially in Israel, that most Jews who believed in Jesus continued to circumcise their children, followed purity laws, and even offered sacrifices (cf. Acts 21:20–26).

Furthermore, in Romans 14:1–15:6 Paul defends the right of the weak (who were probably mainly Jewish Christians) to observe days and to eat foods that were clean. Paul almost certainly thinks here of the Sabbath and of the food laws of the Old Testament. He forbids those who are strong to impose their convictions on the weak. Instead they must love and accept those who differ with them.

Nanos is unconvincing, however, when he argues that Paul always kept the Torah. Paul observed the law when he ministered to the Jews so that he could win them to Christ (1 Cor. 9:20). Even here Paul insists that he is not under the law, which means that he doesn't believe he is obligated to obey its prescriptions. The next verse (9:21) demonstrates, on the most natural reading, that Paul did not keep the law when he evangelized those who were without the law. When Paul evangelized the Gentiles, he would presumably eat with them, and he would eat their food even if it was unclean.

Galatians 2:11–14 calls into question even more fundamentally Nanos's claim that Paul and other Jewish believers always observed the law.[24] Space precludes a detailed treatment, but Peter and the rest of the Jews were regularly eating with the Gentiles before the men from James arrived. Almost certainly the men from James advised Peter to desist from eating with the Gentiles since they were eating unclean foods, that is, foods prohibited by the Old Testament (Lev. 11; Deut. 14). Paul rebuked Peter after he stopped eating with the Gentiles because the latter was acting hypocritically, for Peter had been living like a Gentile previously (Gal. 2:14), which means that he did not observe purity laws when enjoying fellowship with the Gentiles.

The issue in Galatians 2:11–14 was of paramount importance for Paul. If Jewish Christians did not eat with Gentile Christians (which means eating unclean food), they were in effect demanding that the Gentiles observe purity laws to belong to the people of God. Hence, they were compromising "the truth of the gospel" and were "forcing" (*anankazō*) Gentiles to live like Jews to belong to God's people (Gal. 2:14). Remarkably, this is the same charge Paul levels against "the false brothers" in 2:3–5. By insisting on circumcision for Gentiles, they were also compromising "the truth of the gospel" (2:5) and were trying to "compel"(*anankazō*) Gentiles to be circumcised (2:3). If Jews and Gentiles were together in a context where Gentiles felt pressured to abide by the law to be saved, Paul insisted that Jewish believers in Christ live like Gentiles, that they forsake purity laws for the sake of the gospel.

I conclude that Nanos's claim that Paul and other Jewish believers kept the Torah isn't borne out by the evidence. In fact, there were situations in which Paul demanded Jews to abandon the Torah for the sake of the Gentiles, so that the Gentiles would realize that salvation is not based on works of law.

---

24. For a fuller discussion see Thomas R. Schreiner, *Galatians* (ZECNT; Grand Rapids: Zondervan, 2011), 135–49.

It is important to add, as noted above, that Paul permitted Jews and presumably others to abide by prescriptions in the Torah if they weren't imposing those requirements on others for salvation (Rom. 14:1–15:6). Nevertheless Paul certainly doesn't demand observance of Torah by Jewish Christians here. Furthermore, those who think such observance is important, even if they don't require it for salvation, are described as "weak in faith" (Rom. 14:1). Paul is free from the Torah himself (cf. also Col. 2:16–23). He thinks nothing is "unclean" (*koinon*), which is contrary to what the Old Testament says about foods (Rom. 14:14). Or, as he says in 14:20, "all food is clean."[25] Hence, one of the fundamental tenets of Nanos's essay doesn't stand up to close scrutiny. Paul didn't believe Jewish Christians should follow the Torah, though he permitted them to keep the law if it did not compromise Gentiles entering into the people of God apart from the law.

Nor is it persuasive to say that Paul was called on the Damascus Road but not converted. Several texts in the Pauline letters describe Paul's call and conversion (Gal. 1:11–17; Phil. 3:2–11; 1 Tim. 1:12–16). Certainly, he emphasizes his calling as an apostle to the Gentiles in Galatians, but calling and conversion are not mutually exclusive. When we put the accounts together that speak of Paul's call in his letters, the evidence that he was also converted is compelling.

We can summarize the evidence of the texts cited above as follows. Before Jesus appeared to Paul, he belonged to Judaism, persecuted God's true assembly, trusted his own righteousness, put his confidence in the flesh, had worldly gain, was unworthy to be an apostle, was insolent, and was a blasphemer. But on the Damascus Road he experienced the grace, mercy, and love of God, gained Christ, was righteous by faith, turned from unbelief to belief, received eternal life, and was saved. Nanos's claim that Paul still belonged to Judaism after his call to proclaim the gospel is unsustainable: Paul speaks of his "my previous [*pote*] way of life in Judaism" (Gal. 1:13). He was called *and* converted.

Nanos rightly emphasizes that true faith leads to works. Some interpreters of Paul have been more "Pauline than Paul" and have minimized the importance of good works. Paul insisted that faith must express

---

25. I think Paul says these things about the food laws of the Old Testament for salvation historical reasons. He believes the old covenant is no longer in force.

itself in love (Gal. 5:6). I also agree with Nanos that a major part of Paul's argument is eschatological. The new age had dawned with the coming of the Messiah, Jesus. Paul's opponents did not recognize the arrival of the eschaton.

Nevertheless, Paul's polemic can't be limited to salvation history. There is an anthropological dimension to his rejection of works of law as well. And actually the new perspective reading also rightly sees that there is an ethnocentric component. We do not have either-or's here but both-and's. For instance, works of law are closely connected with "boasting" in Romans 3:27–28, which indicates that some were tempted to boast about their adherence to the law and to trust in their obedience as a basis of their justification. Similarly, Paul is concerned that Jews would exclude Gentiles, and thus he reminds his readers that justification is by faith both for Jews and Gentiles (Rom. 3:29–30).

Is Paul anti-Jewish here? Absolutely not. Boasting is not a Jewish problem but a human problem. If God's chosen people have this problem, then no one is exempt. And that is what the Pauline gospel teaches us. We are all prone to pride, and we must renounce any reliance on ourselves or on our works and cast ourselves utterly upon the grace of God in Jesus Christ.

The interpretation proposed here is verified by Romans 4:1–8. Paul moves from "works of the law" (*erga nomou*, Rom. 3:20, 28) to "works" (*erga*). Paul specifically states that if Abraham did the requisite works, he could boast (4:2). The anthropological dimension of the text cannot be waved away. Paul counters here the notion that one can be justified on the basis of works performed, insisting that justification is by faith instead by appealing to Genesis 15:6 (Rom. 4:3; cf. Gal. 3:6–7).

Romans 4:4–5 gives the example of one who expects wages because of work performed, contrasting this with the truth that God justifies the ungodly. Justification is granted not to those who work but to those who believe. Romans 4:4 is directed against those who expect a wage, a payment, a reward for their work. Apparently some believed that their works warranted a reward. Otherwise, Paul would not bother using the illustration. Paul doesn't waste his time responding to problems that don't exist. Paul teaches that no one receives justification by works since all are sinners (1:18–3:20). The only hope for the ungodly is the work of Jesus Christ as the crucified and risen Lord who died to atone for sins (3:21–26).

The example of David in Romans 4:6–8 also demonstrates that Paul's polemic cannot be restricted to Gentiles becoming proselytes. Paul cites Psalm 32, where David praises God for the blessing of forgiveness of sins. "Righteousness apart from works" here (Rom. 4:6) doesn't relate to becoming a proselyte, for David was already circumcised and followed purity laws. David's sins centered on his murder of Uriah and his adultery with Bathsheba. David celebrates the forgiveness granted to sinners who don't fulfill God's standards. Paul teaches that human beings must not trust in their works for justification or salvation, for a reliance on works leads to human boasting instead of trusting in the grace of God (Rom. 11:5–6; Eph. 2:8–9).

Nor does Nanos interpret Galatians 5:3 correctly. He thinks Paul informs the Galatians that they have to obey the entire law if they are circumcised. The false teachers (he calls them "influencers") didn't tell the Galatians such, for all they wanted was for the Galatians to become proselytes and get circumcised. The outside teachers weren't asking them to be subject to the entire Torah. But Paul, according to Nanos, instructs the Galatian Gentiles that they would have to obey the whole law (as Paul was doing) if they accepted circumcision.

This reading is wrong, I would suggest, at nearly every point. It is doubtful that the opponents only wanted the Galatians to be circumcised. It was instead the first step in subjecting themselves to the entire law (Gal. 4:21). Nor is it plausible, as I point out above, to think that Paul himself always observed the Torah. Nanos doesn't think Paul's argument makes sense otherwise. But actually the verse makes good sense if we read it as follows. Paul reminds the Galatians that if they submit to circumcision, they must keep every part of the law to be saved. But he has already taught them that perfect obedience is necessary for salvation (Gal. 3:10; cf. 2:16). Such perfect obedience is impossible, and so subjecting themselves to the law is an impossible burden. They must rely solely on the cross of Christ for salvation.

Finally, near the end of his article Nanos suggests that Jews who do not believe in Jesus but abide by the Jewish covenant may still be saved. I don't think this reading fits with what Paul wrote about the Jews (1 Thess. 2:13–16).[26] Further, Paul's discussion about the Jews

---

26. I am unpersuaded that this text is interpolated by a later author or scribe.

in Romans 9 – 11 clarifies that they must believe in Jesus Christ to be saved. E. P. Sanders in an important article demonstrates that Paul believed that Jews must put their faith in Jesus for salvation.[27] Near the end of that article Sanders indicates that he disagrees with Paul, but rightly says that Paul did not offer the Jews a special way of salvation by keeping the Torah. Paul demanded that Jews believe in Jesus Christ to experience eschatological salvation.

Nanos helps us understand how many Jews feel about Paul in his article, and he has some good observations and insights that should be integrated into our view of Paul. His desire to see people get along with each other in a friendly way is also salutary. But such a desire may also cause him to miss what Paul truly says, even if it does not fit with our cultural conceptions. Paul did not hate the Jewish people; rather, he deeply loved them. He believed they needed to trust in Jesus to experience eternal salvation. The cross was an offense in Paul's day. I think it still is.

---

27. E. P. Sanders, "Paul's Attitude toward the Jewish People," *USQR* 33 (1978): 175 – 87.

LUKE TIMOTHY JOHNSON

It is easy to agree with Professor Mark Nanos on several of the main points of his essay. No one can any longer deny the disastrous and deadly effects of the long history of interpreting Paul from a crypto-Marcionite perspective, with anti-Semitism built into the structure of Pauline interpretation. Nor can it be denied that to the extent classical Christianity constructed itself on this misreading of Paul, its tendency has been to define Christianity in terms of opposition to Judaism, so that, as Nanos helpfully observes, the "othering" of Judaism has been an essential component in the process of Christian self-definition. Finally, Nanos is certainly correct that Christian supersessionism has not only required Jews to perpetually play the role of foil, but it has demanded as well that Jews submit to being defined in "Christian" terms rather than in terms inherent to that tradition. The tragic results of such a distorted version of Christianity and of such a reductionistic reading of Paul should by now be evident to everyone.

As a Roman Catholic scholar who has never much understood, much less been locked into, such a distinctly Protestant form of either/or — Catholicism traditionally embraces the "both/and" — and especially as a scholar who learned Judaism from great Jewish scholars (especially Henry Fischel and Judah Goldin), I find this manner of reading Paul wrong-headed, although defining Christianity on such a misreading has long been evident. Indeed, when E. P. Sanders's book on *Paul and Palestinian Judaism* launched what has come to be called "the new perspective," I saw what some regarded as an epochal breakthrough as a long-overdue statement of the obvious. Speaking of the new perspective, I also agree with Nanos — and in this regard also Campbell — that its appropriation by mediocre scholars to advance still another form of binary opposition has not fundamentally improved the conversation with regard to Judaism.

Three other assertions of Professor Nanos equally deserve ready assent. First, Paul was a Jew whose allegiance was first and foremost to "those of my own race" (Rom 9:3) and whose hope was that "all Israel be saved" (11:26). Paul's "conversion," therefore, should not be seen as a change of religion — there was as yet no such thing as "Christianity" — but as a turn of life from persecutor to apostle because of an encounter with the risen Lord.

Second, Paul was in his own life a Torah-observant Jew; at the very least, he had absolutely no problem with Jewish believers observing the commandments. Concerning the consistency of his own observance, his statements in 1 Corinthians 9:19–23 legitimately give rise to some doubt.

Third, Paul's language about the law and the commandments are in the context of defending the legitimacy of Gentile believers entering the new creation without the obligation of being circumcised or observing the entire range of laws; the Decalogue and the law of love from Leviticus 19:18, however, are obligatory for such Gentile believers. In sum, Paul neither abandons his own Jewish identity and allegiance nor engages in a critique of "Judaism" as a "religion of works" as opposed to a "religion of grace."

But does Professor Nanos entirely avoid constructing his own binary opposition? While observing that Christianity did not yet exist in the time of Paul, he uses language that seems to suggest that "Judaism" did. Although he states, "As a historian, I uphold the view that we should strive to get our history as correct as we possibly can regardless of our opinion of the figures and events," and although he gives a passing glance to "the breadth of ideas and practices within first-century Judaism," Nanos fails to take seriously the historical realities. What has come to be called "formative Judaism," based on the convictions of the Pharisees and the interpretive skills of the scribes, emerged as dominant only after the destruction of the temple and achieved classic form only with the composition of the Mishnah, about 200 CE. Yet this "Judaism" seems to be the one that Nanos assumes to be normative in the time of Paul.

Furthermore, we know from extant literature, including Paul's letters, that Jews appeared in the first century in a variety of forms shaped by geographical, linguistic, and cultural factors, as well as in a variety of ideological positions that led them to disagree on the most fundamental issues, not excluding what constituted Torah (and in what language) and what hermeneutical standpoint for its interpretation was the best. By no means were the premises of the Pharisees that eventually became standard considered the norm among all Jews in the first century; not least among the contributions that the Qumran compositions have made is to confirm the highly contentious character of the Jewish conversation concerning the character of God's people. It is anachronistic to assume for this earlier period the more uniform state of Judaism after 100 CE.

Indeed, the Paul who declares himself a Pharisee (Phil. 3:5) — the earliest historical character we know to so describe himself — and more advanced in the traditions of his ancestors than any of his contemporaries (Gal. 3:14), himself displays elements of the varieties of Jewish life in the first century. He shows the scholars his ability to interpret Scripture through haggadic (Rom. 9–11) and halachic midrash (Gal. 3); but the text he so interprets is the Greek Septuagint rather than Hebrew. And he shows himself in Galatians 4:21–30 equally willing to employ the sort of allegory that would be found in Aristobolos or Philo.

Moreover, Paul is entirely at home in the apocalyptic view of history associated with Palestinian Jewish texts, and he speaks of an experience of ascending to the third heaven that clearly echoes the language used for descriptions of ascent to the heavenly throne-chariot in Merkabah mysticism. Paul also deploys language ("children of light and darkness," "new covenant," the community as God's temple) that is found particularly in the writings from Qumran. If Nanos had asked the question, "What kind of Jew was Paul?" with a genuine historical interest, he would find in him all the complexity of Jewish experience and thought in the period of the early empire.

And if he had looked more closely still, he would have seen that Paul the Jew was also — like James the brother of Jesus — a moral teacher with as much grounding in the discourse of Greco-Roman popular philosophy as in the specific tropes of Torah. Paul is a Jew, moreover, who confidently uses the various rhetorical forms associated with ancient letters; he is as at home with diatribe as he is with midrash. It will not do to appraise "Paul the Jew" without adequately assessing all the diverse components found in this specific Jew of the first century; above all, one cannot simply measure Paul against the frame of a later rabbinic ethos and practice, as though it was obvious what "Judaism" was in the first century.

Paul cannot be collapsed into any standard measure for being Jewish in the first century most of all because, alone among the Jews of whom we can speak with any confidence, Paul displays what can only be called a prophetic consciousness. The language he uses in Galatians 1:15–16 to describe the revelation of God's Son to (or in) him unmistakably alludes to the prophetic calls in Isaiah 49:1 and especially Jeremiah 5:1–10. Like Isaiah, Paul can declare that he has seen the Lord (1 Cor. 9:1; see Isa. 6:1); like Isaiah's servant, he can declare that he has the Spirit of the Lord (1 Cor. 7:40; Isa. 61:1); like Jeremiah, his authority is to build up and not to tear down (2 Cor. 10:8). There is no way to avoid the conclusion that when Paul speaks of himself as proclaiming in the Lord Jesus Christ a new covenant that is superior to that made through Moses (2 Cor. 3:7–18), or a new creation (2 Cor. 5:17; Gal. 6:15), or when he speaks of Christ as the new Adam (Rom. 5:12–21; 1 Cor. 15:45–49), the basis of a "new humanity" (Eph. 2:15–16; 4:24; Col. 3:10–11), he is being far more than a good Jew; he is proclaiming a message that challenges the very basis of Judaism and has revolutionary import and effect.

A vision of Paul that draws from only four of the letters (Romans, Galatians, 1 Corinthians, Philippians) and Acts does not satisfy, even when it is a "Jewish view," for as I have suggested, the entire range of letters was written by this first-century Jew and must be taken into account. Can Paul's view of the Mosaic covenant be assessed without consideration of 2 Corinthians 3? Are the responses to those "wishing to be teachers of the law" in 1 Timothy or those "from the circumcision party" in Titus utterly irrelevant? Is Paul's statement in 1 Thessalonians 2:14–16 to be dismissed, or should it be held in tension with Romans 9:1–3? Is the vision of Ephesians concerning the unity of Jews and Gentiles in the church not part of the Paul read within the Christian community? Progress in conversation among Jews and Christians regarding Paul will not significantly advance so long as the same narrow selection of data and the same narrow selection of issues and the same narrow definitions are operative.

DOUGLAS A. CAMPBELL

Mark Nanos has framed "the problem" in this relation clearly and helpfully, although I will suggest in due course that he should frame his accusations still more precisely. It is a complex difficulty, so he expertly teases out several aspects within it in the first part of his essay.

The basic problem Nanos points to is that the description of Judaism generated by much interpretation of Paul—i.e., by *Paul's* reconstructed description of Judaism—is unfair and deeply so. (And, sadly, it is then transmitted as an authoritative account to his Christian readers.) There seems to be some strange need in Paul's thought to describe Judaism harshly. Its motives are presented as negative. It is conditional and contractual in its mentality and soteriology. It is "legalistic" in the sense that it is oriented by a divine *law*, which of course it does not obey. So it rightly ought to expect only divine punishment. We could put all this a little more technically and suggest that according to Nanos, Paul's thought seems to *require* a *negative Jewish Other* (and this definitive Other then defines any non-Jewish non-Christian "others" in harsh terms as well, although Nanos does not emphasize this implication).

This is part of its warp and woof. Indeed, it does not seem able to *work* as a *system without* this Jewish Other. Of course Nanos goes on to point out that this Jewish Other is rather unfair. Jews certainly do not seem to be motivated by the mercantile motives Christians supply to them. They want to love and respect and obey God, and so on.

Part of the problem is the pervasive translation of *nomos* in Paul as "law." Nanos points out that this signifier is much better rendered as Torah or "teaching." The translation "law" skews interpretation toward

---

28. Space constraints forbid responding here in detail to Nanos's positive proposals about Paul as a Torah-observant Jew, which I find utterly ingenious but ultimately unpersuasive. Suffice it to say that he tends to overlook the negative statements about the Torah in Paul, suggesting its observance is universally problematic in some sense; see esp. Rom. 7:5–25 and Phil. 3:1–11; also Rom. 1:16; Gal. 4:12a.

a legalistic account of Judaism and encourages bald forensic and even political analogies for Judaism. Translated as teaching, however, Christians grasp straightaway that the key issues are ethical and instructive, not mercantile and legalistic. But the usual accounts of Paul's thinking seem to rely on the inaccurate translation.

The harsh "Other" is (supposedly) judged deeply deficient by Paul, and law-observance is also to be universally and completely abandoned. And Nanos goes on to point out how this erases Israel from Christian history, the church *displacing* God's covenant people from the OT — a shocking outcome once one considers it carefully, not the least because of the way it calls the fidelity and competence of God into question. Some of the appalling historical consequences of this sort of thinking then hardly need to be spelled out.

Nanos repeatedly points to the occasional positive comments on Paul's Torah observance that can be found in the sources. Accounts of Paul's posture toward Judaism and Torah generally marginalize this material, but it is present and some account must be taken of it.[29]

Nanos also notes how the protests of the letter of James against any dichotomy between faith and other ethical practices (i.e., "works") make good sense. Faith operating in isolation from other practices is an oddly truncated ethic, and Paul's letters repeatedly say as much; the apostle is constantly enjoining a range of right actions on his converts (i.e., multiple right actions or deeds in addition to faith). So Nanos in effect makes a request here obvious to any Jew for an explanation concerning how faith and the rest of Paul's Christian ethic connect together, although in doing so he is really asking for Paul's Christian interpreters to provide an account of his critique of the Torah (if they are committed to this) that can integrate ultimately with a meaningful ethic. Nanos is, of course, echoing here a standard Catholic complaint with certain readings of Paul.

In addition Nanos observes that the "new perspective" on Paul does not advance the apostle's interpretation as much in relation to these problems as its advocates probably hope. Rather, *it tends to generate the same or directly analogous difficulties*. So, instead of constructing the

---

29. See 1 Cor. 7:17–20; 9:20; perhaps also Gal. 5:11; and Acts 16:3; 18:18; 20:16; 21:24–26; 24:17; and 28:20; many of these texts are noted by Nanos.

Jewish Other in terms of legalism, the interpreter tends to be accused of a form of racism — hardly a big step forward.[30]

Now I basically agree with all this. And I am worried that Christian interpreters of Paul continue to deal with these difficult problems largely by denying them — by denying that they are real difficulties, when clearly they are, or by asking Christians, at the end of the day, simply to privilege their own identities over against this strange and insensitive (de)construction of the Jewish outsider. It is especially troubling, moreover, that this happens after ample scholarly warning *and in a post-Holocaust situation more generally*. Moreover, if these problems persist in Christian readings of Paul, I worry that they fundamentally compromise any witness by Paul to a gospel that is ostensibly grounded in divine benevolence revealed to the world through Jesus Christ. Indeed, outsiders frequently seem to intuit that this last claim on the part of certain Christian evangelists is not really true, given their other commitments.

It is a great relief, then, when we realize that we can begin to resolve these problems satisfactorily by grasping that they are generated almost entirely by the Melanchthonian reading of Paul (see my response to Schreiner for what this is). More precisely, these difficulties come from the determination to read Paul *forward*, which the Melanchthonian construal is strongly committed to. (It is not the only way to read Paul forward, but it is a widespread one.)

Let me elaborate. Paul is going to supply a soteriology at some point — a theory of how people get saved, along with definitions of what they are saved from, how, and what for and to. But if Paul's account of all this is constructed forward, then the construction of the problem must *precede* and *ground* the construction of the solution. The Christian solution will build directly on the definition of the pre-Christian outsider, who biographically, historically, and textually for Paul is a Jew. Moreover, this Jewish outsider will probably be held to occupy an unpleasant and impermanent state, and self-evidently so, so that the solution appears necessary, universal, and compelling. Otherwise

---

30. Nanos also subverts an ancillary explanation that new perspective advocates sometimes propose — that Paul is pushing beyond the particularism of Judaism to a more universal gospel. Nanos points out that Judaism and Christianity are both as particular and universal as each other.

there would be no need to become a Christian! (Other progressions are technically possible at this point—from positive to still more positive situations—but are not so compelling in relation to the Pauline data.)

In short, everything in the solution will depend on the construction of the problem, and that will work best if it is a harsh one. (And a ghastly law of proportionality seems to be at work here: the harsher the construction of the problem in terms of the Jew, the more powerful the impetus into the Christian state and the more obvious and hence firmer the supposed truth of that state—and the heavier the wrathful judgment that falls on the recalcitrant.)

Now the Melanchthonian reading will deliver these considerations in spades for the reader of Paul. The Jew (representing all non- and unbelievers), crushed by the perfect demands of the law and fearing pending punishment, ought to reach out and grasp the solution in the form of a gospel that offers salvation by way of a much easier route—through faith alone. This faith appropriates the kinder, gentler Christian contract within which punishment is redirected onto Christ and away from the deserving sinner, and only the foolish and immoral will resist this self-evident progression—and will presumably go on to soak up any punishment falling on them within history in anticipation of the fearful punishment due at the end of history. Meanwhile the entire construction is in mercantile, self-interested, and legalistic terms—that is, in conditional and contractual terms. This is how the problem is—and must be—constructed in order to generate the Christian solution of salvation by faith alone.

The Torah, moreover, must function throughout as a law, inscribed in the cosmos and the hearts of humanity as well as in the Old Testament Scriptures, which primarily establishes culpability before the divine sovereign. And those who disobey it paradigmatically but refuse to become Christians (i.e., most Jews) are excluded from salvation and hence erased in historical terms. The model is only interested in those who are saved by faith alone, that is, those in the church. Jews are exemplary of Everyman in his sinful state. And they are consequently cast into outer darkness. And we now come to some of Nanos's key difficulties.

It is *very* difficult to give any account of the texts that report Torah-observance by Paul as an apostle. Really, these just have to be marginalized. Historical-critical scholars, using tools long honed for just these sorts of tasks, can achieve this in relation to Acts without too much difficulty—although such moves are not possible for more scripturally reverential scholars like Schreiner. But Paul's own occasional statements have to be interpreted as tiny lapses, or perhaps just not mentioned at all.

The ethical difficulties of this model are also widely known. It is indeed still unclear to me how this model generates any decisive ethical traction. The traditions using it tend to switch models at this point and appeal to "sanctification," which operates in a different way but is firmly committed to Christian ethics. Hence Nanos's queries about ethics and about how faith is ultimately combined with other right practices are accurate. The Melanchthonian model can't really make sense of all this data in Paul. And its appeal to other models to answer these questions effectively concedes the point.

Finally, Nanos is right to sense behind the new perspective a mere recapitulation for much of the time of the troublesome forward dynamic already doing most of the damage within Pauline interpretation in its crisp Melanchthonian form. The new perspective still works forward. And since the underlying problem is prospectivism, and since the new perspective tends not to recognize this, it generally fails to resolve the Jewish questions. These problems have merely been transposed into another interpretative key, so to speak. A legalistic, individualistic, and quite generic account of the problem in legal terms has been replaced by a more corporate and historicizing account that generates its evangelistic and soteriological leverage through charges of inappropriate ethnocentrism and particularity. But these are still charges, and serious ones at that. So Nanos is right in my view to suggest that the positive proposals by new perspective scholars are usually not a step forward— although it is their unwitting aping of the Melanchthonian reading that hampers them.

In sum, then, we can hopefully see by now that Nanos is actually frustrated almost entirely by a particular reading of Paul—the Melanchthonian (or Lutheran) account. Hence his legitimate frustrations are simply a sign for me that *this particular reading* of Paul is *wrong*. Paul just could not have been this nasty and misguided—or, at least, we should exhaust our other options before embracing this desperate expedient. Hence Nanos's Jewish concerns really end up adding grist to my mill, namely, to the suggestion that we abandon Melanchthonian constructions and try to read Paul in a consistently apocalyptic way.[31] Only that construal offers us a way forward in relation to these important and painful Jewish questions—a construal that can move forward because it has learned to think backward.

---

31. I provide a short sketch of these dynamics in ch. 7 of *The Quest for Paul's Gospel* (London: T&T Clark [Continuum], 2005), 132–45; and I articulate the critical relationship between an apocalyptic approach to Paul and salvation-history in ch. 3 (56–68). A brief account of how my *Deliverance of God* is addressing "the Jewish agenda" is provided in my essay "An Attempt to be Understood," *JSNT* 34 (2011): 162–208, esp. 164–74.

CONCLUSION

I have noticed a general trend in the genre of "views" books that there is often a tendency toward superficial resolution. That is, that interactions among the contributors lends itself to flattening out the distinctive approach of the contributors, resolving some of the divisions at a superficial level, reducing differences to haggling over definitions, and reaching bland conclusions to what was were initially intrepid debates. The sharp corners of the debaters often get blunted by the exchanges. Not so in this book. Although one can identify several convergences among our contributors, the differences between them, in their reading of Paul, have been laid bare and are often stark.

This volume illustrates the different ways of reading Paul and the divergent meanings that writers can elicit from Paul for their respective audiences. The validity or invalidity of those readings must be left up to subsequent readers who can themselves adjudicate upon the textual warrant, historical resonance, cultural relevance, and theological utility of those readings. To enable readers here to make up their own minds on what was argued, I want to recap what our contributors stood for and what they stood against in these exchanges.

The Main Points of Contention

Everyone agreed that Paul sees a form of *salvation* as intimately bound up with what God did in Jesus Christ. For Schreiner, Jesus saves primarily from the consequences of sin through his substitutionary death on the cross. For Johnson, salvation is primarily about a liberation and transformation that Jesus effects by his death and by his risen life being imbibed into his followers. For Campbell, salvation is a triune act applied by Son and Spirit that brings participation in the story of Christ. For Nanos, his Paul sees Gentiles needing to be saved from idolatry and immorality through Israel's Messiah. From my perspective, what we find here are different ways of construing salvation, based on whether salvation is about the rectification of believing individuals (Schreiner), the preference for rennovative and restorative metaphors for salvation over forensic ones (Johnson), the attempt to prosecute a christocentric and even trinitarian view of salvation (Campbell), or else a saving act that incorporates non-Jews into a Jewish story of salvation (Nanos). These are not entirely incommensurable, but they do emphasize different things in different ways.

Everyone agreed that *Jesus* is close to the center of Paul's mission and message. Schreiner identifies Jesus' lordship, divine lordship no less, as a central ingredient in Paul's depiction of Jesus. Johnson depicts Paul's Jesus as the gateway to a new creation, a restorer of Israel and renewer of creation. Campbell, in Barthian terms, regards Jesus as the self-disclosure of God, so that what we see of Jesus is to be true of God. Nanos sees Paul as announcing that through Jesus' resurrection, the period Israel awaited has begun — a period when those from the nations can also experience God's mercy and join alongside the people of God. Again, we find here remarks that are not always incompatible, but different elements are picked up and emphasized.

Everyone approached Paul's letters with, or with a view to, a certain *framework*. For Schreiner, eschatology, the "now" and "not yet," provides the organizing principle behind Paul's thought. According to Johnson, the framework for Paul is how he negotiates the cultural complexities of his Jewish heritage and the Greco-Roman environment. For, Campbell, the matrix of apocalypticism explains the narrative and participatory dimensions of Paul's theology. Nanos believes it is crucial to grasp the Jewishness of Paul, his appropriation rather than his denunciation of his Jewish heritage, as the framework to understand Paul. Schreiner and Nanos both underscore the importance of eschatology, though they do very different things with it. Nanos and Johnson both plot Paul as engaging the complexities of Jewish and Greco-Roman culture, but again, they see Paul as working through it with diverse strategies.

Everyone endeavored to demonstrate Paul at least had a vision for the *churches*. In Schreiner's eyes, Paul wanted to show his converts how they stand in continuity with God's purposes and plans made known to Israel. For Johnson, the vision was to enable churches to foster their own unique identity in the Greco-Roman world and simultaneously hold onto their Israelite religious heritage. For Campbell, Paul wanted the churches to be a pneumatic brotherhood that cultivated Christlikeness

Michael F. Bird • 213

in the context of a believing community. For Nanos, he sees Paul as urging the churches (which are subgroups within the synagogue communities) to live in light of the age to come while simultaneously promoting positive relations with non-Christ-believing Jews.

The Unfolding Debate

Thomas R. Schreiner

Schreiner's "Reformed" view received some detailed responses. Campbell appreciates Schreiner's placement of Christology as central to Paul, but he calls Schreiner on not being sufficiently christocentric or Reformed enough in his reading of Paul. Campbell minces no words as he labels Schreiner's approach as "Melanchthonian" and even "Arian," since he locates the center of Paul's theology in law, retributive wrath, and human failure, rather than on love, election, and Christ. Campbell believes that Schreiner's reading of Paul advocates an impoverished Christology and a ghastly approach to the Jewish people.

Johnson contests Schreiner's claim as to whether the fulfillment of Scripture can really be so central for Paul, since it is not central in all of Paul's letters, and some of Paul's readings of the Old Testament are radical and subversive in the eyes of his Jewish contemporaries. Johnson also thinks that for Paul sin is more cosmic and social rather than simply individual. That in turn leads to Johnson's further protest against Schreiner's preoccupation with substitutionary atonement and forensic justification on the grounds that they represent a needless narrowing of Paul's richer description of salvation.

Nanos believes that Schreiner is perpetuating a Protestant exegesis that is decidedly anti-Jewish. Finding fault with Schreiner's methodology, he discusses comments made by Schreiner in his recent Galatians commentary, which expose the a priori biases against historical criticism that Nanos seeks to challenge. In contrast, Nanos believes that Paul was proudly forthright about his own Jewish heritage and held out a more positive place for the Jewish people than Schreiner envisages.

Luke Timothy Johnson

Coming now to Catholic scholar Luke Timothy Johnson, Schreiner expresses his enthusiastic approval for Johnson's ascription of authentic

Pauline authorship to all thirteen Pauline letters and also welcomes Johnson's sketch of experience and tradition in Paul. However, he detects a few lacunas in Johnson's approach, including a failure to fully explore Paul's theological depth and not properly wrestling with Paul's perspective on the law. Schreiner also contests Johnson's belief that Paul envisages election as corporate rather than individual.

Campbell appreciates much in Johnson's approach, especially the triangulation of Christ, salvation, and church, but opines that Johnson still edges into "Melanchthonian" categories. Campbell is also less inclined to a sympathetic reading of the Pauline household codes that Johnson offers since they seem out of step with Paul's egalitarian ethics.

Nanos compliments Johnson for his integration of Jewish and Greco-Roman contexts in reading Paul. Yet Nanos questions whether Paul really did regard Jesus as the divine "Lord," identifiable with the Jewish God. Nanos also objects that some of Johnson's remarks about salvation seem to be anachronistic and do not reflect Paul's broader concerns. He wishes to emphasize too that Paul does not simply want that Jewish Christ-believers remain Torah-observant; rather, Paul would have insisted on it according to Nanos. In fact, Nanos dissents from Johnson that Paul expected Jewish Christ-believers to give up their Jewishness during shared meals, since Nanos believes that Paul expected the exact opposite to occur.

Douglas A. Campbell

That brings us now to Douglas Campbell's "post-New Perspective" view, which prompted some forthright push-back from the other contributors. To begin with, Schreiner genuinely appreciates Campbell's trinitarian themes and trumpeting of divine grace. Even so, Schreiner wonders if Campbell's approach is in fact hyper-Calvinist or even über-Reformed. Schreiner believes that his own approach might have more affinity with Irenaeus, Athanasius, the Gregories, and Calvin, not the least on the theme of judgment. Schreiner also objects that Campbell's reading of Paul's Adam-Christ association does not permit an all-inclusive soteriology since Paul still envisages judgment for those in Adam.

Johnson (like Schreiner) contests whether Romans 5–8 is the best test case for Paul's theology since it brackets out wider currents and themes from the rest of Paul's letters. Johnson even wonders if Campbell's reading is not so much a "post-New Perspective" that helps us to engage the question of Paul and the Jews, as much as it is a Nicene reading that ignores the Jewish issues altogether.

While Nanos heartily endorses the term "post-New Perspective," he remains unconvinced that Campbell actually represents what it could or should be. When it comes to Paul's ethics, Nanos believes that Campbell universalizes remarks by Paul that are often specified for non-Christ-believing Jews or Christ-believing Gentiles, not necessarily for both. Though Campbell claims to represent a post-New Perspective, Nanos believes that he rehearses the same missteps rather than showing a new way forward, such as wrongly equating circumcision and Torah observance.

Mark D. Nanos

Finally, the Jewish approach of Mark Nanos inspired a mixture of affirmation and questioning. Schreiner expresses grave remorse for what Christians have done to Jews over the course of history, and he welcomes Nanos to what has all too often been a very Christian conversation. Despite that, Schreiner is not convinced that Paul was in fact Torah-observant, and Schreiner thinks that Paul was in a sense converted on the road to Damascus. What is arguably Schreiner's most grievous concern is that he thinks that Nanos does not sufficiently account for Paul's remarks about the law as focusing on a human problem of guilt and corruption as opposed to a social problem of Jewish and Gentile relations.

Campbell is highly sympathetic to Nanos's reading of Paul, especially in not pitting Paul *against* Judaism, though Campbell believes that Nanos's frustrations are more with a "Melanchthonian" (i.e., Lutheran) reading of Paul rather than with a robustly Protestant one.

Johnson begins his response by noting that the Catholic tradition has not had the Protestant inclination towards a law-gospel antithesis, so he is naturally sympathetic to Nanos's Jewish reading of Paul as it avoids any sense of crypto-Marcionism. However, Johnson objects that Nanos continues to perpetuate a number of needless binary oppositions of Jewish versus non-Jewishness in Paul. He feels that Nanos has not fully appreciated the variegated forms of Judaism or noted the similarities of Paul's Jewishness to Greco-Roman discourse.

A Final Word

Finally, I want to thank our contributors for their hard work. Their initial essays were stimulating, and the subsequent exchanges have been engaging and entertaining. They have encouraged all of us to go back to the letters of Paul, their contexts and co-texts, and to investigate who the apostle to the Gentiles was and what he stood for. Furthermore, each of these contributors forces us to question our assumptions, to test our interpretations, and to think about what the implications for reading Paul mean for the communities we belong to. In the learned and erudite work put into this volume, we have seen a fine example of the type of conversation that Paul would have appreciated. We are given direction to "test everything" and to "hold fast to what is good" (1 Thess. 5:21 NRSV).

SCRIPTURE INDEX

SUBJECT INDEX